EUROPEAN APOSTASY

PAWEL BIELAWSKI

EUROPEAN APOSTASY

THE ROLE OF RELIGION IN THE EUROPEAN NEW RIGHT

ARKTOS
LONDON 2025

ARKTOS

⊕ Arktos.com ⓕ fb.com/Arktos ⊙ ⓘ arktosmedia ⊠ arktosjournal

Copyright © 2025 by Arktos Media Ltd.

All rights reserved. No part of this book may be reproduced or utilised in any form or by any means (whether electronic or mechanical), including photocopying, recording or by any information storage and retrieval system, without permission in writing from the publisher.

ISBN
978-1-917646-31-4 (Paperback)
978-1-917646-32-1 (Hardback)
978-1-917646-33-8 (Ebook)

Translation
Jafe Arnold

Editing
Constantin von Hoffmeister

Layout and Cover
Tor Westman

CONTENTS

Acknowledgements vii
Introduction ix
Methodology xvii

1. Alain de Benoist and GRECE: A Pathway of Thought 1
    Childhood 1
    Adolescence 4
    Adulthood (to 1968) 6
    GRECE and May '68 14
    Summary 17

2. The *Nouvelle Droite*: The Evolution and Anatomy of Ideas 25
    The Ideational Evolution of the *Nouvelle Droite* 25
    Ideological Anatomy 33
    1. The Theological Level 35
    2. The Philosophical Level 39
    3. The Political Level 61
    Summary and Clarifications 85
    Is the *Nouvelle Droite* "Fascism"? 91
    Positioning the *Nouvelle Droite* on the Left-Right Axis 93

3. Paganism: The "Religion of Europe" 97
    What Paganism Is Not 102
    Cosmocentric-Polytheistic Monism 106
    World-Affirming Ethnic Religion 111
    The Hierophany of Nature 114
    God and Man: Ontic Closeness 117
    How to Be a Pagan (Today) 121

4. Christianity: The "Bolshevism of Antiquity"................125
   Theocentric-Monotheistic Dualism......................132
   A World-Rejecting Universalist Religion..................136
   Totalitarian Egalitarianism............................140
   Western Christianity: The Result of Syncretism.............143
   Summary..148
   Monotheism as the Germ of Secular Totalitarianism..........153
5. The *Nouvelle Droite*'s Political Theology....................157
   Desacralisation, Rationalisation, Secularisation.............159
   The Idea of Progress: The "Faith" of Modernity..............164
   The Ethnocidal Ideology of Human Rights..................179
   Liberalism: The Negation of Democracy...................192
   America: Anti-Europe.................................206
   Modernity: Secularised Christianity.....................216
6. The *Nouvelle Droite* and Islam...........................219
7. The *Nouvelle Droite* and Related Currents...................235
   The *Nouvelle Droite* and French Integral Nationalism..........235
   The *Nouvelle Droite* and Integral Traditionalism.............239
   The *Nouvelle Droite* and Dependism.....................247
   The *Nouvelle Droite* and Third Positionism................252
   The *Nouvelle Droite* and the Fourth Political Theory..........255

Conclusion..265

Bibliography..273

ACKNOWLEDGEMENTS

I WISH TO THANK my doctoral supervisor, Dr. Rafał Łętocha, for his scholarly care for the present work and all of his helpful instructions over the course of writing it. I would also like to thank Dr. Jacek Gulanowski and Dr. Mateusz Waśko for their assistance and their remarks on the subject-matter of this work.

I also wish to thank the three reviewers of my dissertation that has now become this book: Prof. Zbigniew Mikołejko, Dr. Ryszard Michalak, and Prof. Adam Wielomski.

Next, I would like to thank Dr. Mariusz Bechta for his editorial labor and faith in successful publishing.

Thanks are also owed to Dr. Tomasz Szczepański for the opportunity to publish my interviews with leading representatives of the New Right in the journal *Trygław*, and for assisting me with writing my first ever scholarly article.

Finally, I would like to offer up thanks to Alain de Benoist himself for the opportunity to meet him in person and for his recommendation of my work.

INTRODUCTION

THE SUBJECT OF the present study is the question of the role and place of religion in the ideology of the *Nouvelle Droite* (or "New Right"), particularly in the works of Alain de Benoist. The focus on Alain de Benoist's thought is dictated by (1) the fact that de Benoist is the main ideologist and *spiritus movens* of the movement, and (2) the broad scope of the *Nouvelle Droite*'s ideational legacy.

Offering a precise characterisation and definition of the *Nouvelle Droite* is no easy task. Besides the fact that the movement itself is not homogenous, it is also characterised by a certain multi-dimensionality. It does not have a strict political, religious, or (counter-)cultural character. The movement comprises elements of philosophy and religious studies, sociology and political science, legal science and even sociobiology. It would be more appropriate to call the movement a "(multi-dimensional) ideational bloc". One could, of course, attempt to point out some kind of main, constitutive element or field that might have conditioned all the rest and imparted its tone. If we look at the *Nouvelle Droite* from such a perspective, then this current can be described as a neo-pagan movement. The very term "New Right", which expressly implies a focus on the sphere of politics, was not coined by the current's own representatives, but rather is a *sui generis* "label" pinned on it by its opponents.

The founder and most important figure of the *Nouvelle Droite* is Alain de Benoist, a philosopher, political scientist, and historian of ideas, who was born on 11 December 1943. De Benoist comes from a family with aristocratic roots. He studied law, philosophy, sociology, and religious studies at the University of Paris, Sorbonne. He is the author of numerous books and publications on a whole array of subjects, ranging from philosophy and religious studies to economic topics. To this day, he remains the most iconic and significant figure of this current.

The birth of the *Nouvelle Droite* can be regarded as the founding of the think tank GRECE (*Groupement de recherche et d'études pour la civilisation européenne* — Research and Study Group for European Civilisation) on 5 May 1968 in Lyon. This think tank saw its main task as changing the intellectual climate in France (and later across Europe) through "metapolitics" (a term which one representative of the *Nouvelle Droite*, Jean-Claude Valla, defined as "the domain of values which are not concerned with fleeting political questions, but which indirectly influence the political consensus"). One important point of reference for the *Nouvelle Droite* is the concept of cultural hegemony formulated by the Italian thinker and Communist activist Antonio Gramsci. Following this Italian Marxist, Alain de Benoist argues that before any political power can be seized, it is first necessary to win the battle over culture. Societal changes are possible only upon changing the ideological superstructure of the opinion-forming elites.

Alain de Benoist's approach to religion, particularly Christianity, is very particular. De Benoist has a decisively negative opinion of the latter, which he considers to be inherently intolerant, oppressive, totalitarian, and inexorably conducive to persecution. His sympathy lies with "paganism", which refers at once to Greco-Roman polytheism as well as to the beliefs of the "barbarian" peoples of the North, towards which he has a positive attitude. De Benoist considers polytheism to be tolerant by nature and non-oppressive. He also appreciates the pagan Greco-Roman heritage and the colossal role that paganism played in the constitution of Europe. In addition, following in the wake of Carl Schmitt's political theology, de Benoist recognises the Enlightenment to have been a secular continuation and, in some sense, fulfilment of Christianity, rather than an antithesis to Christianity. Political liberalism, the idea of "progress", human rights, and the linear concept of time — all of these, in Alain de Benoist's opinion, should be seen as derived from Christianity, i.e., they are Christian ideas in secular form.

The *Nouvelle Droite* represents a favourable topic for study not only because it is an undoubtedly interesting current, but also by virtue of its far-reaching, multilayered, unorthodox, and ambiguous character, which decisively resists all the worn-out schematics. It cannot be reduced to simple, crude propaganda, and the current itself has aimed to maintain an academic-scientific level of discourse. The movement has handed down an extraordinarily rich and broad ideational legacy (which, given that the movement still exists to this day, is inevitably only growing). Alain de Benoist himself is the author of dozens of books, hundreds of articles, and the subject of hundreds of interviews. Moreover, the current has spread beyond France. It has since found footholds in, among other countries, Belgium, Germany, Italy, England, and the United States of America.

The aim of the present work is to study the role played by religion in Alain de Benoist's thought, that is, the place and function that religion fulfils in this French thinker's ideo-political concepts. This study intends to show how Alain de Benoist sees the development of religion in Europe, how he frames the respective roles of paganism and Christianity, and how he assesses and interprets the latter in terms of their influence on European history and civilisation, particularly with regards to how the Christian religion translates into modern political ideas. In view of the intersections between the domains of religion, politics, culture, and civilisation in this context, the present work's study of Alain de Benoist's thought requires an interdisciplinary approach that combines elements of philosophy, religious studies, and political science.

The fundamental research aim of this work is to answer the question of the role that religion plays within the totality of the *Nouvelle Droite*'s ideational system. In order to answer this question, this work poses auxiliary questions. First, what role, according to Alain de Benoist, has

Christianity played in the history of Europe? Second, what, according to him, was "paganism" in pre-Christian Europe, and how did it differ from Christianity? Third, what, according to this French author, were the long-term consequences of Christianity's adoption in Europe, and how do they translate into the political sphere?

This introductory chapter describes the methodology applied in this study, presents its research questions, and elaborates on certain terminological questions. The first chapter presents Alain de Benoist's path of thought, i.e., the path of his intellectual development up to the founding of GRECE. The second chapter is dedicated to presenting the ideational foundations of the *Nouvelle Droite* by way of outlining and discussing the totality of its system on the theological, philosophical, and political levels. It also presents an outline of the gradual evolution of the *Nouvelle Droite*. The third chapter presents Alain de Benoist's vision of "paganism". The fourth chapter is dedicated to the *Nouvelle Droite*'s perspective on Christianity. The fifth chapter presents the *Nouvelle Droite*'s political theology, whereupon the author attempts to answer the question of how the New Right's "paganism" translates into its views in the political sphere. The sixth chapter has a comparative character: it compares the *Nouvelle Droite*'s concepts to other, similar ideological currents. The final chapter summates the research carried out up to this point and defines the place and role of religion within the totality of the *Nouvelle Droite*'s system.

The *Nouvelle Droite* current has been met with a considerable amount of scholarly studies, particularly in the countries of Western Europe. The most complete and exhaustive work on Alain de Benoist's thought is, without a doubt, *Sur la Nouvelle Droite* ["On the New Right"], authored by Pierre-André Taguieff.[1] When it comes to Francophone literature, it also bears mentioning *Les paganismes de la Nouvelle Droite (1980–2004)* ["The Paganisms of the New Right

---

1 Pierre-André Taguieff, *Sur la Nouvelle Droite* (Paris: 1994).

(1980–2004)"], which belongs to the pen of Stéphane François,[2] as well as *Les intellectuels de la Nouvelle Droite et la religion. Histoire et idéologie d'un antichristianisme de droite (1968–2001)* ["The Intellectuals of the New Right and Religion: The History and Ideology of an Anti-Christianity of the Right"], authored by Olivier Moos.[3] In the English language, noteworthy publications include Tamir Bar-On's *Where Have All the Fascists Gone?* and *Rethinking the French New Right: Alternatives to Modernity*,[4] Tomislav Sunic's *Against Democracy and Equality: The European New Right*,[5] and Michael O'Meara's *New Culture, New Right: Anti-Liberalism in Postmodern Europe*.[6] In Poland, the *Nouvelle Droite* is severely understudied. Barely a few strictly scholarly articles have appeared, among them Jakub Stobiecki's "Alain de Benoist and the French New Right — Founders of the Right-Wing Metapolitical Strategy"[7] and several articles in Polish by the present author: "From Traditionalism to Futurism: Guillaume Faye's Archeofuturism", "Alain de Benoist's Organic Democracy as an Alternative to Globalist Liberal Democracy", "Human Rights, the Civic Religion of the West: The Perspective of the European New Right"; "Revolt against the Unipolar World, or Anti-Colonialism 'from the Right': The Perspective of Alain de Benoist's New Right", "The 'Bolshevism of Antiquity', or Christianity as a 'Revolution': Selected Aspects of the Perspective of

---

2 Stéphane François, *Les paganismes de la Nouvelle Droite (1980–2004)*, PhD dissertation (2005) [https://theses.hal.science/tel-00442649/].

3 Olivier Moos, *Les intellectuels de la Nouvelle Droite et la religion. Histoire et idéologie d'un antichristianisme de droite (1968–2001)* (Freiburg, 2005).

4 Tamir Bar-On, *Where Have All The Fascists Gone?* (London/New York: 2016); idem, *Rethinking the French New Right: Alternatives to Modernity* (New York: 2013).

5 Tomislav Sunic, *Against Democracy and Equality: The European New Right* (London: Arktos, 2011).

6 Michael O'Meara, *New Culture, New Right: Anti-Liberalism in Postmodern Europe* (London: Arktos, 2013).

7 J. Stobiecki, "*Alain de Benoist i Francuska Nowa Prawica — twórcy prawicowej strategii metapolitycznej*", Przegląd Politologiczny 2 (2003), 27–36.

Alain de Benoist's New Right".[8] The popular-scholarly articles in Polish worthy of mention include Jarosław Tomasiewicz's "Against Equality and Democracy: The New Right in France",[9] Marek Konopko's "New Right, New Culture, New Paganism",[10] Ryszard Mozgol's "We Choose the 'Third Way': Alain de Benoist on the 'Decolonisation' of Europe",[11] Alexey Dzhermant's "The European New Right and the Belarusian Perspective",[12] Krzysztof Tyszka-Drozdowski's "Alain de Benoist: Above Left and Right",[13] an interview with Adam Wielomski on this subject,[14] and my own interviews with Alain de Benoist and Tomislav Sunic.[15] The above-mentioned Wielomski also dedicated a chapter to

8   Paweł Bielawski, "*Od tradycjonalizmu do futuryzmu. Archeofuturyzm Guillaume'a Faye'a*", Athenaeum 58 (2018), 60–71; idem, "*Demokracja organiczna Alaina de Benoist jako alternatywa dla globalistycznej demokracji liberalnej*", Politeja 46(61) (2019), 481–502; idem, "*Prawa człowieka — religia obywatelska Zachodu. Perspektywa Europejskiej Nowej Prawicy*", Athenaeum 66 (2020), 138–149; idem "*Bunt przeciwko jednobiegunowemu światu, czyli antykolonializm „z prawa". Perspektywa Nowej Prawicy Alaina de Benoist*", Społeczeństwo i Polityka 3(64) (2020), 5–21; idem, "*„Bolszewizm starożytności", czyli chrześcijaństwo jako „rewolucja". Perspektywa Nowej Prawicy Alaina de Benoista — wybrane aspekty*", Studia Religiologica 54(2) (2021), 181–194.

9   J. Tomasiewicz, "*Przeciwko Równości i Demokracji: Nowa Prawica we Francji*" in idem, *Między faszyzmem i anarchizmem. Nowe Idee dla Nowej Ery* (Pyskowice: 2000), 25–28.

10 M. Konopko, "*Nowa Prawica, Nowa Kultura, Nowe Pogaństwo*", Fronda 8 (1997), 57–64.

11 R. Mozgol, "*Wybieramy „trzecią drogę". Alain de Benoist o „dekolonizacji" Europy*", Templum Novum 11/12 (2011–2012), 7–9.

12 A. Dziermant, "*Europejska Nowa Prawica i perspektywa białoruska*", Pressje 22–23 (2010), 132–146.

13 K. Tyszka-Drozdwoski, "*Alain de Benoist. Ponad lewicą i prawicą*", Pressje 5 (2019), 45–51.

14 A. Wielomski, "*Rozmowa z dr A. Wielomskim*", interview by T. Szczepański, Odmrocze 8/9 (2004), 78–81.

15 Alain de Benoist, "*Wywiad z Alainem de Benoist*", interview by Paweł Bielawski, Trygław 16 (2015), 31–36; T. Sunic, "*Wywiad z Tomislavem Suniciem*", interview by Paweł Bielawski, Trygław 16 (2015), 37–48.

Alain de Benoist's thought in his *Killers of the West: The Nietzschean-Heideggerian Right and Left*.[16]

Many of Alain de Benoist's works have been translated into European languages (English, Spanish, Italian, German, and Russian). Only one title has appeared so far in Polish: *Against Liberalism*, translated by Krzysztof Tyszka-Drozdowski.[17] To this day, there is no synthetic, scholarly work on Alain de Benoist's thought on the Polish market. Filling this gap is one of the aims of the present work.

On the whole, the French-language works can be treated as reliable. They exhibit relative objectivity and are as exhaustive as possible. When it comes to English-language works, however, the majority of them are far from objective. Rather, they are expressly one-sided. Firstly, the majority of them reduce the *Nouvelle Droite* to the strictly political layer, almost completely ignoring the philosophical and theological levels. Secondly, their perspectives are expressly reductionist and critical. The analyses they contain ultimately boil down to attempts to prove that the *Nouvelle Droite* is a variant of fascism. The present work takes a different direction.

---

16 A. Wielomski, *Zabójcy Zachodu. Prawica i lewica nietzscheańsko-heideggerystyczna* (Warsaw: 2022).

17 Alain de Benoist, *Przeciw liberalizmowi* (Warsaw: 2022).

METHODOLOGY

B EING A WORK in the field of the political science of religion, the present study is necessarily interdisciplinary. The pioneer of the discipline of the history of ideas, Arthur O. Lovejoy, discerned that historical studies of ideas figure under different names: the history of philosophy, the history of science, ethnography, the history of language, the history of literature, the history of economy, the history of education, historical sociology, and the history of religions.[1] He believed that cultivating the history of ideas within the field of one, narrow specialisation is artificial, but not entirely arbitrary.[2] Such an approach can lead to neglecting essential content that goes beyond any individual scientific discipline.[3] He also emphasised the weight that historical context carries for a work's content and the need to refrain from treating a work in separation from any historical context.[4] A similar opinion was expressed by another historian of ideas, Quentin Skinner,[5] who analogously argued that the context of an historical work should not be passed over even if (but not only because) it is not possible to reconstruct what a given writer was claiming in a manner that is completely free from our own "prejudices" (or "pre-judgements",

---

1 A. O. Lovejoy, *Essays in the History of Ideas* (Baltimore: 2019), 1.
2 Ibid., 2.
3 Ibid., 7.
4 A. O. Lovejoy, "Reflections on the History of Ideas", *Journal of the History of Ideas* 1(1) (1940), 14.
5 D. Łysiak, "*Znaczenie i rozumienie w historii idei. Program Quentina Skinnera*", *Przegląd Prawniczy Uniwersytetu Warszawskiego* 2/2018 (2018), 59.

vide Hans-Georg Gadamer). The very fact of using a given terminology takes place within the scope of a paradigm (whether conscious or not). According to Skinner, one possible danger in the history of ideas is when source materials are studied with paradigms adopted in advance.[6] One practical example of this would be what is called the "mythology of doctrines", or finding in the thought of an author under study a doctrine which the author himself does not necessarily represent. One example of such would be interpreting scattered remarks as exemplifications of some kind of monolithic doctrine from previous history.[7] According to Skinner, every researcher should pose the question to himself: "If all the writers are claimed to have *meant* to articulate the doctrine with which they are being credited, why is it that they so signally failed to do so, so that the historian is left reconstructing their implied intentions from guesses and vague hints?"[8] One can protect oneself from such an approach by being conscious of the paradigms at play and by focusing on what the given thinker really wanted to say. Skinner regarded the most important methodological note to be the thesis that it cannot be said of any creator of ideas that he intended or accomplished something that he himself never would have accepted as an authentic description of what he intended to accomplish.[9] The decisive majority of English-language works on the *Nouvelle Droite* seem not to heed the dangers pointed out by Skinner at all.

Next, it bears underscoring the difference between political science *sensu stricto* and the political science of religion. The former usually focuses on facts, dates, names, etc. In other words, it revolves around concrete details that are perceptible to the naked eye. The task of the political science of religion, in turn, is to reach those facts that cannot be grasped by the naked eye — beliefs, convictions, ideas. Bogumił

---

6 Ibid., 60.
7 Ibid., 61.
8 Q. Skinner, "Meaning and Understanding in the History of Ideas", *History and Theory* 8(1) (1969), 10.
9 Łysiak, "*Znaczenie i rozumienie w historii idei. Program Quentina Skinnera*", 68.

Grott did a great job of formulating this in his article "The Function of Knowledge Derived from Religious Studies in Political Science Studies: Considerations in the Context of Selected Nationalist Doctrines": "Restricting ourselves only to historical events and the institutional forms of state organisations and other strictly political affairs [...], without taking into consideration the systems of values that create types of cultures out of the soil they were born out of, poses a problem that has not been exhausted and described to any satisfactory extent."[10] François' *Les paganismes de la Nouvelle Droite (1980–2004)* and Moos' *Les intellectuels de la Nouvelle Droite et la religion. Histoire et idéologie d'un antichristianisme de droite (1968–2001)* serve as good examples of this difference between political science and the political science of religion. The first focuses on conveying as many facts and details as possible, and in this regard it is necessarily longer. The second, meanwhile, has a more holistic character and prioritises comprehensive understanding by concentrating more on ideas than on facts.

The present work likewise intends to avoid the reductionist framing which, in the present author's judgement, is an inadequate approach in the case of such a complex phenomenon as the *Nouvelle Droite*. After all, the *Nouvelle Droite* is a multi-dimensional intellectual current, and totally focusing on only one aspect (for example, the political sphere) obscures and disfigures more than it clarifies in the picture of this subject. At the same time, this work's ambition is more about shedding light on, structuring, and understanding the topic rather than maximally exhausting it (which, given the immensity of source material, would be a backbreaking task). In this regard, this work adopts a hermeneutic perspective which takes into consideration the approach

---

10 Bogumił Grott, *Funkcja wiedzy religioznawczej w badaniach politologicznych. Rozważania w kontekście wybranych doktryn nacjonalistycznych*" in B. Grott and O. Grott (eds.), *Wiedza religioznawcza w badaniach politologicznych* (Radzymin: 2015), 17. Bogumił Grott is the author of the term "political science of religion" (*politologia religii*). He first used this term in a research project on the significance of religious factors in the ideas and programmes of political parties conduced at Jagiellonian University in 1992–1993.

of Hans-Georg Gadamer. This German philosopher's formulation of hermeneutics constitutes a development of the method of his mentor, Martin Heidegger. Drawing on his predecessor's thought, Gadamer presents the notion of the hermeneutic circle, which he describes in the following manner:

> A person who is trying to understand a text is always projecting. He projects a meaning for the text as a whole as soon as some initial meaning emerges in the text. Again, the initial meaning emerges only because he is reading the text with particular expectations in regard to a certain meaning. Working out this fore-projection, which is constantly revised in terms of what emerges as he penetrates into the meaning, is understanding what is there.[11]

If the priority is understanding, then it is essential to approach the text in a way that is as open as possible, without disfiguring its interpretation by theses which are presumed in advance.

According to the author of *Truth and Method*, understanding lies in creating ever more and ever better projections and constantly revising them. Understanding consists not in an abstract framing of a topic under study, but in the active experience of the subject which, in Gadamer's opinion, is dynamic and constantly points out new perspectives. No text is interpreted exclusively with reference to the context in which it appeared. The condition of the possibility of understanding is the existence of a horizon of thought that is shared by the text and its receiver.[12] It is impossible for the reader to free himself from the convictions that constitute his ways of thinking. However, the reader is capable of changing these convictions under the influence of the text:

---

11 Hans-Georg Gadamer, *Truth and Method*, 2nd ed., trans./ed. Joel Weinsheimer and Donald G. Marshall (London: Bloomsbury, 2020), 279.

12 M. Maszkiewicz, "*Hermeneutyka i teoria intertekstualności jako metodologia badań modernizmu w poezji serbskiej drugiej połowy XX w. na przykładzie cyklu „Deset soneta nerođenoj kćeri Ivana V. Lalicia""* Adeptus. Pismo Humanistów 6 (2015), 4.

> The interpreter's own thoughts too have gone into re-awakening the text's meaning. In this the interpreter's own horizon is decisive, yet not as a personal standpoint that he maintains or enforces, but more as an opinion and a possibility that one brings into play and puts at risk, and that helps one truly to make one's own what the text says.[13]

Therefore, it bears emphasising that understanding is no ordinary historical reconstruction; rather, it concerns the creation of a certain new quality that brings together the meaning contained in the text and the consciousness of the receiver who retrieves this meaning. This process of removing the distance between the time of a text's appearance and the present of its interpretation is, as Gadamer termed it, a "fusion of horizons", that is, the fusion of the historical horizon of the text and the contemporary horizon of its receiver.[14]

To summarise, the present work situates itself in the domain of the political science of religion understood as a subdiscipline of religious studies,[15] and it brings the latter into connection with certain elements from the philosophy of religion.

The objects of this analysis are primary source texts, with detailed consideration paid to the works of Alain de Benoist. In connection with the fact that the *Nouvelle Droite* is still currently active as a movement, it was necessary for this work to demarcate a chronological caesura. Hence, the following timeframe has been adopted to suit this work: the beginning is 1968, when GRECE was founded, and the end is 2006, when Alain de Benoist's last essential book on the subject of

---

13 Gadamer, *Truth and Method*, 406.

14 Z. Pawłowski, "*Metoda historyczno-krytyczna i analiza narracyjna w perspektywie założeń hermeneutycznych*", *Biblica et Patristica Thoruniensia* 11 (2018), 165.

15 For the sake of clarity, let it be said that I am not hereby suggesting that the political science of religion is solely a subdiscipline of religious studies. To the contrary, one can even more often encounter it as a derivative of political science. I consider attempts to finally establish whether the political science of religion is derivative of political science or religious studies to be baseless and pointless. Both religious studies and political science should be treated as the "parents" of the political science of religion.

religion was published, namely *Jésus et ses frères et autres écrits sur le christianisme, le paganisme et la religion* ["Jesus and His Brothers, and Other Writings on Christianity, Paganism, and Religion"].[16] Some sporadic references will also be made to later works. The present work carries out a tri-leveled analysis: the first level consists of the publications of Alain de Benoist (with special attention paid to those on the topic of religion) and other thinkers of the *Nouvelle Droite* who followed de Benoist's line of ideas; the second level consists of interviews with Alain de Benoist (with the aim of more precisely clarifying certain contents of his books); the third level consists of questions posed directly to Alain de Benoist.

This work employs a hermeneutic perspective with the intention of uncovering and bringing into relief the inner meaning of Alain de Benoist's works and pointing out their connections to other texts from the *Nouvelle Droite* circle alongside other currents to which the French author refers. Unlike the majority of hitherto works on the *Nouvelle Droite*, which have treated this phenomenon primarily as a political current, we have adopted an anti-reductionist perspective, which is further qualified by the detailed analysis paid to questions pertaining to the topic of religion. Topics from the domains of urban sociology, the positive sciences, etc., were excluded insofar as such would have been bound up with digressing from the religious studies character of the work at hand. This study also applies the comparative method for the sake of comparing the *Nouvelle Droite* to different as well as related ideational currents.

Terminology

The original term in French is *Nouvelle Droite*. In English translations, the term "European New Right" is often used. The additional qualification of "European" is essential, especially in English, for the sake of

---

16 Alain de Benoist, *Jésus et ses frères et autres écrits sur le christianisme, le paganisme et la religion* (Paris: 2006).

distinguishing the *Nouvelle Droite* from the Anglo-Saxon New Right, which is a strictly conservative-liberal political movement that has nothing in common with the former. The *Nouvelle Droite* is a multidimensional ideational bloc in which politics is only one component element. One could, of course, attempt to point out some kind of main, constitutive element or field that might have conditioned all the rest and imparted its tone. If we look at the *Nouvelle Droite* from such a perspective, then it could be defined — although such would still be a certain simplification — as a "neo-pagan movement".

The term "European New Right" is more often employed as a useful shorthand or simplification; however, as Tomislav Sunic (one of this milieu's most well-known representatives) suggests, such a term was pinned on the movement by its left-wing opponents in the 1970s. Sunic himself does not support the term, instead preferring "New School", "New Tradition", or "Archeofuturism",[17] and at one point he even proposed the term "European Leftist Conservatives".[18] In any case, Sunic writes, "The authors and the ideas presented here are critical of socialism, liberalism, and various other forms of egalitarian beliefs, including the Judaeo-Christian origins of modern democracy".[19]

Apart from the explicitly politically-leaning terminology used by Sunic, the *Nouvelle Droite* is decidedly not a political movement in the conventional sense. It certainly has nothing in common with the so-called Anglo-Saxon "New Right",[20] which is by all means a political movement (Janusz Korwin-Mikke can be considered a representative of this current in Poland). Rather, the *Nouvelle Droite* is a school of thought, an intellectual current, or a metapolitical movement.

---

17 Sunic, "*Wywiad z Tomislavem Suniciem*", 37.
18 Sunic, *Against Democracy and Equality*, 44.
19 Ibid.
20 It should be pointed out, however, that there are representatives of the *Nouvelle Droite* active in the Anglo-Saxon world, such as Greg Johnson, John Morgan, Michael O'Meara, Troy Southgate, etc.

For the sake of the greatest possible terminological precision, it bears dwelling on each of the three notions that make up the name "European New Right", i.e., "European", "New", and "Right". The meaning of the first term is rather clear. The central question of the *Nouvelle Droite*, the question that animates the whole movement, is the problem: "What is Europe?" It is certainly not the "West", as Sunic writes: "It is beyond doubt that the terms West (*l'Occident*) and Westernisation (*occidentalisation*) have undergone a semantic shift. Over the last 40 years, in French they've taken on a negative connotation associated with globalism, vulgar Americanism, thuggish liberalism, and 'market monotheism'."[21]

In this context, then, "European" is a synonym for "continental", that is "non-Anglo-Saxon", and is supposed to be opposite to the "West". The clear differentiation between "Europe" and the "West" is meant to underscore the United States' strong political and cultural penetration of Europe. The entirety denoted by the "West" is understood to mean America and Americanised Europe, the latter of which is seen *sui generis* as a cultural colony of the former. The very notion of the "West" implies a lack of European subjectivity under the decisive dominance of the US.

"Europe" *sensu proprio* is Europe based on its own identity, culture, and axiology, distinct and free from American influences. These influences are multidimensional, i.e., they are not only in the sphere of the economy or politics, but also on the level of philosophy, religion, and, as follows, identity. The *Nouvelle Droite* does not view Europe exclusively in geographical terms. Rather, Europe is a civilisational entity constituted by kin peoples (mainly of Indo-European heritage) and shaped by Greek thought and Roman institutions. This finds reflection in a specific mentality, long-formed institutions and traditions, as well as a common heritage in the broad sense.

---

21   T. Sunic, "*Zachód przeciwko Europie*", *Szczerbiec* 149 (2013), 16.

The term "Right" in the context of the *Nouvelle Droite* is quite debatable and ambiguous. The majority of the conventionally understood European Right would strongly object to the "right-wingness" of this current. Louis Pauwels, the former editor of *Le Figaro* and a sympathiser of the *Nouvelle Droite*, stated: "My positions are those of what we can call the 'new right' and which have nothing to do with the bourgeois, conservative, and reactionary right".[22] Sunic claims that "we are not traditionalists, we are not conservatives in the Catholic sense of the word, modern conservatives, whatever that might mean. [...] Some of my worst enemies are so-called conservatives."[23] It bears keeping in mind that the *Nouvelle Droite* opposes classical French nationalism as well as typically right-wing conservative liberalism along with its cult of capitalist commerce.[24] Why "Right", then?

To put it as simply as possible, the "Right" in *Nouvelle Droite* means no more no less a rejection of egalitarianism.[25] As Alain de Benoist himself put it, he is situated "on the Right" (broadly understood) because the Left represents an egalitarian concept of the world which he does not share and which he defines as the main ideological enemy.[26] From the perspective of the *Nouvelle Droite*, egalitarianism is not so much an ideology or doctrine as much as it is a certain vision of the world, or rather a concept of the world, which is bound up with a specific mentality, a certain mental type. Egalitarianism is a type of transhistorical and meta-doctrinal mentality. It manifests itself as a disposition that can take on different ideological or doctrinal forms in history, forms which can be most heterogenous and even contradictory. Egalitarianism, nevertheless, is their common denomination, and it is seen as something negative because (1) it is foreign to the European spirit (ancient European communities were by nature "organic" and

---

22 Bar-On, *Where Have All The Fascists Gone?*, 84–85.
23 Sunic, "*Wywiad z Tomislavem Suniciem*", 38.
24 Taguieff, *Sur la Nouvelle Droite*, 19.
25 Ibid., 215.
26 Ibid., 214.

therefore hierarchical) and (2) it is of (Judeo-)Christian origin, which is to say that, since "Christianity originated outside of Europe", it is not properly European, for "every people should live by its own rhythm" and "every culture should develop on the basis of the schemata of thought that it itself originated."[27]

Taguieff, the author of a study on the New Right, describes two types of the *Nouvelle Droite*'s self-definition. The first (presented in the above paragraph) is described as a "positional definition", since it defines the *Nouvelle Droite* as "not left" or "anti-left". The second is termed a "conceptual definition", which refers to the *Nouvelle Droite*'s anti-egalitarianism/anti-Christianity.[28] What is essential in this second definition is that anti-egalitarianism and anti-Christianity are treated as synonymous (sic!). For the sake of clarification, let us give the floor to Alain de Benoist:

> The *minimum minimorum* will evidently be to define any current that rejects the left in an *explicit* manner as being of the right. I would like to introduce a restrictive nuance, however. I hereby define *the right*, by pure convention, as the consistent attitude to view the diversity of the world, and by consequence the relative inequalities that are necessarily the product of this, as a positive thing; and the progressive homogenisation of the world, extolled and effected by two-thousand years of egalitarian ideology, as a negative thing. [...] In other words, in my eyes the enemy is not 'the left' or 'communism' or even 'subversion', but rather this *egalitarian ideology* whose formulations, religious or lay, metaphysical or supposedly 'scientific', have continued to flourish for over two thousand years, whose 'ideas of 1789' were but a step, and of which communism and the current subversion are the inevitable outcome.[29]

---

27 Ibid., 73.
28 Ibid., 218.
29 Alain de Benoist, *View from the Right — Volume I: Heritage and Foundations*, trans. Robert A. Lindgren (London: Arktos, 2017), 43; Alain de Benoist, *Vu de droite: Anthologie critique des idées contemporaines* (Paris: 2001), 16.

What, then, is "new" in the *Nouvelle Droite*? Its innovativeness can be formulated fundamentally on two levels: content and method. Besides certain right-wing traits, such as its praise for order, hierarchy, tradition, authority, and its rejection of utopia, the *Nouvelle Droite* nevertheless departs from the orthodox understanding of the right (in content) by its specific pairing of anti-Christianity and anti-egalitarianism. Anti-Christianity constitutes the historical grounding of its anti-egalitarianism, which is the core of the *Nouvelle Droite*'s "right-wingness" *vel* "anti-left-wingness". Thus, anti-Christianity and anti-egalitarianism flow into one. This specific cluster and reduction has its source in the (Nietzschean) genealogical method's grasp of the Judo-Christian roots of the "egalitarian cycle".[30] Defining their right-wingness by means of positioning themselves in opposition to the cluster-pair of Christianity-egalitarianism is therefore the "new" in the "New Right".

When it comes to method, the newness here is based on what could be described as a theoretical taste. The "old right" is characterized as having "lacked culture", i.e., as being indifferent or even averse to the sphere of ideas, culture, intellectualism and intellectuals. The lack of any refined theory or doctrine became one of the reasons for the right's defeat in the cultural field within the past half a century, or even the last two centuries. As Alain de Benoist remarks:

> A right-winger is driven by enthusiasm or indignation, astonishment or disgust, but never reflection. Instead, he reacts. Hence his nearly always emotional reactions to events. Always staying on the surface of phenomena, content with the information in the press, taking up a narrow point of view on every matter, lacking any insight into causes, his naive, even childish manner of reacting is striking. When you point the moon out to them, many right-wingers will look at your finger. History becomes impossible to understand, even when a right-winger constantly refers to it. Hence the popularity of naive conspiracy theories that can lead to genuine madness. Social problems are explained in terms of obscure manipulations by

---

30 Taguieff, *Sur la Nouvelle Droite*, 216.

'unseen conspiracies', 'dark alliances', etc. Because the right is not interested in ideas, it has a tendency to reduce everything to people. Right-wing political movements are above all associated with their founders and they rarely manage to survive without them. Disputes on the right are largely quarrels between individuals repeating the same rumours and slanderous accusations. Analogously, the right's opponents are never systems or ideas, but categories of people put in the role of scapegoats (Jews, *métèques*, 'bankers', Masons, foreigners, 'Trotskyites', immigrants, etc.). The right has difficulty understanding any system that is void of a subject: the systemic effects of the logic of Capital, its structural tensions, the geneses of individualism, the significance of ecological threats, the effects of technological development, etc. The right does not understand that one needs to fight people not because of who they are, but because they support harmful systems of thought and values. In reducing struggle to the level of individuals who aren't liked for who they are, the right tends towards xenophobia or something worse. The right is the great loser of history. It has lost nearly every battle to which it committed itself. The last two centuries for the right are a streak of one defeat after another. This suggests that the victory of its opponents is to a large extent a result of the right's own weaknesses. [31]

At any rate, it needs to be clearly said that the label "European New Right" should be treated with a far-reaching distance. Alain de Benoist does not consider himself to be "right-wing" since at least 1986, nor does he consider himself to be "left-wing". He prefers to speak of himself as a person with "left-wing ideas and right-wing values". He also often highlights the uselessness of the Right-Left axis in describing the contemporary political and ideological spectrum.[32]

Nevertheless, for the sake of summation (while bearing in mind that such is a far-ranging simplification), it would be best to recall the subtle distinction drawn by Alain de Benoist himself in 1977, when he

---

31 A. de Benoist, "*Intelektualna pustka starej prawicy*", *XPortal* [https://xportal.pl/?p=11030] [accessed 14/06/2021].

32 Ibid.

emphasised that his ideas are situated "to the right" (*à droite*) but are not — ontologically and genetically — "of the Right" (*de droite*).[33]

To suit the requirements of the present dissertation, I distinguish between the *Nouvelle Droite* in the strict sense and in the broad sense. I take the *Nouvelle Droite sensu stricto* to be the ideational legacy of GRECE as worked out in *Éléments* and *Nouvelle École*, especially taking into account the work of Alain de Benoist (as the movement's real *spiritus movens*) and those who have followed his line of ideas. I take the *Nouvelle Droite sensu largo* to be the legacy of those who have drawn on the foundations worked out by the GRECE, but with certain obvious divergences in their views in relation to the "Alain de Benoist line" (for example, Guillaume Faye's "Archeofuturism"). The present study focuses on the *Nouvelle Droite sensu stricto*.

---

33   de Benoist, *Vu de droite*, 15; idem, *View from the Right*, vol. I, x.

CHAPTER I

ALAIN DE BENOIST AND GRECE: A PATHWAY OF THOUGHT

ALAIN DE BENOIST describes himself as a passionate and engaged intellectual, but above all as a theoretician who writes mainly on the philosophy of politics and the history of ideas.[1]

Childhood

Alain de Benoist was born on 11 December 1943 in Saint-Symphorien, a small town near Tours, in the very same clinic where Charles Maurras would die 10 years later.[2] De Benoist was born into a bourgeois family of Belgian heritage and aristocratic roots who were naturalised in 1678 as result of the Treaties of Nijmegen.[3] Alain de Benoist says that as a child he had clear blonde hair, was full of energy, but was shy, introverted, and very sensitive.[4] He had a good relationship with his parents, although his father (also named Alain) was often absent from home.[5] Due to his father's work, the whole family moved to Paris when Alain was six years old.[6] He saw his grandparents on his

---
1   Alain de Benoist, *Mémoire vive* (Paris,: 2012), 11.
2   Ibid.
3   Ibid., 13.
4   Ibid., 19–20.
5   Ibid., 21.
6   Ibid., 17.

mother's side, who lived in Rennes, once or twice a year.[7] His grandparents on his father's side had gone their separate ways earlier. Alain de Benoist kept in contact with his grandmother, Yvonne de Benoist, from the house of Druet — and this contact was, as Alain de Benoist says, quasi-permanent. He regularly vacationed at the Avanton castle, his grandmother's summer home. This grandmother was the most important person for him in his childhood, and she exerted the most significant and constant influence on him, including on matters of education.[8] He describes her as eccentric, with a strong personality and much literary and artistic experience. She took him to gardens, parks, and the museums of Paris, and introduced him to painting. As Alain de Benoist puts it, she lived in a state of "permanent exaltation":

> She helped me understand the meaning of the saying '*noblesse oblige*': belonging to the aristocracy does not mean that one has greater privileges or additional rights, but only a greater amount of obligations, more to do than what is obligatory, and to feel more responsible than others. To act in a noble manner [...] is to never be satisfied with oneself, to never think in categories of utility.[9]

As for his grandparents on his mother's side, de Benoist remembers them as being simple people. Thanks to them and their surroundings, he learned how life looks for the "popular class" and how inter-class relations look in reality.[10] The young Alain de Benoist was shocked by the contemptuous manner that common folk were treated, including by his own grandmother. He recalls that she — as was often the case with people from her stratum — was convinced that she was above people from "the people." The very word "people" always had a pejorative sense for her.[11] Her mannerisms towards servants, which were supposed to

---

7 Ibid., 21.
8 Ibid., 22.
9 Ibid., 23.
10 Ibid., 27.
11 Ibid.

underscore social differences, were a clear reflection of this. As Alain de Benoist shares in one anecdote, his grandmother bought two types of candies — cheap ones for the village children and expensive, high-quality ones for him:"When I protested, she responded: 'Those kids are from the people!' I adamantly demanded to share 'candies with children from the people'. Then, in the countries of the Third World as well as among the good French bourgeoisie, I constantly noticed the treatment of servants as lesser beings, as objects. This arrogance and disdain always aroused my ire and disgust."[12]

Alain de Benoist describes himself as a child who was talented in the humanities, but not in the hard sciences.[13] He supposedly taught himself how to read and write on a typewriter. His father had to bring a letter to school explaining that the young de Benoist himself had done his homework on the typewriter.[14] He got started with reading with the books of Jules Verne, Jack London (although not Alexandre Dumas), and the Grimm bothers. Greek myths had the greatest impression on him: "If I had to go to some unpopulated island with only one book, it would be the *Iliad*."[15]

When it comes to religion in the family, de Benoist describes his parents as average practicing Catholics and his father's grandmother as deeply devoted.[16] In his high school years, de Benoist discovered the works of Friedrich Nietzsche, who made a colossal impression on him.[17]

---

12   Ibid., 27–28.
13   Ibid., 32.
14   Ibid., 33.
15   Ibid., 35.
16   Ibid., 46.
17   Taguieff, *Sur la Nouvelle Droite*.

Adolescence

Alain de Benoist describes his youth as incredibly politicised. Like many of the boys of his generation, he was "burning to defend a cause".[18] At the age of 16, half of his fellow students at the Louis-le-Grand lycée were affiliated with a political party. The majority of them were of socialist or communist persuasion. Political engagement was something natural for him. He says that the left seemed to be more interesting in terms of culture and intellect than the conservative right. He was drawn to the theme of class struggle: he couldn't stand the "money system" or "bourgeois philistinism".[19] On the other hand, getting engaged on the left (as he saw in the activism of his peers) seemed to him to be the new form of conformism. He didn't want to be like the others.

De Benoist took an interest in philosophy — he discovered Aristotle, Plato, Descartes, Leibniz, Kant, Hegel, Nietzsche, Marx, Bergson, and Sartre.[20] Philosophy "opened his eyes" and provided points of orientation. The key philosopher of his youth was, of course, Friedrich Nietzsche. Besides the fact that there was a "Nietzschean left" (Bataille, Palante, Klossowski, Deleuze), Nietzsche's thought drew him away from the far left. Among other things, he liked how Nietzsche "called on us to fight against bourgeois conformism from above, not from below".[21] He saw Marxism as a relic of Christian thought, or rather its secularisation. The idea that all people are of identical dignity was shocking to him. In de Benoist's eyes, egalitarian humanism lacked a heroic dimension.

---

18 de Benoist, *Mémoire vive*, 52.
19 Ibid.
20 Ibid., 53.
21 Ibid., 57.

In 1961, de Benoist joined the *Federation des etudiants nationalistes* (FEN, Federation of Nationalist Students),[22] led by François d'Orcival, which was the legal student offshoot of an older organisation, *Jeune Nation* (Young Nation),[23] whose official aim was to "fight against the Marxist takeover of the university" and to support French Algeria.[24] Besides publishing activities, FEN members dabbled in classic activism: handing out leaflets, putting up posters, organising meetings, street fights with political opponents, and taking part in demonstrations. De Benoist recounts: "I loved the electrifying atmosphere of demonstrations, the movement of crowds, the way in which slogans were chanted, clashes with the police, the smell of tear gas. In February 1961, during a demonstration at Place de l'Étoile, I was arrested... My mother who came to pick me up was also arrested!"[25]

In ideological terms, the FEN's important positions were informed by Jacques Ploncard's *Doctrines du nationalism*, George Sorel's

22 The *Fédération des étudiants nationalistes* was a French nationalist students' organisation that was anti-democratic (anti-egalitarian) and anti-communist. Founded by François d'Orcival (a former member of *Jeune Nation*) under the pseudonym "Amaury de Chaunac-Lanzac", the organisation existed from 1960–1967. It was affiliated with *Jeune Nation*, of which it was a legal offshoot. In its later years, it largely adopted the ideological line of *Europe-Action* (with due consideration for the generational age difference) and published a periodical entitled *Cahiers universitaires* ("University Journals"), in which de Benoist was published under the pseudonym "Fabrice Laroche". See Taguieff, *Sur la Nouvelle Droite*, 11, 111–112, 114, 122.

23 *Jeune Nation* was a French nationalist organisation that was integralist and neo-Pétainist. Existing from 1950–1958 (delegalised on 15 May 1958), it arose on the initiative of the Sidos brothers, Pierre and Jacque, and was led by the former. The organisation was significantly influenced by Dominique Venner. See Taguieff, *Sur la Nouvelle Droite*, 113–114.

24 de Benoist, *Mémoire vive*, 61–63.

25 Ibid., 64.

Reflections on Violence, and Vladimir Lenin's *What Is to Be Done?*[26] Instead of "comrade", FEN members addressed each other as "friend".[27]

Adulthood (to 1968)

After finishing high school in 1961, Alain de Benoist enrolled in law studies at the Sorbonne. He also studied philosophy, religious studies, and sociology. He studied up to the bachelor level, but he didn't attend his exams because he didn't want to "collaborate with the system" — which, as he later stated, was completely foolish.[28]

The year 1962 was the beginning, as Alain de Benoist himself defines it, of the *Europe-Action*[29] period. In that year, Dominique Venner[30] was released from prison and decided to found a publishing

---

26 Ibid., 64–65.

27 Ibid., 65.

28 Ibid., 68.

29 *Europe-Action* was a French far-right organisation that was pan-European and anti-immigration. It existed from 1963–1967 and was centred around the journal of the same name. Led by Jacques de Larocque-Latour (pseudonym "Coral"), it was de facto overwhelmingly influenced by Dominique Venner. Its membership included Venner's supporters from *Jeune Nation*, members of the FEN, and remnants of the Secret Army Organisation (OAS). The organisation's programme advocated a "European nationalism" based on the solidarity of White nations, as opposed to classical French nationalism, as well as "biological realism", i.e., biological racism and eugenics. It staunchly opposed Arab-African immigration. Alain de Benoist was one of the group's main collaborators; its members included many future GRECE-ists, such as Pierre Vial, Jean Mabire, Jean-Claude Valla. See Taguieff, *Sur la Nouvelle Droite*, 11–12, 45, 122; R. Cousin, "*Europe-Action*" [https://www.memoiresdeguerre.com/article-europe-action-43458265.html].

30 Dominique Venner (1953–2013) was a French historian and writer. He served as a soldier in Algeria and was a member of the terrorist Secret Army Organisation (*Organisation de l'Armée Secrète*, OAS). He published numerous historical works, such as *Histoire et tradition des Européens* (2002) and received a prestigious award from the French Academy for his book on the Red Army (*Histoire de l'Armée rouge*, 1981). At the age of 78, he shot himself in the Notre-Dame Cathedral in France as an act of protest against what he

house, Saint-Just, and a magazine, *Europe-Action*.³¹ While in prison, Venner had edited a fundamental text that would be released in 1962, the pamphlet *For a Positive Critique*,³² which, according to Alain de Benoist, had a capital influence on their milieux and on himself. The text was a kind of self-criticism of the right, and it was the first to draw a distinction between "nationals" (*nationaux*) and "nationalists" (*nationalistes*), the difference being that the latter are revolutionaries while the former are not. He compares the former to oxen and the latter to bulls. Maintaining a critical position towards the "reactionary right", which was interested exclusively in current affairs, Venner emphasised the importance of long-term formational work to be carried out by conscious and "ideologically structured" activists.³³

What was new in Venner's thought (in relation to the old *Jeune Nation*) was, above all, (a) pan-Europeanism, (b) anti-Christianity, and (c) a quasi-biological conceptualisation of society.³⁴ De Benoist says that the idea of European nationalism found fertile soil in him, as he was not a supporter of classical "Franko-French" nationalism and shallow chauvinism.³⁵ The pan-European orientation of nationalism, the critique of egalitarianism, and calling into question Christian values, which were often described as "oriental" and as responsible for the "fall" of Western man, where what attracted the young de Benoist.³⁶

Alain de Benoist recounts:

---

saw as the "criminal dismantling of European cultural identity". See *"Kim był samobójca z Notre Dame? Dominique Venner: Nacjonalista, który wybrał śmierć samuraja"*, Polska Times [https://polskatimes. pl/kim-byl-samobojca-z-notre-dame-dominique-venner-nacjonalista- ktory-wybral-smierc-samuraja/ar/9o1651/2].

31 de Benoist, *Mémoire vive*, 76.
32 See Dominique Venner, *For a Positive Critique* (London: Arktos, 2017).
33 de Benoist, *Mémoire vive*, 76.
34 Ibid., 77.
35 Ibid.
36 Taguieff, *Sur la Nouvelle Droite*, 186.

When I cross a border, I breathe! This explains my love for voyages and knowing other cultures. Europe, for its part, has always attracted me. In the 1960s, I saw it as a third force, equally as far away from the Eastern bloc as from America. I admire its rich history, the diversity of its components, as well as the polyphony of its landscape. [...] The term 'European nationalism' was certainly unfortunate. A Europe turned into a nation-state — on the basis of the Jacobin model — would be a catastrophe. Nevertheless, it spoke to our feelings on the necessity of leaving French nationalism in order to adopt a somewhat broader perspective [...], to take up as our own [...] not just any singular [mono-national — P. B.] history, but a culture and civilisation from which all European cultures are derived. [...] In *Europe-Action* [...] Christianity was above all defined as a religion that is 'foreign' to Europe by the fact of its roots. This is a perspective that I certainly wouldn't take today: there are non-European religions which seem to me to be better than Christianity. In one way or another, anti-Christianity didn't shock me at all.[37]

A materialistic-biological racism was also present in this ideology, and although it didn't shock Alain de Benoist, he later acknowledged that he was not a fervent supporter of such, and that he now regards such as an error. At the time, however, our French author accepted the idea of race as a fundamental subject of history, although the question of the differences between races was more essential to him than the question of a hierarchy of races.[38]

Europe-Action strongly emphasised the opposition between the West and the Orient. Everything that was Western was regarded as good, and everything Eastern as bad. "East" was taken in broad terms as encompassing the Middle East, India, and the Far East. The term "oriental" was perceived as unambiguously pejorative.[39]

The above-described ideological course (including the critique of Christianity and old French nationalism, which was formulated explicitly in the fifth issue of *Europe-Action*) caused an uproar among the

---

37   de Benoist, *Mémoire vive*, 78.
38   Ibid., 79.
39   Ibid., 78.

cadre. This resulted in a rift in the movement, although the decisive majority supported Venner's new line. The same happened among FEN members, who from that point on became a quasi-branch of *Europe-Action*, but without losing organisational autonomy.[40]

Starting in 1965, Alain de Benoist was increasingly interested in the philosophy of science, archaeology, linguistics, and religious studies. He read Georges Dumézil, Mircea Eliade, Gustave Le Bon, Célestina Bouglé, Félix Dantec, Jean-Marie Guyau, Théodule Ribot, Herbert Spencer, Raymond Ruyer, and Georges Matisse. This was the time when, as a result of his studies in philology, exegesis, dogmatic theology, and, above all, studies on the origins of Christianity, that Alain de Benoist's ideational formation began to take on its pronounced anti-Christian component.[41]

The central figure for him then was Louis Rougier.[42] The latter had rather broad scientific interests, but for de Benoist his most essential works were those on Christianity, of which he was unambiguously critical, as he was an advocate of the Greco-Roman civilisational heritage and identified with Celsus, who accused Christians of being a subversive sect.[43] Rougier's works underscored profound differences between "Middle Eastern" and "European" axiology. As de Benoist recounts, Rougier unconditionally loved Greco-Roman culture, which he appraised above all for its tolerance: "Having no single God, it also had no imposed truth, no dogma, no schisms, no heresies, no

---

40 Ibid. 80.
41 Ibid., 94.
42 Louis Rougier (1889–1982) was a French philosopher, epistemologist, and historian of civilisations who lectured at the University of Caen. He was a member of the Patron's Committee of GRECE and the *Nouvelle École*. He was a rationalist, a supporter of logical positivism, and an anti-Gaullist. His works include *Le génie de l'Occident* [The Genius of the West] (1969), *Le conflit du christianisme primitif et de la civilisation antique* [The Conflict of Early Christianity and Ancient Civilisation] (1977).
43 J. Bartzel, "Louis Rougier", *Myśl konserwatywna* [https://myslkonserwatywna.pl/louis-rougier/].

anathemas, no crusades."[44] Although he was not one of the founders of GRECE, Rougier exerted a significant influence on the *Nouvelle Droite*'s critique of Christianity and maintained constant contact with Alain de Benoist.[45]

According to de Benoist, 1966–67 marked the end of the *Europe-Action* period. At the end of 1966, *Europe-Action* and the Saint-Just publishing house collapsed due to financial troubles.[46] The same happened to the *Mouvement nationaliste du progrès* (MNP)[47] / *Rassemblement europeen de la liberte* (REL),[48] which suffered disgraceful electoral defeat.[49] On 2 July 1967, Venner announced his definitive departure from politics.[50]

As for the question of whether his activism proved to be a waste of time, Alain de Benoist responds:

> It wasn't wasted time. Activism is a school, one of the best there can be. It is a school of discipline and posture, exaltation and enthusiasm, a school of self-dedication. It is also a crucible of friendship, and there are few like it:

---

44 de Benoist, *Mémoire vive*, 94–95.

45 Ibid., 96.

46 Ibid., 97.

47 The *Mouvement nationaliste du progrès* was a French nationalist political grouping that had a pan-European profile and was an offshoot of *Europe-Action*. It was established in January 1966 by leading members of *Europe-Action* (Dominique Venner, Jean Mabire, Pierre Bousquet, etc.) with the participation of young members from the FEN (Alain de Benoist, François d'Orcival, Georges Schmeltz). In November 1966, the MNP regrouped into a political party, *Le Rassemblement européen de la liberté*. See Taguieff, *Sur la Nouvelle Droite*, 11.

48 *Rassemblement européen de la liberté* was a French political party that existed from 1966–1969; it unsuccessfully participated in the March 1967 elections. Within it, an informal group centred around Alain de Benoist (including activists from the FEN and some of the editors of *Cahiers universitaires*, such as Jacques Bruyas, Vincent Decombois, Jean-Claude Bardet, Jean-Claude Valla, Pierre Vial) would later form the backbone of GRECE, which was founded in 1968. See Taguieff, *Sur la Nouvelle Droite*, 11, 13–14.

49 Ibid., 11.

50 de Benoist, *Mémoire vive*, 97.

joint activism creates ties that pass the test of time and, sometimes, prevail over everything. One does, of course, harbour many illusions, believing that if only one squeezed one's fist tighter, the more men could be mobilised, but this also harbours a sense of meaning of one's own existence. However, it is a school which one needs to know when to leave: there is nothing funnier than old activists repeating the same slogans as decades ago [...]. Activism has its limitations. It has its drawbacks. An activist is not only someone who completely offers himself up, which is a good thing; he is also a partisan in the worst sense of the word. He repeats a catechism and refers to a collective 'we' which absolves him of any personal reflection. The 'good activist' is a 'true believer' who prefers answers to questions, for he needs certainties. [...] He does not belong to those who seek truth, but to those who seek faith. And, like all believers, he sets aside any critical thinking so as to bask in his sectarianism.[51]

Seeing the downfall of activism, Alain de Benoist decided to start from scratch.[52] He was 23 then. In early autumn 1967, he spent a week in a hotel in Denmark, on the Baltic coast, in order to hone his ideas and think through his next steps: "Pursue a 'theoretical' existence, as Aristotle said, but how?"[53] Alain de Benoist had no intent of creating a "catechism"; instead, he endeavoured to propose a pathway of thought.

A few weeks later, he organised a meting with around 200 colleagues in an old barn in Vendée, on the same grounds that the FEN had used for training camps.[54] It was at this meeting that the idea of creating the magazine *Nouvelle École* appeared.[55] It would be a journal

---

51   Ibid., 83–84.
52   Ibid., 103.
53   Ibid., 104.
54   Ibid.
55   *Nouvelle École* defined its two main tasks as follows: (1) providing a forum for the study and analysis of diverse topics advanced by, among others, world class scholars, the aim being to discover and establish a certain number of leading principles for the philosophical, scientific, and juridical life of the West; (2) fighting for freedom, which for European civilisation is a key value, and unmasking those who call into doubt the centuries-old values of the Weset, its originality, creativity, significant contribution, and position — *Nouvelle École* 1

containing exclusively theoretical texts, not on current affairs. The title was meant to refer to Georges Sorel and his "new school" of revolutionary syndicalism, as well as to insinuate its academic-scholarly character. Issue 0 (on Marxism) was followed by issue 1 in February 1968, which was published by the cottage industry method.[56] De Benoist initially envisioned *Nouvelle École* as a "flagship" publication that could direct the "fleet" of a greater number of specialised journals aimed at defined targets, i.e., an archeological journal, a religious studies journal, a journal on the hard sciences, etc. However, none of the latter ever came out.[57]

According to Alain de Benoist, his collaborators convinced him that, in addition to the journal itself, a certain organisational structure was needed. He suggested that the acronym of such an association have an obvious symbolic meaning. Moreover, he opted for the logo to refer to Celtic-Irish art and to be sufficiently complicated so as to not be copiable and paintable on walls.[58] The *Groupement de Recherche et d'Études pour la Civilisation Européenne* (Research and Study Group on European Civilisation), or GRECE, was provisionally constituted in January 1968 in Nice.[59] The official founding congress was held in Lyon on 4–5 May 1968, and the organisation was registered in January 1969.[60]

(1968) in Taguieff, *Sur la Nouvelle Droite*, 166–167. Starting in 1970, *Nouvelle École* had a Patron's Committee that included representatives of the radical right like Jean Mabire and Ronald Gaucher, as well as scholars, writers, and philosophers, such as the British geneticist Cyril Dean Darlington, the scholar of religions Mircea Eliade, the sociologists Julien Freund and Jules Monnerot, the philosopher Louis Rougier, professor of history Marcel Le Daly, the writers Arthur Koestler, Louis Pauwels, Thierry Maulnier, and Raymond Abellio. See P. Milza, *Fascisme français. Passé et présent* (Champs: 1987), 372–373.

56 Taguieff, *Sur la Nouvelle Droite*, 166–167.
57 de Benoist, *Mémoire vive*, 105.
58 Ibid., 105–106.
59 Taguieff, *Sur la Nouvelle Droite*, 165.
60 Ibid.; de Benoist, *Mémoire vive*, 105.

During the creation of GRECE, de Benoist initially invited old FEN activists. Their meeting in Lyon in May 1968 was attended by 36 people (including, among others, Alain de Benoist, Jacques Bruyas, Pierre Marcenet, Jean-Jacques Mourreau, and Jean-Pierre Toni), of whom 27 from FEN and *Cahiers Universitaires* became the "founding group".[61] Already a year later, three-fourths of them had left the ranks of the association, as they weren't interested in working on ideas.

Alain de Benoist initially envisioned GRECE as a kind of synthesis of the Frankfurt School, *Action Française*, and the *Centre National de la Recherché Scientifique*.[62] "Evidently, however", he recalls, "it was necessary to lower expectations."[63] Nevertheless, GRECE rather quickly caught wind in its sails, and in the early '70s branches appeared in Paris, Bordeaux, and even on the island of Reunion.[64] In addition to *Nouvelle École*, autumn 1968 saw the founding of a second periodical, *Éléments*, at first for internal use, but later changed into a magazine for the broader public.[65] The '70s also saw the publication of other specialist periodicals, such as *Nouvelle Éducation*, directed by Fabrice Valclérieux, which was intended for teachers, and *Nation-Armée*, for military men, on the initiative of Philippe Conard. In addition, symposia, conferences, and educational seminars were organised on diverse topics: philosophy, the life sciences, religious studies, archaeology, psychology, social sciences, etc.

GRECE was constituted as a centralised, hierarchical structure centred around Alain de Benoist himself. Besides founding members, one could join the think tank as a titular member, an affiliated member, or as an assistant member. Membership type was connected to the order in which members joined the organisation as well as with

---

61 de Benoist, *Mémoire vive*, 106.
62 The *Centre National de la Recherché Scientifique* is France's equivalent of other countries' Academy of Sciences.
63 de Benoist, *Mémoire vive*, 109.
64 Ibid., 108.
65 Ibid., 109.

their level of active engagement and loyalty. The GRECE leadership was structured in the form of a pyramid consisting of a Command, Cente, and Chancellery (the top). The think tank was governed by two secretariats — one responsible for studies and research, and the other for administrative-financial questions. There also existed a disciplinary commission that wielded a range of possible sanctions (admonition, reprimand, public condemnation, disciplinary suspension and expulsion). Thanks to this, GRECE structures turned out to be relatively durable and stable, and leadership changes were small.[66]

GRECE members saw themselves *sui generis* as a new social (counter-)elite, which by way of working in the sphere of culture could effect a revaluation of the common norms current in political and cultural life. Discarding the combination of loud, confrontational, militaristic nationalism, racism, and authoritarianism that was typical of the radical Right, the organisation adopted the strategy of a slow, long-term process of winning public opinion. In order to achieve this goal, it adopted the principle of acting within socially accepted boundaries and not, as a point of programme, creating a strictly political movement, but rather a quasi-academic research institute and cultural organisation that did not (at least openly) posit political aims. The aim was to create an intellectual counter-cultural movement against the Left that had managed to dominate the sphere of culture.

GRECE and May '68

It bears paying attention to the fact that the emergence of GRECE cannot be treated as a *sui generis* right-wing reaction to May '68, given that the provisional secretariat of GRECE had already been constituted on 15 January 1968,[67] and the first official issue of *Nouvelle École* is dated February-March 1968. The founding meeting of GRECE took

---

66 J. Stobiecki, "*Alain de Benoist i Francuska Nowa Prawica — twórcy prawicowej strategii metapolitycznej*", Przegląd Politologiczny 2/2003 (2003), 28.

67 Taguieff, *Sur la Nouvelle Droite*, 10.

place before the eruption of May '68, and the latter began only halfway into May. The appearance of the New Right cannot, therefore, be seen as a reaction to the New Left, even though one might notice certain similarities between the two movements. Rather, the matter at hand was a new generation that wanted to stake out its relation to the old order, create its own particular discourse, and gain its own voice. As Alain de Benoist recalls:

> May 1968, as is too often forgotten, was above all the last great general strike of the working class, and I, as a faithful reader of Sorel, could only be happy about this. I felt sympathy for the anarchists, but above all for the Maoists who hoped to import 'cultural revolution' to France [...]. In that period, I wasn't yet ready to analyse and draw conclusions out of the whole turmoil. Only later did I realise that there were essentially two different May 68s. On the one hand, there was the radical critique of the consumer society, the society of the spectacle, and commercial values, and I sympathised with it. On the other hand, there was the pseudo-revolution of 'desire' [...] which, under the cover of radical slogans, concealed the individualism of a spoiled child. Unfortunately, the second tendency gained the upper hand. The 'desirous' of May quickly figured out that it was capitalism and the consumer society that could give them the best opportunity to satisfy their drives. Of course, they passed to the side of the market society and the principles of economic liberalism [...] and were the natural successors of the 'liberalisation of customs'. The 'converted' subsequently became the propagators of 'humanitarianism' and the ideology of human rights. There is an evident kinship between the '*bobos*'[68] and the second May '68. Towards these people I feel only disgust.[69]

As for these "converts", Alain de Benoist outright calls them "traitors". He recounts that many former May '68 leaders ("left-wing revolutionaries" in their time) landed in comfortable positions in ministries and

---

68 Bobo (*bourgeois bohème*) is a pejorative term for a (usually young) person from the French middle class with left-liberal political beliefs. The Polish equivalent is *leming*, i.e., "young, educated person from a big city".

69 de Benoist, *Mémoire vive*, 107–108.

other state institutions.[70] Although he did not share their ideals, de Benoist felt a certain dose of sympathy for those days' dissidents. A word of clarification is required here. De Benoist drew a fundamental distinction between two types of rightists in those times. The first, although they didn't exude sympathy for bourgeois society, still regarded communism as worse.[71] The second, for whom bourgeois society was enemy number one, saw communists more as competitors than sworn enemies.

> I fought against Marxism as a false idea, but I was never a rabid anticommunist. I am convinced that anyone who wants to overthrow bourgeois society is objectively an ally, or in the very least has convergent aims. [...] In a situation when the 'radicals' are fighting amongst themselves [...], the capitalist world can sleep peacefully: its enemies are squabbling amongst themselves.[72]

Our French author believes that the May '68 revolt was less of a rebellion against the spirit of the times than a product (side effect) of it, as it did not call anything into doubt on a fundamental level. The revolt provoked unrest, but riots should not be mistaken for revolution. The dissent was not against the system of values of French society. It was about society supposedly having betrayed these values. The point was to bring these values — Freedom, Equality, Fraternity — back to life. "The thought never occurred to them that, besides 'authority', the very 'content' itself could be called into question."[73] Only the *Nouvelle Droite* became the first to do so.

What the French thinker shared with the protesters of the day was their distaste for the liberal-capitalist status quo and the desire

---

70 Alain de Benoist, "*Mai 68*" in idem, *C'est-à-dire. Entretiens — Témoignages — Ex plications*, vol. 2 (Paris, 2006), 241).

71 "Left with no choice, they became the system's guard dogs." — de Benoist, "*Mai 68*", op. cit., 238.

72 Ibid.

73 Alain de Benoist, *Les Idées à l'endroit* (Paris: 1979), 287.

to create a new, anti-liberal, anti-materialist order.[74] For de Benoist, the main enemy was and is liberalism, which is at present the most dangerous variant of egalitarianism.[75]

Summary

The creation of GRECE was the result, and an attempt to respond to, a series of disastrous failures suffered by the French national right: the delegalisation of *Jeune Nation*, the collapse of the *Organisation de l'Armée Secrète*, the electoral catastrophe of the *Mouvement nationaliste du progrès / Rassemblement européen de la liberté*, as well as the de facto collapse of *Europe-Action*.[76] As Jakub Stobiecki has observed, the appearance of GRECE can also be considered a response to the failure of the French right *sensu largo*, i.e., to the question "what is to be done?" in the face of France's defeat in the Algerian War and the right's loss in the parliamentary and presidential elections. These events compelled a serious reevaluation of hitherto activities, views, and *modi operandi*. The new generation realised that change was needed in the ideological field, as the doctrinal sterility had already caused a lack of effectiveness in both the theoretical and practical field. GRECE was supposed to remediate all of this.[77]

In Taguieff's opinion, there is no doubt that Alain de Benoist was responsible for an ideological and strategic pivot in 1968–69, the culmination of which was the founding of GRECE.[78] His definitive role was marked by two publications: *Les Indo-Européens* (1965) and *Qu'est-ce que le nationalisme?* ["What Is Nationalism?"] (1966), the latter of which redefined nationalism as a concept of the world based on the

---

74 Bar-On, *Where Have All The Fascists Gone?*, 62.
75 Alain de Benoist, "L'ennemi principal" in *Éléments pour la civilisation européenne* 41 (1982), 39.
76 Taguieff, *Sur la Nouvelle Droite*, 10–11.
77 Stobiecki, *Alain de Benoist i Francuska Nowa Prawica*", 28.
78 Ibid., 14.

"natural facts of life", which implied distinguishing between human races, cultural differences, and incongruent systems of values:

> A race constitutes a single whole which [...] contains all kinds of individual differences. Objective studies of history show that only the European race (the white, Caucasian race) has been constantly developing since the moment it appeared [...] unlike the races that have been in stagnation and therefore practically going backwards. The main reason for the progress of the European race lies in the fact of the cumulation of its scientific and technological achievements which have constituted Western civilisation. The European race has no absolute superiority. It simply has the greatest capacity for progress in the evolutionary sense [...]. Racial factors are statistically hereditary, and every race possess a psychology proper to it. This psychology is the source of its value.[79]

The above biological-racial notion of a people reveals a clear ideational affiliation with the "European nationalism" put forth by Dominique Venner and clearly contrasts the classical French nationalism of Charles Maurras or Maurice Barrès. Yet, it would be erroneous to define GRECE as merely a prolonging of *Europe-Action*. Apart from certain similarities, the differences between the "schools" of Venner and de Benoist are evident and clear. At the very outset, it needs to be remembered that GRECE has existed incomparably longer than *Europe-Action* (the latter existed for barely five years, the former is more than 50 years old), hence even a cursory comparison of both groups must bear in mind the progressive ideational evolution of GRECE. It's also noteworthy that, contrary to appearances, Venner was not one of the founders of GRECE, and neither was he a representative of the *Nouvelle Droite sensu stricto*, even though, on the other hand, there is no doubt that *Europe-Action* prepared the ground for GRECE, and Venner himself can be recognised as a precursor of the *Nouvelle Droite*. The ideational divergence between *Europe-Action* and GRECE is fundamentally rooted in two fields: content and method.

---

79 Alain de Benoist, *Qu'est-ce que le nationalisme* (Paris: 1966), 8–9, quoted in Taguieff, *Sur la Nouvelle Droite*, 15.

Although anti-egalitarianism was mentioned in the previous chapter as being constitutive of the *Nouvelle Droite*, it was not, however, decisive, since opposition to egalitarianism was widespread throughout the French radical right in the '60s-'70s. On the level of content, it was the development and deepening of the radical critique of "Judeo-Christianity", and the accompanying redefinition of "paganism" (along with the later adoption of the Dumézilian trifunctional model as a normative fact) that distinguished Alain de Benoist's ideological line in the midst of other right-wing anti-liberal and anti-democratic groups.[80] The discovery of Georges Dumézil's research allowed them to reformulate hitherto European-nationalist doctrine as "Indo-European", and to pass from the doctrine of "defending the West" to "Indo-European heritage", which was supposed to be the basis of the specificity of a certain "mentality" (see *Nouvelle École* 21–22 from October 1972-February 1973). This transition and this concentration on (Indo-)Europeanness allowed for the creation of a new antithesis: Europe vs. the West (symbolised by the US) instead of the West vs. the East. This ideational metamorphosis would fully crystallise only in the late 1970s.[81]

Along with this change on the level of ideas, there also came a change in method and strategy. All of the undertakings in which Alain de Benoist had taken part up to this point were typical radical right-wing projects, i.e., they concentrated strictly on the political sphere, activism, and had a basically anti-intellectual character, their publications being of a political-pamphleteer tone. First of all, with the founding of GRECE, de Benoist broke with anti-intellectualism and introduced — through the publishing houses he directed — a scholarly-academic discourse; second, he completely resigned from activism and party politics in favour of being active in the sphere of culture and

---

80 Ibid., 186.
81 Ibid., 174.

ideas, working through a "metapolitical"[82] strategy, one also known as "Gramscianism from the right" or "right-wing Gramscianism".[83] De Benoist points out:

---

82 J. Bartyzel, *"Metapolityka"* [http://www.legitymizm.org/ebp-metapolityka]: "Metapolitics (German *Metapolitik*, French *métapolitique*, Italian *metapolitica*, Spanish *metapolítica*, from the Greek *metá*, "beyond", "after", and *politiká*) is the interdisciplinary, theoretico-practical knowledge of the pre-political foundations and final aim of politics as considered from the standpoint of viewing human culture as a whole in the light of natural law as well as with reference to that which is supra-natural; [metapolitics] also intentionally describes the rules of political order necessary for the existence of a good society; in other words, it is a philosophy of politics which contains a theory of being (metaphysics), a theory of knowledge (epistemology) and a theory of values (axiology), and thus also usually passes into political theology."

83 Antonio Gramsci (1891–1937) was an Italian politician, writer, philosopher, and Marxist theoretician. He is most well known for his concept of cultural hegemony, which overturned the orthodox Marxist order of the relations between base and superstructure by recognising the primacy of the latter. Gramsci described how the bourgeoisie uses cultural institutions to maintain power in capitalist societies. In his opinion, it is not violence but cultural power and ideology that is key to maintaining power. Cultural hegemony propagates norms and values in such a way that they are seen as "normal" and "common sense". See P. Śpiewak, *Gramsci* (Warsaw: 1977), 80–81: "In continuing the discussion on Gramsci's views on revolution, it is necessary to […] dwell on the problem of the intellectual […]. Along with the formation of a sense of internal solidarity within a given dependent class, there is also an awakening of its own consciousness of its historical personality, and there emerges an intelligentsia stratum that is specific to this group. It gives this class a full feeling of the uniformity of its aims and aspirations, develops its consciousness of its economic, social, and political role in the State, works out a strategy of political struggle, and creates a class ideology. Gramsci called the group of intellectuals who directly identify with this class's interests organic intellectuals. Hence, for instance, the capitalists create their own organisers of economic life, theoreticians of political economy, and organisers of culture. […] The aim of the journal *L'Ordine Nuovo* was to create a group of working class intellectuals, to work out a strategy of revolutionary struggle and philosophical doctrine, and to shape public opinion. Organic intellectuals are an active group of activists and thinkers who are directly bound to the interests of their class and who openly operate in favour of this class, seizing and maintaining political and cultural hegemony within the State."

[The term 'metapolitics'] is often misunderstood, especially by those who are convinced that "metapolitics" is merely another means of politics. In reality, just as metaphysics does not have much in common with physics, so is metapolitics situated, without a doubt, beyond politics. This term is by no means new, as it can be found in 1784 in Jean-Louis de Lolme, a student of Montesquieu. Joseph de Maistre defined it in 1814 as the 'metaphysics of politics' [...]. I used the term to justify intellectual work in the eyes of those who [...] were constantly still too attached to the political perspective. I proceeded from the assumption that there is no effective action without a well-structured theory ('One cannot put the cart in front of the horse'). The French Revolution as we know it would not have happened if its roads had not been cleared by the philosophers of the Enlightenment; there would be no Lenin without Marx, and so on.[84]

In short, metapolitics is "the domain of values which do not involve immediate political issues but which act indirectly on the political consensus".[85] The "metapolitical" strategy is based on the assumption that acquiring cultural and ideological hegemony is a prior, necessary condition of gaining political power. Hence the weight of "cultural struggle" and the central role of intellectuals (instead of politicians or activists). It is this conviction, this will of ideological counterattack against the cultural left, that was the cornerstone of GRECE.[86] The *Nouvelle Droite* de facto became — against the backdrop of the broader landscape of the French right — a third voice alongside conservative liberalism and revolutionary nationalism.[87]

To sum up, GRECE departed from the line of *Europe-Action* on two fundamental levels: (a) its philosophical interests were above strictly political ones; (b) its metapolitical strategy, or its cultural offensive against the "intellectual terrorism" of the New Left.[88] The *Nouvelle*

---

84 de Benoist, *Mémoire vive*, 111–112.
85 Jean-Claude Valla, quoted in Michael Walker, "Spotlight on the French New Right", *The Scorpion* 10 (1986).
86 Taguieff, *Sur la Nouvelle Droite*, 165.
87 Ibid., 164.
88 Ibid.

Droite's innovativeness lies in that it was a group that decided — in contrast to other right-wing groups — to take up the struggle against the left in the field of ideas and culture. GRECE was supposed to fill the "gap" or the "intellectual vacuum" of the "old right". As Alain de Benoist says:

> The right has never been fond of intellectuals. It is not strange that the expression 'left-wing intellectual' has long since been a tautology. For many right-wingers, intellectuals are simply intolerable. They imagine them to be prudes sprawled on long chairs picking the wings off flies, splitting hairs, and publishing books that are invariably described as boring and indigestible. This kind of thinking is widespread in many milieux [...]. We can define the intellectual as a person who wants to understand and wants others to understand as well. The right very often does not even try to understand. It ignores the possibilities created by mental effort. In effect, right-wing culture today is a phenomenon that practically doesn't exist. It persists only in closed circles and among marginal publishers and newspapers, which only right-wingers recognise to be the right newspapers. The ostracism to which the right has been subjected is not the only factor that has led to this [...][89]

According to de Benoist, cultural power (exerted by intellectual elites, creators of culture, scholars, journalists, etc.) has become more important than political power, as those who control culture and the media are in a position to shape collective consciousness and — as follows — political preferences. The only thing that the right can do in such a situation is to establish the priority of seizing "cultural hegemony". This is a necessary condition for eventually seizing political power.[90] From the *Nouvelle Droite*'s perspective, the main cause of European right-wing conservative groups' lack of success was that they didn't manage to "successfully infiltrate the cultural level of society in order to introduce another 'counter-ideology' to the masses".[91] If the right is supposed to gain power, then it would need in advance to create a

---

89 de Benoist, "*Pustka intelektualna starej prawicy*".
90 Alain de Benoist, *Orientations pour des années décisives* (Paris: 1982), 12.
91 Sunic, *Against Democracy and Equality*, 70.

refined doctrine on a high theoretical level and work out a cultural strategy with the aim of undermining the cultural hegemony of the left. Unlike the left (which always appreciated the role of cultural institutions), the right naively thought that everything boils down to the economy, hence there is no point in attaching too much importance to culture. In the *Nouvelle Droite*'s appraisal, appreciating the weight of culture and political myths is key to seizing and maintaining power.

In connection with this, the *Nouvelle Droite* adopted Antonio Gramsci's understanding of the role of the intellectual. This Italian communist did not see the intellectual as any ordinary expert. Instead, he outlined the concept of the "organic intellectual" who is not only an expert, but a tribune of the people, a representative of the opinion-creating elite. According to Gramsci, intellectuals are the "officers" of the ruling class whose task is to uphold cultural hegemony. In other words, the intellectuals' role is to shape the consensus that is "given" by the masses (as shaped by these intellectuals). From this perspective, political struggle (or, more broadly, the process of acquiring power) is to be seen as a total process encompassing not only parliamentary politics, but also the spheres of education, the media, science, etc.

The liberal right's great mistake was their absolutisation of the economic question and their virtually complete neglect of the sphere of culture. The *Nouvelle Droite* current, in line with the Gramscian perspective, believes that promoting an intellectual counter-culture inside the current liberal system is key to gaining cultural hegemony.[92]

---

92 Ibid., 71.

CHAPTER II

THE *NOUVELLE DROITE*: THE EVOLUTION AND ANATOMY OF IDEAS

The Ideational Evolution of the *Nouvelle Droite*

THE *Nouvelle Droite* is a difficult current to unambiguously classify because, among other reasons, it has undergone fundamental changes over the course of its existence. One could even say that it has undergone a kind of evolution. As Alain de Benoist himself has said, periodisation is necessary for understanding the current.[1] He divides the history of the *Nouvelle Droite* into three basic periods:

> 1. The early period, which covers the 1970s, was the period of "systematic exploration of the ideological landscape" with inevitable ambiguities and a certain theoretical fluidity; this period concluded with the end of collaboration with *Figaro-Magazine* (at the turn of the '70s-'80s).
>
> 2. The middle period lasted up to the founding of the periodical *Krisis* in 1988, and was above all a period of "clarification and working through".
>
> 3. The mature period, which started in the 1990s (and is still ongoing), saw the *Nouvelle Droite*'s intellectual creativity attain "its highest level".[2]

Taguieff, for his part, distinguishes four periods of the *Nouvelle Droite*:

---

1 de Benoist, *Mémoire vive*, 112–113.
2 Ibid., 113.

1. 1968–1972 was the first period in which a doctrinal corpus begin to take shape, the emphasis falling on inequality (inter-individual and inter-ethnic) and genetic determination. A positivistic and scientific perspective dominated. The foremost themes were: hereditary intelligence, physical anthropology, and "scientistic raciology" (or simply biological racism). Marxism-Leninism and communist movements were positioned as the main enemy.

2. 1972–1979 was the period of the "first doctrinal fixation", where the emphasis fell on elitism, hierarchy, and the destructive influence of "Judo-Christianity" on the culture of Europe. Doctrinal particularity was constituted by consolidating anti-egalitarianism, "European paganism", and a kind of "Nietzschean neo-aristocratism" appended with a "differentialist anti-racism" (1975) and the "'scientific' doctrine of European cultural identity" (the integration of Georges Dumézil's work into the *Nouvelle Droite*'s corpus of ideas), which led to the birth of a "culturalism of the right". Egalitarianism of monotheistic origin was designated as the main enemy.

3. 1979–1983. This period was the moment of doctrinal readaptation (the beginning of which can be seen in the publication of de Benoist's *Les idées à l'endroit*[3]), where the emphasis fell on the diversity of cultures and identities, which are appraised as inherently good within the framework of ethnopluralism and "radical cultural relativism" borrowed from (far) left thought. "Western universalism" was contested and assessed as "ethnocidal". Signs of an ideological "de-rightisation" could be seen for the first time in decisive opposition to liberal capitalism and economism and the rejection of (socio-)biological reductionism. An explicit "anti-totalitarianism" crystallised and was followed by developing the "differentialist" theme, i.e., defending the "cause of peoples" (*la cause des peuples*) and the "rights of peoples" against "human rights" (which are rejected for being an ideological instrument of "Western imperialism"). The main enemy became the United States, which symbolised "occidentalism, Americanism, Atlanticism, universalism, cosmopolitan liberalism, and market ideology".

4. 1984–1987 was the period of a second ideological fixation, the main themes of which were: "differentialist third-worldism", "right-wing postmodernism", and the category of the sacred (*sacrum*), the latter of which was seen as the foundation of "deep" European identity. Although there was an abundance of tendencies and a kind of "blurring of the basic consensus",

---

3   "Ideas Set Straight".

among the leadership cadre of the *Nouvelle Droite*, a certain dominating orientation[4] took shape that was centred around defending autochthonous identities and roots and underscoring the cardinal value of cultural differences against all homogenising currents and ideologies (such as in the guise of the "American-Soviet condominium"). The *Nouvelle Droite* positioned itself as advocating diversity and tolerance against "imperialist uniformity and the deculturation of peoples". The main metapolitical goal was upholding the existing differentiation of cultures with the aim of preserving diversity in the world. There appeared the postulate of an alliance between Europe (liberated from American influence) and the Third World against two (hostile) blocs: the Western-liberal and Eastern-communist.[5]

In turn, Stéphane François distinguishes three periods in the evolution of the *Nouvelle Droite*:

1. 1968–1979 — the first period is characterised by European "nationalism", the critique of egalitarianism in the guise of Christianity, a non-linear concept of time (whether circular or cyclical) inspired by Nietzsche's thought, praise for paganism (of Indo-European provenance), anti-universalism, anti-occidentalism, equating the West with the United States, anti-liberalism, and regionalism. The years 1968–1972 clearly stand out for their pro-Western racialism, scientism, strong anti-Marxism, anti-technocratism, and "romantic vision of revolution". In the latter (sub-)period, GRECE was still under the strong influence of *Europe-Action*.[6]

2. 1979–1989 — in the second period, the *Nouvelle Droite* adopted a more "holistic" direction, a more clear-cut affirmation of paganism and anti-occidentalism came to the fore, the West was identified with deculturation-Americanisation, and there appeared the postulate of organic democracy and differentials. GRECE exhibited a hostile attitude towards materialism, capitalism, globalisation, the consumer society, and the US. Modern individualism was contrasted to the holism of traditional societies (Louis Dumont), while the critique of egalitarianism was somewhat softened, since an overly systematised anti-egalitarianism could lead to affirming social Darwinism in the guise of liberal capitalism, axiomatising interest and

---

4 First and foremost, Alain de Benoist and Guillaume Faye.
5 Taguieff, *Sur la Nouvelle Droite.*, 68–69.
6 Stéphane François, *Les paganismes de la Nouvelle Droite*, 24–25.

market competition as mechanisms of selections. Alain de Benoist gradually departed from Nietzsche's thought in favor of Heidegger. In the early '80s, as a project of renovating its discourse, the *Nouvelle Droite* committed itself to promoting its own peculiar neo-paganism,[7] which supposedly resulted in an anti-totalitarian and "tolerant" attitude. In the second half of the '80s, the role of the *Nouvelle Droite*'s main enemy (instead of Judeo-Christian egalitarianism) was assumed by liberal utilitarianism.[8]

3. 1990-present — explicitly far-right inspirations disappear in favor of a more "left" orientation. Alain de Benoist describe his views as anti-individualist, anti-nationalist, anti-ethnocentric, anti-capitalist, localist, and communitarian. In 1991, a manifesto was published for the first time,[9] which postulated: strong identities against rootlessness; the right to difference against racism; cooperation against immigration; gender against sexism; autonomy from the bottom vs. the "New Class" (Christopher Lasch); a federal Europe against Jacobinism; strengthening democracy against depoliticisation; the division of labor as opposed to the logic of capital; organic economy vs. the cult of market values; local communities vs. Gigantism; cities of a human scale vs. megalopolises; integral ecology against demonic productivity; independence of thought and returning to the discussion of ideas.[10]

The above classifications do not exhibit any significant differences. Both of the academic works cited were published when the *Nouvelle Droite* had already adopted its "later" guise (Taguieff's in 1995, François's in 2005). Like Alain de Benoist, François divides the *Nouvelle Droite*'s corpus into three basic periods. By comparison, Taguieff assigns more weight to certain nuances. However, the creation of as many as four phases in the *Nouvelle Droite*'s evolution does not seem to be sufficiently justified. The last two phases outlined by Taguieff do not manifest any fundamental differences. The fourth phase he proposes

---

7   Ibid., 46.
8   Ibid., 49.
9   Alain de Benoist and Charles Champetier, "*Manifeste. La Nouvelle Droite de l'an 2000*", *Éléments pour la civilisation européenne* 94 (1999), 11–23.
10 François, *Les paganismes de la Nouvelle Droite*, 60–61.

is more of a development or complement of the third phase rather than something completely separate. What might eventually have some grounds would be his perception of the "(sub-)period" in the beginning of the *Nouvelle Droite* (1968–1972), when GRECE was still strongly influenced by *Europe-Action*. On the other hand, the essence of the early period *sensu largo* (from 1968 to the turn of the '70s and '80s), as Alain de Benoist points out, was the search for their own ideational path and (out of necessity) a certain fluidity. In this regard, dividing the *Nouvelle Droite*'s evolution as a current into three periods seems to be the most optimal variation.

To sum up, GRECE in its initial period was still clearly influenced by *Europe-Action* ("European" nationalism, defending the West, scientism, anti-Marxism, etc.); not long thereafter followed the clarification of its first proper features, i.e., its merging of "European paganism" and anti-egalitarianism and, likewise, its equating of Christianity with egalitarianism. This was the early period of "wandering and searching" (1968–1979). Subsequently, it adopted a holistic, anti-totalitarian (supposedly stemming from "paganism"), and differentialist (the emphasis being more on diversity/pluralism than on hierarchy), and (populist-) democratic position, and it began to concentrate its critique on liberalism more than egalitarianism. This was the transitional period (1979–1989) in which the ideational specificity of the *Nouvelle Droite* took shape. The last (or rather latest) phase in this evolution is marked by an obvious "left" turn (of an alter-globalist shade), wherein right-wing elements (like ethnocentrism, nationalism, hierarchy, etc.) have been subject to significant blurring or even elimination. Although he remains critical towards mass immigration, Alain de Benoist accepts the right of the immigrant population to preserve its own culture and presence in the public space (in contrast to the homogenising "Jacobin" centralism).[11] This is the mature phase in which the the

---

11   Alain de Benoist, "*Racisme et xénophobie*" in idem, *C'est-à-dire*, vol. 2, 213.

Nouvelle Droite's ideas took on their final form and essentially haven't undergone any further ideological formation (from 1990 to present).

The evolution of the *Nouvelle Droite*'s ideological corpus ranges from a rather explicit right-wing orientation[12] to a more ambiguous creature. In 1972–1979 there came the first reformulation of the doctrine, in which the *Nouvelle Droite* departed from (typically right-wing nationalist) anti-communism and the idea of defending the West and distanced itself from racism. Communism is still seen negatively, but it's not seen as the principal enemy;[13] it is no more than another crystallisation of egalitarianism — a symptom, not a cause. The West, in turn, is not seen as something that should be defended at any cost; rather, it is seen as an entity that is an effect of cultural-mental "colonisation" from which Europe needs to liberate itself. As Taguieff notes, the change in position towards Marxism constituted a touchstone of the originality of GRECE against the backdrop of other French groups on the nationalist right.[14] Also in this period, de Benoist took a stand "against all racisms" — equally against biological racism and the racism that hides under the mask of "anti-racism". On the one hand, he rejects the possibility of an objective hierarchy between races (which is always assessed from a subjective perspective), and on the other hand he draws attention to how egalitarian and anti-racist (as well as racist) ideologies are responsible for various types of massacres and genocides.[15] The borderline point that concludes this period and gives way to the new period can be taken to be the publication of *Les idées à*

---

12   Let us underscore that this right-wingness, according to the *Nouvelle Droite*, boils down to its opposition to egalitarianism.

13   On this question, certain minor differences can be noticed inside GRECE. For example, for Jean-Claude Valla, Marxism-Communism remains the most harmful of the egalitarian political doctrines, whereas for de Benoist (from 1981–1982, and especially from 1974–1975), American liberal capitalism is enemy number one.

14   Taguieff, *Sur la Nouvelle Droite*, 78.

15   Alain de Benoist, "*Contre tous les racismes*", *Éléments pour la civilisation européenne* 8–9 (1975), 14.

l'endroit (1979), in which Alain de Benoist still explicitly opposes egalitarianism and raises the question of elitism, but, nevertheless, there are already obvious symptoms of the later evolution.

The early 1980s were the moment of another doctrinal reformulation. In Alain de Benoist's publications from this period one can notice an already gradual marginalisation of anti-egalitarianism in favour of defending the pluralism of cultures.[16] The *Nouvelle Droite* has not, of course, departed from the critique of egalitarianism, but the latter has become decisively less explicit. Instead, to the fore has advanced the critique of all forms of uniformisation and cultural homogenisation, as well as the mixing of cultures and ethnoses. *Nouvelle Droite* thought is increasingly less biological and more concentrated on culture and history.[17] Difference (*différence*) becomes a cardinal value, the anti-totalitarian idea par excellence. Differentiation becomes the *Nouvelle Droite*'s "obsession" instead of anti-egalitarianism. The idea of an alliance between Europe and the Third World (against the liberal-capitalist hegemony of the US) appeared in 1984. In 1985, de Benoist's *Démocratie: le problème* was published, in which he speaks out decisively in favor of direct democracy.[18] In 1986, de Benoist renounced any affiliation with the right and reformulated his own position.[19] Instead of left and right, he sees a dispute between those who want a unidimensional world and defend human rights (of the abstract human) and those who advocate a pluralistic world and defend the rights of peoples and their cultural integrality.[20]

Since the 1990s, as François argues, GRECE has increasingly resembled something in the likes of a "new left". Christopher Lasch and Jean-Calude Michéa, among others, have become inspirations for the current. In 2004, Alain de Benoist described himself as an

---

16   Taguieff, *Sur la Nouvelle Droite*, 246–247.

17   Ibid., 87.

18   The same year saw an issue of *Éléments* dedicated to the topic of democracy.

19   Alain de Benoist, *Europe, Tiers Monde, même combat* (Paris: 1986), 8.

20   Ibid., 17.

anti-individualist, anti-nationalist, anti-ethnocentrist, and anti-capitalist who adheres to localist and communitarian positions.[21] As already mentioned, in the last phase of GRECE's evolution he upheld the right of immigrant communities living in France to preserve their cultural "difference" while retaining civil rights. François cites in this context the case of Arnaud Guyot-Jeannin (a representative of the young generation of GRECE), who has said that on the question of immigration the *Nouvelle Droite* currently takes a moderate position, which he describes as "identitarian differentialism". Rejecting the xenophobia and racism of the right as well as the "immigrationism" and "assimilationism" of the left, he argues that immigrants are not the reason why the French live in a state of decadence—the decadence of the French is the reason why some immigrants cause problems.[22] In other words, the Republic does not have the right to demand that immigrants renounce their own roots in the name of homogenising assimilation. This forced assimilation is the cause for social unrest. The separate identity of immigrants should be recognised and respected. According to the differentialist credo, every people has the right to preserve its own identity and particularity.

The simplest way to summate the ideational evolution of the *Nouvelle Droite* is to describe what this current defines as its main enemy. Initially, the main enemy was egalitarianism. In the later phase, the forefront was taken over by the motif of the right to difference (*droit à la différence*). It was then, in Tagiueff's opinion, that the *Nouvelle Droite*'s doctrine lost its clarity and transparency. For the latter researcher, the essence of the problem of the *Nouvelle Droite*'s later phase of ideational evolution is the contradiction between explicit hierarchy and implicit egalitarianism (in the guise of hyperpluralism).[23] The right to difference implicitly puts all cultures on equal standing,

---

21 François, *Les paganismes de la Nouvelle Droite*, 60.

22 Ibid., 62.

23 Taguieff, *Sur la Nouvelle Droite*, 297.

yet the idea of hierarchy (the Indo-European trifunctional model) is at the origin of the *Nouvelle Droite*. At the same time, the critique of the Christian West shifts into a critique of the West per se, of which America is supposed to be the highest stage.[24]

Both François and Taguieff note certain weaknesses in the last phase of GRECE's doctrinal evolution.[25] The *Nouvelle Droite*'s unconventionality is seen as going too far, and its inconsequentialness and lack of consistency are taken to have caused a relative utopianness as well as a loss of express clarity that disoriented hitherto supporters of the movement. Moreover, the ideational convergence with the New Left (from 1977–1978) caused a break in ranks: some GRECE members (Jean-Claude Bardet, Jean-Jacques Mourreau, and Pierre Vial,[26] among others) joined the then increasingly popular Front National of Le Pen. Guillaume Faye left GRECE in 1986. Starting in the mid-1980s, *Nouvelle Droite* was increasingly marginalised.[27] In the 1990s, GRECE became a de facto apolitical organisation, one symbol of which can be seen in 1993: the new editor-in-chief of *Éléments*, Charles Champetier, rejected the label "New Right" and changed it to "New Culture".[28] Our ensuing reconstruction of the *Nouvelle Droite*'s ideological framework is based on taking this last phase of doctrinal evolution as the most representative.

Ideological Anatomy

According to Jarosław Tomasiewicz, the ideological array of the *Nouvelle Droite* has three main sources: (1) the philosophy of Reaction, i.e., Friedrich Nietzsche, Julius Evola, Oswald Spengler, Ernst Jünger,

---

24 Ibid.
25 François, *Les paganismes de la Nouvelle Droite*, 63; Taguieff, *Sur la Nouvelle Droite*, 296.
26 Taguieff, *Sur la Nouvelle Droite*, 284.
27 Ibid., 297.
28 Ibid., 284.

and Carl Schmitt; (2) the accomplishments of contemporary science, particularly anthropology, sociobiology, ethology (especially Konrad Lorenz); and (3) Indo-European mythology as represented by Mircea Eliade, Louis Rouger, and Georges Dumézil.[29]

According to Tomislav Sunic, the ideological foundations of the *Nouvelle Droite* are constituted by "the Presocratic thinkers, Homer, the *Iliad*, and the *Odyssey*—this is the fundamental starting point for the 'New Right' [...] We have Nietzsche in philosophy, Oswald Spengler in historiosophy, Vilfredo Pareto in sociology, Carl Schmitt in law [...] and let's not forget the tragics, starting with Sophocles and Euripides".[30]

Alain de Benoist himself describes his path of ideas as beginning with his youth's fascination with Nietzsche and then (in the early 1960s) his discovery of Louis Rougier's thought. Both of the latter were admirers of Greco-Roman antiquity as well as opponents of Christianity. Back in the 1960s, de Benoist strived to somewhat distance himself from Rougier's thought on account of his economic liberalism, positivism, and scientism. De Benoist considerably revised his reading of Nietzschean thought under the influence of reading Martin Heidegger,[31] who became one of his main points of reference. When it comes to the sphere of religious studies, de Benoist names his main inspirations as Walter F. Otto, Mircea Eliade, Gilbert Durand,

---

29 Tomasiewicz, "*Przeciwko Równości i Demokracji: Nowa Prawica we Francji*", 26.
30 Sunic, "*Wywiad z Tomislavem Suniciem*", 37.
31 de Benoist, *Jésus et ses frères*, 267: "Reading Heidegger led [me] to a serious revision of the Nietzschean thinking that had, despite everything else, retained its power in certain aspects the whole while (the 'spherical' concept of history, the concept of the 'Great Midday'), but was dubious in other respects (the *Übermensch* and especially the 'will to power', which Heidegger rightly interpreted as the 'will to will' that is derived from the metaphysics of subjectivity and lies at the very foundations of modernity). I'll also add that reading Heidegger, besides the help it offered in ridding myself of any 'Promethean' inclinations, taught me to distinguish between metaphysics and ontology."

Claude Levi-Strauss, and Georges Dumézil.³² Among other important sources of inspiration, he names German sociology (Max Weber, Georg Simmel, Ferdinand Tönnies, Werner Sombart), the thinkers of the German Conservative Revolution, some Catholic authors (Charles Péguy, Georges Bernanos, Emmanuel Mounier), some Jewish authors (Hannah Arendt, Leo Strauss, Martin Buber), as well as the American communitarians (Charles Taylor, Michael Sandel).³³

1. The Theological Level

1. Neo-Paganism

The *Nouvelle Droite* does not aim to literally recreate old cult practices. From this current's point of view, such would be rather pointless. However, all the cult practices of ancient paganism were expressions of the epoch and of a certain type of mentality, sensitivity, and the specific character of man's relation with the world — and such enabled the crystallisation of these institutions of the ancient world instead of others. Attempts at recreating old religious practices in unchanged form are devoid of sense, especially taking into consideration the fact that the mentality connected to these practices has disappeared. Thus, the first step is to attempt to recreate the old conceptual structures, worldview, and axiology — this is the *sine qua non* condition of any constructive reference to European paganism.

Therefore, this current's representatives present an approach to paganism that is more philosophical than confessional, more conceptual than strictly religious. Moreover, the *Nouvelle Droite* does not refer to

---

32 During my personal conversation with Alain de Benoist on 2 October 2018, he called Dumézil and Eliade his main reference points. It is worth mentioning that the Polish mediaevalist Aleksander Gieysztor adopted a similar strategy of drawing on the works of Dumézil and Eliade with the aim of reconstructing the religion of the ancient Slavs. See A. Gieysztor, *Mitologia Słowian* (Warsaw: 2006).

33 de Benoist, *Jésus et ses frères*, 266–268.

a specific pagan tradition, but rather to paganism "as such", seeking out common themes and ethoses that would unify the image of reality of the various historical, pre-Christian societies while taking into special consideration the Indo-European heritage.

1.1 Christianity: The Greatest Catastrophe in the History of Europe

Tomislav Sunic states:

> Monotheism is the greatest catastrophe that has ever befallen European peoples on the philosophical level — significantly worse than communism, significantly worse than liberalism — as it produced [...] this monotheistic way of thinking [which] has ruined our feeling of tolerance. [...] The problem with Christianity, like with every other monotheism, is that it is very exclusionary — anyone who isn't with me is against me.[34]

In the perspective of the *Nouvelle Droite*, thus, Christianity is the biggest catastrophe in the history of Europe. It alienated European peoples from their authentic, indigenous spirituality (Indo-European, monistic and polytheistic). Moreover, it implanted in the European mentality the germs of the egalitarianism that the *Nouvelle Droite* sees as something extraordinarily negative. According to them, Christianity initiated a catastrophic identity crisis among Europeans.

According to Alain de Benoist, identity is dialectically constituted by "positive confrontation with the Other".[35] The essence of monotheism, however, is radical rejection of the Other — in principle, Christianity rejects everything that is non-Christian.[36] The Christian is incapable of "moving on with the agenda" whenever confronted with the existence of something or someone that does not fit into the schema of one God and one Truth. The doctrinal rejection of the

---

34 Sunic, "*Wywiad z Tomislavem Suniciem*", 39.
35 Moos, *Les intellectuels de la Nouvelle Droite et la religion*, 46.
36 Louis Rougier, *Le conflit du christianisme primitif et de la civilisation antique* (Paris: 1977), 57–58.

Other causes a "crumbling" of the monotheistic identity itself. The only way to deal with this identity crisis is to liquidate this difference (for example, through conversion or physical elimination of the Other). Besides the very negation of difference, there is a "hypertrophic ignorance of one's own indigenous identity".[37] Olivier Moos describes this inclination to liquidating any difference as "the passion of totalitarian uniformisation".[38] The *Nouvelle Droite* sees all the religious wars that have taken place in Europe as consequences of the adoption of Christianity and its intolerant opposition, uniformisation, and "totalitarian" spirit.

With paganism the matter is completely different. In de Benoist's opinion, paganism is inherently tolerant. Pre-Christian European religions were closed within their own ethnos, and the concept of conversion to religion was something completely foreign to those societies. As the French thinker states, "Only paganism can accept that different cities have different gods."[39] This is a very important thread in *Nouvelle Droite* thought, which finds its translation on the political level as well. The current programmatically rejects monotheistic logic (*tertium non datur*): "We do not oppose intolerance with intolerance. Instead of pitting Hellenes and Nazarenes against teach other, we prefer to fight against the word of Paul that there will be 'neither Jew nor Greek'. We are ready to fight for the right of peoples to worship their gods."[40]

1.2 The Clash between the Indo-European and Judeo-Christian Mentalities

The starting point of the whole of the *Nouvelle Droite*'s thought is a constitutive meta-thesis that sounds as follows: there exists a fundamental

---

37 Moos, *Les intellectuels de la Nouvelle Droite et la religion* 46.
38 Ibid.
39 Alain de Benoist, *On Being a Pagan*, trans. Jon Graham (Atlanta: Ultra, 2004), 148.
40 Alain de Benoist, "L'addition n'a pas été payée", *Éléments pour la civilisation européenne* 36 (1980), 2.

and insurmountable contradiction between the Judeo-Christian (monotheistic) and Indo-European (polytheistic) mentalities which ultimately always leads to them "clashing".

The civilisation that we know today as "Western" or "Latin" was created under the influence of this contradiction and tension between two opposing sources, which provoked the above-mentioned "identity crisis" that has been ongoing for centuries. In other words, the "West" is a synthesis of the heritage of Indo-European polytheism and Judeo-Christian monotheism. Alain de Benoist argues that it was only a matter of time until an unavoidable "friction" broke out between both elements (e.g., the return to ancient aesthetic in the Renaissance, the abundant references to paganism in Romanticism, etc.).

Christianity today is undergoing a deep crisis — it is no longer the official doctrine that defines the values of Europe, but only one among other possible opinions. However, although the churches are empty, this does not at all mean that Christianity has completely disappeared. It has influence in a secular form, in the guise of the ideology of progress, the ideology of human rights, and egalitarian universalism.[41] Even modernity itself is "Christian truths put in our heads."[42]

Kazimierz Krzysztofek and Marek Szczepański have argued:

> No one denies the dynamism of the West in the civilisational sphere, but besides the economic element, it is seen above all in the sphere of utilitarian consumer culture, the industries of entertainment and technology; however, one can notice increasingly strong symptoms of spiritual exhaustion. [...] The condition of the vitality of a system is the maintenance and enrichment of the cultural resources it draws upon. In the meanwhile [...]. The West has over-exploited these resources.[43]

---

41 de Benoist, "*Wywiad z Alainem de Benoist*", 32.

42 Ibid., 34.

43 K. Krzysztofek and M.S. Szczepański, *Zrozumieć rozwój. Od społeczeństw tradycyjnych do informacyjnych* (Katowice: 2005), 263.

The only way for Europe to regain its spiritual strength and overcome the present civilisational-spiritual crisis is to rediscover the pagan Indo-European roots of European culture. This does not mean literally returning to old cult practices; rather, Alain de Benoist believes that "the mental universe of the old European religions can be a source of constant inspiration for us".[44]

In the context of religion, the three key ideas of the *Nouvelle Droite* can be defined as follows:

(1) Rejecting "Judeo-Christian" values, especially monotheism, egalitarianism, and universalism, which are seen as having subverted the ancient world;

(2) Turning to the pre-Christian religiosity of Europe, drawing on the Indo-European trifunctional model (per Dumézil);

(3) Rejecting religious universalism (along "pagan rules" — every city has its own gods) and, consequently, recognising the value of "difference" (*différence*), that is, a pluralism (descriptive and normative) of peoples and values ("political polytheism"), which is connected to recognising the particularities of cultures (along with their specific traits) as irreducible wholes.[45]

2. The Philosophical Level

2.1 The Crisis of Modernity

Alain de Benoist writes: "All critical thought attempts to put the age in which it develops in perspective. The present is a pivotal period — a

---

44 de Benoist, "*Wywiad z Alainem de Benoist*", 32.
45 Moos, *Les intellectuels de la Nouvelle Droite et la religion*, 4.

turning point or an *interregnum*, characterised by a major crisis: the end of modernity."[46]

What is "modernity"? Modernity has been the civilisational paradigm of the West for the past three centuries. It is constituted by the following five processes:

(a) Individualisation — the destruction of traditional forms of communal life;

(b) Massification — the adoption of a standardised lifestyle and behaviour;

(c) Desacralisation — the replacement of religious narratives about the world with scientific interpretation;

(d) Rationalisation — the dominance of instrumental reason, the free market, and technological efficiency;

(e) Universalisation — expanding a monolithic model of society, which is regarded as having no alternative, across the whole globe.[47]

The sources of modernity are older than might seem to be the case. In de Benoist's opinion, they lie in Christian metaphysics, out of which modernity takes shape merely through the rejection of the transcendent dimension (while retaining the rest). All of the elements that come together to constitute modernity could already be found in Christianity itself. Individualism was already present in the notion of individual salvation and the individual relation with God, a relation which is beyond all earthly relations. Egalitarianism was derived from the concept that all souls are equal before God. The ideology of progress was taken from the conviction that history has an absolute beginning and a final end, and, as such, happens according to God's plan. Universalism, in turn, is a natural consequence of faith in a single

---

[46] Alain de Benoist and Charles Champetier, "Manifesto for a European Renaissance", in Sunic, *Against Democracy and Equality*, 209.

[47] Ibid.

revealed truth that is applicable always and everywhere, regardless of geographical area and cultural context. All of these concepts were secularised by the Enlightenment, which gave rise to the constitution of the Western modernity that we know today.

Christianity, the Enlightenment, and modernity have many common traits. One emerges from the other in a necessary and unavoidable fashion — this is Alain de Benoist's argument. The basis of all of these phenomena — egalitarianism, individualism, and liberalism — is, in a word, "universalism", or "individuo-universalism".[48] This individuo-univeralism is assessed unambiguously and critically as having caused the disintegration of traditional, collective identities and their cultures, reducing everything and everyone to being consumers in one big, homogenous, world market. Alain de Benoist calls this the "ideology of the same" (*l'idéologie du même*): "This situation worries me, and I call it the ideology of sameness [...] Its central point is the assumption that we are all one humankind, brothers and sisters of the same family. Differences between us might exist, but they are inessential and must gradually be uprooted or reshaped into something in the likes of folklore."[49]

Modernity is dominated by two basic motivations or desires: freedom and equality. In the perspective of the *Nouvelle Droite*, however, these two values have been betrayed, having been "cut off from the communities which protected them".[50] The postulate of equality was never fully implemented. Communism betrayed it by creating the most criminal system in history. Capitalism trivialised it by legitimising egregious economic and social inequalities in the name of egalitarianism. Modernity promises much, such as in the form of the "ideology of progress", but it does not fulfil these promises. It gives rise to ever more

---

48 Alain de Benoist, "Alain de Benoist answers Tamir Bar-On", *Journal for the Study of Radicalism* 8(1) (2014), 144.

49 Alain de Benoist, "*Nowoczesność jako wróg tożsamości*", *Szczerbiec* 151 (2019), 10.

50 de Benoist and Champetier, "Manifesto", in Sunic, *Against Democracy and Equality*, 210.

and ever new needs whose fulfilment is reserved for an insignificant minority. The unfulfilled promises made to the majority incite social rage. Unfulfilled promises, connected with the rapid tempo of social, civilisational, and technical changes, along with the depreciation of the past and tradition, cause a big dose of resentment, frustration, anxiety, and uncertainty. "The more the world is subject to uniformisation, the greater grows the inclination towards rebellion. Thus, the impulse that leads to the homogenisation of the planet creates new kinds of divisions. At times, the resistance might take on extreme forms — for example, terrorism."[51]

Modernity, the era of the "end of ideology" and the "end of history", with its focus on instrumental reason and the myth of constant economic (material) growth, creates a spiritual vacuum that is unprecedented in the Western world, and the spread of anxiety leads to living in a world that is stripped of both past and future.

De Benoist and Champetier write in the *Manifesto*:

> Thus, modernity has given birth to the most empty civilisation mankind has ever known: the language of advertising has become the paradigm of all social discourse; the primacy of money has imposed the omnipresence of commodities; man has been transformed into an object of exchange in a context of mean hedonism; technology has ensnared the life-world in a network of rationalism — a world replete with delinquency, violence, and incivility, in which man is at war with himself and against all, i.e., an unreal world of drugs, virtual reality and media-hyped sports, in which the countryside is abandoned for unliveable suburbs and monstrous megalopolises, and where the solitary individual merges into an anonymous and hostile crowd, while traditional social, political, cultural or religious mediations become increasingly uncertain and undifferentiated.[52]

The present crisis is just modernity progressively exhausting itself. Yet, it constantly tries to "pull along" its universalist utopia in the guise

---

51 de Benoist, "*Nowoczesność jako wróg tożsamości*", 10.
52 de Benoist and Champetier, "Manifesto", in Sunic, *Against Democracy and Equality*, 211.

of "liberal globalisation". This model is presented as the one and only one that is universal for the whole world. Humanity is therefore seen as a sum of rational individuals striving to fulfil their own interests, individuals who are implicitly the same in their aspirations, emotions, motivations, morality, etc. In this perspective, the differentiation of the cultures and peoples of the world hinders human unity and, in this regard, all such differences are seen as contingencies, coincidences, or even harmful anachronisms. The ultimate end of the project of modernity is, according to Alain de Benoist, the uprooting of individuals from their particular communities and subjecting them to one, universal, common *modus vivendi* and *operandi*. In practice, the most effective means of achieving this is shaping society along the model of the market.[53] This is liberal, global capitalism.

Alain de Benoist states: "It would be a mistake to see capitalism only as an economic system. It is also an 'anthropological' system in the sense that it creates a specific model of man, *Homo oeconomicus*, a producer-consumer oriented exclusively at maximising personal benefit."[54]

2.2 The Human: A Being Rooted in Time and Space

Being human always means being-in-the-world. As de Benoist and Champetier write:

> From the socio-historical viewpoint, man as such does not exist, because his membership within humanity is always mediated by a particular cultural belonging. [...] All men have in common their human nature, without which they would not be able to understand each other, but their common membership in the species always expresses itself in a single *context*. [...] They do not exist in the real world other than as concretely rooted people.[55]

---

53 Ibid., 210.
54 Alain de Benoist, "*Czas Rewolucji Duchowej. Rozmowa z Alainem de Benoist*", *Szczerbiec* 151 (2016), 13.
55 de Benoist and Champetier, "Manifesto", in Sunic, *Against Democracy and Equality*, 216.

The *Nouvelle Droite* does not particularly dwell on the nature of the human being as a species (with the exception of biologically belonging to *Homo sapiens*), unlike the classical left and right, both of which proceed from initial theses on human nature in general regardless of point of view. In the *Nouvelle Droite*'s vision, man is always "thrown" into the context of a specific culture, tradition, people, ethnic group, etc., and one cannot speak of a person outside of this context, as this context is what makes him a person as such. The *Nouvelle Droite* underscores the fact that no person participates in "humanity" directly, but always indirectly, by way of a specific culture. De Benoist writes:

> Man has a certain nature, but his specificity lies elsewhere. In other words, 'man in the state of nature' or man constituted 'exclusively' by the state of nature 'does not exist'. His specificity is his culture — culture which does not annul the presupposition of his natural [biophysiological] structure, but which, building on it, constitutes a new level of reality [... that is] completely human [...] Man is a 'being of [a specific] culture'. He is an 'historical being'. His historicity is implicated by his culture, because 'nature' remains unchanging, whereas culture is constantly evolving.[56]

Different cultures present different answers to fundamental questions, as each culture has its own "centre of gravity". This is also why every attempt to unify them will end up destroying them. In this regard, the idea of absolute existence, of a universal law that would ultimately resolve all religious, moral, and political dilemmas would be, according to the *Nouvelle Droite*, completely baseless. It is this type of (monotheistic) mentality that is the source of any totalitarianism.[57]

While the classical right (on the basis of Christian ethics) sees man as a being that is deeply tainted by original sin, and is therefore inclined towards evil, and while the Enlightenment sees man as good in nature, the *Nouvelle Droite* says that "by nature, man is neither good nor

---

56 de Benoist, *Les idées à l'endroit*, op. cit., 96.
57 de Benoist and Champetier, "Manifesto", in Sunic, *Against Democracy and Equality*, 216.

bad".[58] This starting presumption de facto situates the *Nouvelle Droite* beyond the typical classification of left and right. Social, customary, and moral norms have no absolute dimension, for they depend on cultural context. The human being does not have a nature that can be separated from his culture, for culture shapes him as a human.[59] De Benoist emphasises that the very notion of culture exists exclusively in the plural (*sic!*), i.e., there is no "universal" culture. Man, of course, is an animal, but it is not his animalness that defines him as a human, but rather only the culture in which he was born and which shaped him as a human. *Homo sapiens* is born, but the human being is not. One *becomes* a human being.[60] [61]

---

58 Ibid., 215.

59 de Benoist, *View from the Right*, vol. 1, 272: "Regarding the 'reality' of man, one can say that it can be apprehended and decomposed into four levels: the *microphysical* level (*energy*); the *macrophysical* level (*matter*); the *biological* level (*life*), and finally a specifically *human* level, characterised by *culture* and *historical consciousness*. Man shares his belonging to the first *three* levels of the universe [...]. Only the last one properly belongs to him."

60 de Benoist, *Vu de droite*, 388: "The idea known to the Ancients: [...] we are not 'born' man — but we can 'become' man."

61 On the question of philosophical anthropology, Alain de Benoist draws abundantly from Martin Heidegger's thought. See J. Galarowicz, *Martin Heidegger — genialny myśliciel czy szaman?* (Krakow: 2014), 133–134: "Why does no essentialist and substantialist anthropology — defining man by indicating his constant and universal essence, structure, and enduring and identical substrate that decided his oneness — manage to reach the truth about man, even if it proclaims his superiority over the rest of nature? Because what decides upon mankind, its dignity and greatness, does not have the character of an essence, structure, or substance [...]: it is not a particular essence that distinguishes him from other beings, but rather his way of existing, of being. 'Dasein' is not something present, given like a thing. It 'is' not, but rather becomes or 'essences' in the face of its possibilities [...]. Man is a dynamic 'reality' deeply permeated by time."

Thus, there can be no talk of "humanity" as something that is any more than a collection of all *Homo sapiens*.[62] From the *Nouvelle Droite*'s perspective, there is no essential or moral "humanity". Such a conviction as to the existence of a common, single, human essence is of monotheistic genesis. Only the Judeo-Christian "monohumanism"[63] demands that the human be seen in this way, as a type. Why? Because, according to monotheistic doctrine, all people are created by one and the same God. The oneness of the human type is, therefore, a reflection of the oneness of God. Christian doctrine proclaims moral oneness for the whole human species while at the same time taking the individual to be a being that is irreducible to political community.

The New Right's philosophical anthropology can therefore be described as "polyhumanism": every people has its own gods, and, as follows, its own standards and moral norms. Given that every people has its own gods, there is no "one human" — there are peoples. This plurality of peoples is seen as a cardinal value. A people and its culture are, according to Alain de Benoist, irreducible wholes and autotelic values.

---

62 The inspiration of Oswald Spengler's thought is very clear here. See Oswald Spengler, *The Decline of the West — Volume I: Form and Actuality* (Legend Books, 2024), 26–27: "'Mankind,' however, has no aim, no idea, no plan, any more than the family of butterflies or orchids. 'Mankind' is a zoological expression, or an empty word. [...] I see, in place of that empty figment of *one* linear history which can only be kept up by shutting one's eyes to the overwhelming multitude of the facts, the drama of *a number* of mighty Cultures, each springing with primitive strength from the soil of a mother-region to which it remains firmly bound throughout its whole life-cycle; each stamping its material, its mankind, in *its own* image; each having *its own* idea, *its own* passions, its own life [...]."

63 Alain de Benoist and Guillaume Faye, "*La religion des droits de l'homme*", *Éléments pour la civilisation européenne* 37 (1981), 6.

2.3 Social Holism: Culture and People as Autotelic Values and Irreducible Wholes

Alain de Benoist asserts:

> There are basically two ways of seeing man and society. Either one sees a fundamental value in the "individual" (and, as follows, in 'humanity' as consisting of the sum of all individuals) — this is the Christian, bourgeois, liberal, and socialist idea; or the fundamental value is 'peoples' and 'cultures', which are primarily pluralistic notions that establish a 'holistic' approach to society. In the first case, humanity, or the 'sum' of all individuals, is 'contained' in every separate individual: first one is a 'human' and only then, as if by accident, is one a member of a culture or a people. In the second, humanity is nothing more than a 'collection' of cultures and folk communities: it is by 'organic belonging' that man is affirmed in his humanity. [...] European civilisation was originally a holistic civilisation; society was seen as a 'community', as an organic whole to which one belongs by 'heritage' and 'kinship'. [...] It was by means of Christianity that individualism appeared in the European mental space along with egalitarianism and universalism.[64]

The starting point here is the (concrete) social bond that is a determinant of individual behaviours. This social bond is not a result of any contract — it is the condition of such. To be part of an organic community does not mean that one's individual identity disappeared — it is the foundation of such. In the holistic conception, the whole is something more than the sum of its parts, and it possesses values which the separate parts do not. To be a human means being a person and a social being. In other words, the individual and collective dimensions are not identical, but they are inseparable.[65] From the holistic perspective, man is constituted by the given socio-historical context.

---

64 de Benoist, *Orientation pour des années décisive*, op. cit., 35–36.

65 de Benoist and Champetier, "Manifesto", in Sunic, *Against Democracy and Equality*, 217: "Human existence is inseparable from the communities and social groups in which it reveals itself. The idea of a primitive 'state of nature' in which autonomous individuals might have coexisted is pure fiction: society is not the result of a contract between men trying to maximise their best interests, but

This means that the individual is secondary to the community that shapes it — or, in other terms, the individual is first a human of a given community and only then "human." This model, which is the most common in world history, is the complete opposite of individualism, which should be seen as specific to the West.[66]

The process of transitioning from holism to individualism began, as de Benoist claims, with Christianity, which "planted the germ of individualism in Europe by affirming the equality of individuals before God and making salvation into an individual affair, thereby loosening the union of individual and social community".[67] In the Christian religion, man is not firstly a social being, but above all a moral being. The individual soul draws its value from the individual's relationship with God, while the equality of all souls before God makes "humanity" a moral category. At the same time, the classic opposition between wisdom and the world becomes radicalised. Morality concerns one's relationship with God (as separate from the world), and thus man (as a moral being) realises his essence, so to speak, apart from the world.[68] This vision of the human being was later taken over by individualism, whose triumph led to the "breakdown of the social bond".[69] Alain de Benoist writes:

> We can say that a society and a people are 'healthy' when they (1) are conscious of their cultural and historical roots, (2) manage to gather themselves around some kind of 'mediator', whether individual or symbolic, that is capable of mustering energy and being a catalyst for the will of fate, and (3) have the courage to 'designate their enemy'. Alas, none of these conditions are fulfilled in the case of liberal-market society, which (1) erases memory,

---

rather of a spontaneous association whose most ancient form is undoubtedly the extended family."

66 Alain de Benoist, "*Critique de l'idéologie libérale*" in idem, *Critiques — Théoriques* (Lausanne, 2002), 15.

67 Alain de Benoist, "*Du lien social*" in *Critique — Théoriques*, 197.

68 de Benoist, *Orientations pour des années*, 36.

69 de Benoist, "*Du lien social*", 196.

(2) extinguishes the subtle and sterilises passion, and (3) does not want to have enemies and believes that it is 'possible' not to have them.[70]

Key to the social philosophers of the *Nouvelle Droite* is that peoples and cultures[71] are regarded as good in and of themselves and as irreducible wholes. In this regard, their hostility towards the modern, individualist-liberal model of the "formal-contractual" society is obvious, as they see the latter as a "disintegrating" factor for traditional cultural communities. De Benoist writes:

> The 'plan' of liberal modernity is the deconstruction of organic communities with the aim of transforming the members of different cultures into individual consumers of a global market, consumers with the same tastes, needs, and preferences — and obedient to the diktat of supply and demand. Modernity is hostile towards ethno-cultural differentiation in that it poses a hindrance to the 'march of progress towards a monolithic humanity'.[72]

Of course, the above entails breaking with the paradigm of "monolithic humanity" and accepting the existence of different races. However, the

---

70 Alain de Benoist, *Orientations pour des années*, op. cit., 52.
71 See Spengler, *Decline of the West*, vol. 1, 141: "A Culture is born in the moment when a great soul awakens out of the proto-spirituality (*dem urseelenhaften Zustande*) of ever-childish humanity, and detaches itself, a form from the formless, a bounded and mortal thing from the boundless and enduring. It blooms on the soil of an exactly definable landscape, to which plant-wise it remains bound. [...] Every Culture stands in a deeply symbolical, almost in a mystical, relation to the Extended, the space, in which and through which it strives to actualize itself." Idem, *The Decline of the West — Volume II: Perspectives of World-History* (Legend Books, 2024), 203–208: "For me, the 'people' is a *unit of the soul*. [...] Neither unity of speech nor physical descent is decisive. That which distinguishes the people from the population, raises it up out of the population, and will one day let it find its level again in the population is always the inwardly lived experience of the 'we.' The deeper this feeling is, the stronger is the *vis viva* of the people. [...] They are neither linguistic nor political nor zoological, but spiritual, units."
72 de Benoist, "*Nowoczesność jako wróg tożsamości*", op. cit., 9.

affirmation of a plurality of races should not be mistaken for racism.[73] The New Right's "ethnopluralism" does not take the Other to mean an enemy. The *Nouvelle Droite* sees the multiplicity of ethnic groups and nations as an "added value", for this "authentic diversity" is what creates the world's richness. The *Nouvelle Droite* wants to preserve this diversity. Western modernity is characterised by a hidden racism in its destruction of this diversity. This happens through, for example, mass immigration (which implies social dissolution and the dilution of the indigenous culture) and imposing the ideology of human rights on non-Western countries (which causes the disintegration of indigenous social institutions). This hidden racism is seen as already making itself known in the very fact of the conviction that the West is de facto ahead of other cultures and therefore reserves for itself the right to judge (consciously or not) the universality of the rights, standards, and norms that are… Western. This is the "ethnocidal ideology of the West"[74] — nominally universalist, but in reality ethnocentric.

Instead of endlessly discussing human rights, Alain de Benoist proposes to raise the topic of the rights of peoples. He argues that it is necessary to put an end to modern proselytism and to recognise that the ideology of human rights is a "Western construct with limited applicability",[75] i.e., a construct that is difficult to implement in cul-

---

73 Ibid., 11: "Accepting the existence of races is something different from racism, but in Europe this is not obvious. Personally, I'm conscious of the significance of race; however, for me it is only a factor, one of many. In my worldview, Europe, race, culture, and identity are of enormous significance and I think in accord with the principles of ethnopluralism about their future in the same way as I would about the future of every other ethno-racial group […] Our identity, the identity of immigrants, and all identities in the world have a common enemy and it is the System that destroys them in every corner of the planet. This System is the enemy, not other peoples. The richness of the world is diversity, authentic diversity."

74 See Alain de Benoist, "*L'idéologie ethnocidaire de l'Occident. Droits de l'homme et droits des peuples*", *Éléments pour la civilisation européenne* 109 (2003), 28–36.

75 Ibid., 34.

tures for which liberal-individualistic thought is something foreign. In the name of what should these cultures adopt a cultural paradigm that is foreign to them? This vision is the foundation of the New Right's "ethnopluralism" or "ethno-differentialism": rootedness against uprooting, the right to differentiation against racism, and cooperation against immigration.

2.4 "Pagan Conservatism": Revolution "from the Right"

Tomislav Sunic states:

> The New Right [...] is for the principles of tradition [...], which does not refer to the old Christian tradition, but rather to a tradition that goes far, far beyond Christianity. My thesis is the following: our European tradition did not begin with *Anno Domini* 1, when Jesus Christ — so-called Jesus Christ — was born. Our tradition goes back thousands and thousands of years earlier and encompasses ancient Greece, ancient Rome, the ancient Slavs [...] This is what the New Right, myself included, are for — we want to regain our heritage not only from the last 2,000 years, but our heritage from thousands and thousands of years before. This means connecting our traditional heritage with our postmodern epoch.[76]

And further:

> There is ample evidence that pagan sensibilities can flourish in the social sciences, literature, and arts, not just as a form of exotic narrative but also as a mental framework and a tool of conceptual analysis. Numerous names come to mind when we discuss the revival of Indo-European polytheism. In the first half of the twentieth century, pagan thinkers usually appeared under the mask of those who styled themselves as 'revolutionary conservatives', 'aristocratic nihilists', 'elitists' — in short, all those who did not wish to substitute Marx for Jesus, but who rejected both Marx and Jesus. Friedrich Nietzsche and Martin Heidegger in philosophy, Carl Gustav Jung in psychology, Georges Dumézil and Mircea Eliade in anthropology, Vilfredo Pareto and Oswald Spengler in political science, let alone dozens of poets such as Ezra Pound or Charles Baudelaire — these are just some of

---

76 Sunic, "*Wywiad z Tomislavem Suniciem*", 37–38.

the names that can be associated with the legacy of pagan conservatism. All these individuals had in common the will to surpass the legacy of Christian Europe, and all of them yearned to include in their spiritual baggage the world of pre-Christian Celts, Slavs, and Germans.[77]

Adam Wielomski defines conservatism as a comprehensive ideational world that defends the social principles and philosophical concepts prior to the Revolution of 1789. The foundational idea of (continental) conservatism is "genuine order" [*prawdziwy ład*],[78] as opposed to

---

77 Tomislav Sunic, "Marx, Moses and the Pagans in the Secular City" in idem, *Postmortem Report: Cultural Examinations from Postmodernity*, 2nd ed. (London: Arktos, 2017), 5.

78 According to Wielomski, the conservative idea of "reality" or "genuine order" is based on 12 fundamental threads: (1) contrasting what is natural and what is "genuine," i.e., a deep scepticism of the human intellect's capacity and ability to project and implement total social change, which is to say that conservatism is a reaction to the post-Enlightenment "bourgeois" world; (2) the conviction that human reason is limited, which is one of the results of original sin; (3) a dislike for "technological rationalism", a resistance to modernisation and change, and thus a general dislike for technology and machines in that they destroy the organic character of the world and man's connection to nature; (4) the belief in supra-temporal values and principles, such as authority, tradition, social hierarchy, property, family, etc.; (5) opposition to the emancipation of the individual from traditional social structures, and instead advocating rootedness instead of emancipation; (6) defending intermediary social bodies, or the institutions that stand between the State and the individual, which pertains to an organic model of society instead of rationalistic uniformisation; (7) emphasis on duties to society, not individual rights—freedom cannot be understood outside of belonging to a group and the possibility of participating in the greater whole; (8) the superiority of the principle of legitimism over the principle of the sovereignty of the people (which is seen as a false principle); (9) hostility towards egalitarianism and democracy in favour of advocating social hierarchy; (10) the idea of de-politicising society, i.e., resisting mass politics—it is the elite (not the masses) that should deal with politics; (11) a specific concept of property, i.e., a sentiment for family property "with which man possesses a mystical, spiritual connection"; (12) negating the linear concept of time in favour of a parabolic model of time, which is bound up with a rejection of the idea of progress. See Wielomski, *Konserwatyzm* (Warsaw: 2007), 26–29. The *Nouvelle Droite* fits well into most of these points.

"empirical order", which is not "real" (in the ontological sense) but is only a "bad dream".⁷⁹ If conservatism is understood in this manner, then the *Nouvelle Droite* could *per analogiam* be called "pagan conservatism". For them, the "genuine order" and "real Europe" is the world of pre-Christian Europe. The revolution that destroyed this world was Christianity. As Sunic argues:

> Jesus Christ was the Bolshevik of antiquity. What he taught in the first century was shocking to many Romans and ancient aristocrats [...] He wanted to create a utopia on earth, but unfortunately we have convincingly seen what came out of Christianity — I have in mind its secular consequences in the guise of liberalism and communism.⁸⁰

Thus, to be more specific, the *Nouvelle Droite* could be attributed to the revolutionary current of conservatism or even the "conservative revolution", which Wielomski describes as "the desire to create a conservative vision of order that in one way or another refers to the principles and ideas of the pre-revolutionary world, but is not merely a reproduction of them, for the world has changed".⁸¹ Alain de Benoist abundantly draws from the ideational heritage of the German Conservative Revolution (Arthur Moeller van den Bruck, Oswald Spengler, Ernst Jünger, Hans Freyer, Werner Sombart, Carl Schmitt, among others). The thesis could even be put forth that the *Nouvelle Droite* is a development or subsequent phase of the Conservative Revolution.⁸² The

---

79   Ibid., 17.
80   Sunic, "*Wywiad z Tomislavem Suniciem*", 39. Cf. Alain de Benoist, *Les idées à l'endroit*, especially the chapter "The 'Bolshevism of Antiquity'", 167–184. The *Nouvelle Droite* was not the first current to see the germs of Bolshevism in Christianity. Cf. Oswald Spengler, *The Hour of Decision: Germany and World-Historical Evolution* (Legend Books, 2023), 97: "All Communist systems in the West are in fact derived from Christian theological thought [...]. Christian theology is the grandmother of Bolshevism."
81   Wielomski, *Konserwatyzm*, 53.
82   Such an opinion seems to be maintained by Lucian Tudor in his *From the German Conservative Revolution to the New Right* (Santiago de la Nueva Extremadura:

similarities are indeed shocking: disdain for the bourgeois world and treating the liberal bourgeois (instead of the Marxist-communist) as symbolic enemy number one; the aspiration to create a "new reality" that would put an end to the "suspension of history" that liberal democracy is; a spherical instead of linear concept of time; the postulate of a transvaluation of all values; the conviction that liberal modernity is a momentary "interregnum"; understanding conservatism to mean certain eternal principles rather than a possible literal return to bygone institutions; activism and taking an interest in the present world and the future instead of a cult of the past.[83]

2.5 Differentialist Feminism

The *Nouvelle Droite* advocates differentialist feminism, i.e., a feminism that recognises equality between women and men while simultaneously recognising the fundamental differences between the genders. De Benoist and Champetier write:

> The modern concept of abstract individuals, detached from their sexual identity, stemming from an 'indifferentialist' ideology which neutralises sexual differences, is just as prejudicial against women as traditional sexism which, for centuries, considered women as incomplete men. This is a twisted form of male domination, which in the past had excluded women from the arena of public life, and admits them today — on the condition that they divest themselves of their femininity.[84]

De Benoist argues that the difference between the genders is one of the most fundamental differences there is, for it assures the continuation of the species. The desire to abolish or ignore these differences is a utopia. Woman and man differ biologically, which is further reinforced by cultural gender. Although every inidividual can make their own

---

2014).

83 Wielomski, *Konserwatyzm*, 54–58.
84 de Benoist and Champetier, "Manifesto", in Sunic, *Against Democracy and Equality*, 232.

life choices, both genders have fundamentally different predispositions that are natural to them and which cannot be reduced to a social construct.[85] The natural differences between the genders cause women to have a natural advantage in some fields and men in others.[86] In their desire to blur the differences between genders, universalist feminists don't take into consideration the fact that universal and abstract values are essentially masculine in nature.[87] Moreover, de Benoist writes, "Those who reject gender particularities are in effect against motherhood, for it is a hindrance to the 'liberation' of woman."[88]

European societies are patriarchal, which means that authority belongs not as much to man as to the father, the head of the family. De Benoist argues that to wish for "liberation" from the family means wishing to destroy the social structure that has created this society. This structure goes back to the roots of our civilisation as it emerged in the Neolithic.[89] In other words, the desire to deconstruct the institution of the family leads to the destruction of our civilisation. De Benoist emphasises that, compared to the cultures of Asia or the Middle East, woman has had a high status in European (pre-Christian) civilisation and was not treated like an object.[90] In Indo-European societies, women participated in cultural life and at times even in political life.[91] The devalorisation of woman in Europe was caused by the influence of the biblical religion. As de Benoist points out, disdain for woman

---

85 Ibid.: "Nonetheless, in general, a large number of values and attitudes fall into feminine and masculine categories: cooperation and competition, mediation and repression, seduction and domination, empathy and detachment, concrete and abstract, affective and managerial, persuasion and aggression, synthetic intuition and analytic intellection, etc."
86 Alain de Benoist, *La Conditioned Féminine* in P. Vial (ed.), *Pour une Renaissance Culturuelle* (Paris, 1979), 105–106.
87 Manifesto 232
88 de Benoist, *La Conditioned Féminine*, 106.
89 Ibid., 108.
90 Ibid., 110.
91 Ibid., 112.

was something common across the works of the Church Fathers.[92] In other words, it is not "patriarchy" itself that is anti-woman, but rather the Judeo-Christian legacy.

Margaret Mead pointed out that differences in gender roles are to a large extent an effect of culture.[93] De Benoist, by contrast, maintains that culture is rooted in nature: "If there exist societies in which the roles of man and woman are different from the ones we know, then there does not exist any society in which these roles would be the same."[94] From de Benoist's perspective, feminism can, roughly speaking, be divided into two kinds. The first aims to defend woman from oppressive stereotypes from the Judeo-Christian tradition. The second wants to level and annual all differences between genders. Of course, Alain de Benoist is decidedly for the first version.

From the *Nouvelle Droite*'s perspective, the difference between genders should be recognised and taken into account in the public space alongside supporting women's rights like "the right to virginity, to maternity, to abortion".[95]

2.6 Integral Ecology: Overcoming Anthropocentrism

Virtually everyone supports reducing the pollution of the environment. The whole question is how to approach this problem and how to solve it. From the *Nouvelle Droite*'s perspective, this problem is rooted

---

92 Ibid., 113. De Benoit assesses Christianity's later "pro-family" position as a compromise between Christianity and the social realities of the Greco-Roman world. At the same time, he underscores that that the Christian pro-family stance does not respect women as women; instead, it is based on a highly abstract notion of woman. Christianity is dominated by a disdain for corporeality and an obsessive exaltation of virginity, which it puts above marriage.

93 See Margaret Mead, *Sex and Temperament in Three Primitive Societies* (New York: 2001).

94 de Benoist, "*La Condition Féminine*", 109.

95 de Benoist and Champetier, "Manifesto", in Sunic, *Against Democracy and Equality*, 233.

in modern anthropocentrism and the ultimate goal of ecology should be to overcome this anthropocentrism.

Both Christianity[96] and classical humanism place man in a privileged position over nature, which is treated like an object and as a basis of resources for exploitation. In other words, nature plays the role of man's servant. The *Nouvelle Droite* proposes a more "partner-like" relationship between man and nature, one based on "the development of a consciousness of the mutual coexistence of mankind and the cosmos".[97] It is for this reason that the current liberal-capitalist model of production and development is called into question, as this system itself underlies the Western concept of development,[98] and it is in turn rooted in the idea of progress (uncritical faith in the emancipatory possibilities of modern science and technology). The problem with this model is that, if it did manage to be effectively implemented across the whole globe (on the same level as it is in the West), then the effect would be "planetary suicide",[99] the total drainage of resources in the name of ever greater production and consumption. Alain de Benoist writes:

---

96 In 1967, Lynn White published the article "The Historical Roots of Our Ecological Crisis", which blamed the ecological crisis on the implementation of the biblical command to "subdue the earth" (Genesis 1:27–28). In turn, Michael Bell saw the ethical basis for the emergence of "assembly line production", that is, technological development that excessively exploits the environment, in Calvinism. In Bell's opinion, it is not enough to change the approach to technology, although one potential resolution could be reviving the legacy of St. Francis of Assisi. See A. Ganowicz-Bączyk, "Narodziny i rozwój etyki środowiskowej", *Studia Ecologiae et Bioethicae* 13(4) (2015), 46; P. Matczak, *Problemy ekologiczne jako problemy środowiskowe* (Poznań: 2000), 75–75. De Benoist would certainly agree with both of them. It is also worth recalling that the French thinker has a more favourable evaluation of the Church when it comes to St. Francis and Bernard of Clairvaux.

97 de Benoist and Champetier, "Manifesto", in Sunic, *Against Democracy and Equality*, 242.

98 Alain de Benoist, "Sur l'écologie II" in *Critiques — Théoriques*, 358.

99 Ibid.

> Instead of the right-left division, ecology puts forth a different, more fundamental division between productivism and anti-productivism, between the quantity of manufactured goods and the quality of life, between happiness as the fastest accumulation of the greatest quantity of material goods and development through self-realisation and self-fulfilment. This is the old opposition between being and having, between the right proportion and 'always more'.[100]

On the one hand, ecology is naturally conservative, as it prioritises quality of life, preserving organic society, and traditional ways of life, as well as underscores the value of biodiversity. On the other hand, it is revolutionary in that it breaks with productivist ideology and the logic of the market.[101]

Alain de Benoist emphasises that at the foundations of ecologism (as a philosophy) we find, above all, a fundamental critique of the idea that the economy should be treated as the key to our destiny. We currently live in an epoch in which the economy has been emancipated from political control and allowed to be deaf to social and environmental issues.[102] Political ecology is the antonym to economic ideology ("productivism") in which society is driven into the role of a producer of material goods that works in accordance with the diktats of the market's self-regulation.[103] Boundaries are an important concept in ecology, for "in a finite world, there are limits to growth".[104] The contemporary production model, however, is constructed as if there were no limits — this "mega-machine" of production knows only one law: maximising profit. Ecological consciousness concerns being attentive to the existence of objective boundaries (to growth, resources, etc.) and the real limitations that make permanent, endless economic growth

---

100 Alain de Benoist, "Sur l'écologie I" in *Critiques — Théoriques*, 338.

101 Ibid., 337.

102 Ibid., 338.

103 Ibid., 339.

104 de Benoist and Champetier, "Manifesto", in Sunic, *Against Democracy and Equality*, 241.

impossible. Thus, changing the existing production-consumption model is a necessity. Getting out of the productivist framework means integrating the notion of boundaries and limits, i.e., ceasing to equate more with better, maximum with optimum, quantity with quality, etc.[105]

It bears emphasising that Alain de Benoist has reservations about the concept of "sustainable development" since, in his opinion, this idea attempts to reconcile ecology with the logic of the market. It has a tendency to see nature and natural resources as a kind of "capital".[106] The fundamental problem, in this French thinker's opinion, is this logic of the market. Protecting the environment cannot be reconciled with the logic of constant, ongoing growth.[107] It is not enough to make the bad effects of capitalism more mild. Rather, the point is to completely break with this logic. Economic hubris and Promethean technology need to be kept in check for the sake of enabling harmonious coexistence between man and nature, as opposites to the model in which man dominates nature. This should enable the creation of a more symbiotic model that can preserve biodiversity.[108] In de Benoist's opinion, it is necessary to rethink everything anew from the foundations, put an end to the hegemony of productivism and instrumental reason, and break with the "religion of growth" and the "monotheism of the market" in order to work on the causes, not only the effects.[109]

These views situate Alain de Benoist close to the current of deep ecology (Arne Neess, George Sessions, Bill Devall, Warwick Fox, Alan Drengson, and Robyn Eckersley), although he himself does not identify with the latter. He does not share the extreme position (the

---

105 de Benoist, "Sur l'écologie I", 339.

106 Alain de Benoist, "Écologie" in idem, *Entretiens — Témoignages — Explications*, vol. 2 (Paris: 2006), 169–170.

107 de Benoist, "Sur l'écologie II", 356.

108 de Benoist and Champetier, "Manifesto", in Sunic, *Against Democracy and Equality*, 242.

109 de Benoist, "Sur l'écologie II", 356.

idea of "wilderness") that sees man as a "parasite" on the body of a primordial pure, "wild nature" — such a standpoint, in de Benoist's opinion, is too dualistic and binary. In turn, the problem with a more moderate approach — the monistic approach, which sees man as only a part of nature — lies in that it does not acknowledge the particularity of man in relation to the rest of living nature, as if in the perspective of a "mystical organicism or naive pantheism".[110] "Nature" is not the same as man, nor is it his opposite. The "trick" is to reject the vision of an ontological chasm between humanity and the rest of the living world while at the same time adopting the perspective of "pluralistic monism", which is based on a "dialectic of oneness and plurality and refers to the ethics of dialogue".[111] De Benoist thinks that Heidegger's thought follows this path.[112] The issue is that man must take on the role of the "shepherd of being" instead of being the "master of beings".

Over recent years, three main currents of environmental ethics have taken shape: anthropocentric (where human interest is the main point of reference), biocentric (where all living beings are the main point of reference), and ecocentric (where all of living and inanimate nature has its own intrinsic value[113]). Alain de Benoist's views can be situated in the latter category.

---

110 de Benoist, "Écologie", 165.

111 Ibid., 166.

112 A similar perspective is shared by Magdalena Hoły-Łuczaj, who interprets Heidegger's thought in the spirit of a radical non-anthropocentrism that comes close to deep ecology. See Magdalena Hoły-Łuczaj, *Radykalny nonantropocentryzm. Martin Heidegger i ekologia głęboka* (Warsaw: 2018).

113 A. Ganowicz-Bączyk, "Narodziny i rozwój etyki środowiskowej", *Studia Ecologiae i Bioethicae* 13(4) (2015), 40.

3. The Political Level

3.1 The Critique of Liberalism

Liberalism as such has never been a monolithic doctrine. There exist different versions and interpretations of liberalism. What, nevertheless, is their common denominator? Firstly, liberalism is understood as an economic doctrine that perceives the market (as implicitly self-regulating) as a paradigm for the entirety of social reality. On the political level, this translates into a desire to limit the role of politics (the State) as much as possible.[114] Secondly, liberalism is understood as a doctrine based on an individualist anthropology, i.e., an anthropology that sees man as "a being that is not necessarily social". These two characteristic traits of liberalism (the separate individual and the market as normative aspects) are antithetical to any collective identities.

The members of organic communities are conscious that they are a part of something greater than themselves and that the community itself is something more than an ordinary sum of individuals. Liberalism, based on individualism, aspires to leave behind all social relations that go beyond the formal contract between individuals. In order for the market to function optimally, it is necessary to erase everything that hinders the free circulation of goods and "human resources", including, for example, state borders. Liberalism is the political expression of modernity par excellence.

The universalist, egalitarian, and individualist basis of liberalism is the result of Christian influence. As in Christianity, man is firstly a moral subject, and only then a political or social one. In the liberal perspective, society is an ordinary sum of atomised individuals linked by a "social contract" that is treated strictly instrumentally, not autotelically.

---

114 From this very same standpoint, Alain de Benoist argues that the expression "political liberalism" is, in a certain sense, contradictory, since liberalism itself is supposed to be inherently "apolitical" (as in Carl Schmitt's understanding).

De Benoist notes:

> From the very beginning Christianity framed man as an individual which — in advance of any other connection — possesses an inner relationship with God and in this relationship strives for salvation by way of personal transcendence. This relationship with God affirms man's value as an individual, which is reflected in a devaluation and degradation of the world. Moreover, the individual is acknowledged to be equal in relation to all other people who also possess individual souls. Egalitarianism and universalism are, therefore, introduced on the highest level: the individual soul attains its absolute value on the strength of its loyal relationship with God, which is shared by the whole of humanity.[115]

A certain "dualist tension" must have appeared when Christianity was in confrontation with the mundane world around it. Being a Christian entailed, to a certain extent, a disdain for the (material) world. Because the soul functions within the body, it couldn't completely cut itself off from the world.[116] To the extent that it could bend the mundane world to its moral demands, "the individual from the world beyond gradually returned to this world, plunged into it, and deeply transformed it."[117] This transformation supposedly happened in three stages. Firstly, mundane life was no longer rejected *en bloc*, but was relativised (Augustine's synthesis of "two cities"). Secondly, in a certain sense, the papacy secularised itself when it achieved political power. Thirdly, from the time of the Reformation, man completely plunged himself into the affairs of the mundane world, where he worked *ad maiorem Dei gloriam* by striving for material success as a manifestation of God's grace.

---

[115] de Benoist, "*Critique de l'idéologie libérale*", 14.

[116] Ibid.: "The individual 'from the world beyond' gradually became tainted by the mundane world."

[117] Ibid.

Individualism and equality originally pertained exclusively to relations with God,[118] hence they initially couldn't operate within the framework of European hierarchical and organic community. Once these ides became secularised, modern individualism was born. The division into the "individual from the world beyond" and the "individual of this world" disappeared.

As a result of this, the "organic community of the holistic type" disappeared. Its place was taken by a collection of separated individuals — linked only by interests and rational contract. To use the terms coined by Ferdinand Tönnies, "community" (*Gemeinschaft*) yielded to "society" (*Gesellschaft*). To quote Alain de Benoist: "The primacy of the individual over the community is simultaneously descriptive, normative, methodological, and axiological."[119] In other words, it is absolute.

Nevertheless, liberalism still had to somehow stake out its stance towards the social question. In this respect, the liberal analysis of society appeals either to contractualism (John Locke), the "invisible hand" (Adam Smith), or the idea of "spontaneous harmony" (Friedrich von Hayek).[120]

Liberals regard the market as the most effective, rational, and just regulator of social life. They don't even question the origin of the market; for them, it is the "natural" model for the totality of social relations. They treat the market as something "natural", something primordially existent, not something created by deliberation or decision. De Benoist draws attention to how this "naturalisation" of presuppositions is typical of any ideology, i.e., ideologies present themselves not as constructs of the human spirit, but as a "simple transcription of the natural order".[121] In connection with the postulated "naturalness" of

---

118 Respectively, the individual soul's relationship with God and the equality of all people before God.

119 de Benoist, "*Critique de l'idéologie libérale*", 15.

120 Ibid., 18.

121 Ibid.

the market, the state is treated as an "artificial" creation, which serves to exhibit the idea that the regulation of social relations by the market is "natural". The economic order created by the market, therefore (in the liberal perspective), is primary before social order — neither of them is intentionally institutionalised by any organ of authority (for example, the State).[122] This order is equated to the "state of nature". Regulated by the "invisible hand", the market becomes the foundation of order as based on impartial, "objective laws" which allow for the regulation of social relations without any need for the existence of a separate organ of power (the "Leviathan").

Alain de Benoist argues that the "invisible hand" is nothing other than a secular avatar of Providence. However, it bears underscoring that Adam Smith did not equate the mechanism of the market and the "invisible hand", for the latter was supposed to mean only the

---

[122] In reality, the opposite is the case. In this context, de Benoist refers to the work of the Hungarian economist Karl Polanyi, who demonstrated that the market is an institution created by the State and that there is nothing "spontaneous" or "natural" in it. Karl Polanyi, *The Great Transformation: The Political and Economic Origins of Our Time* (Boston: Beacon Press, 2001), 145–147: "There was nothing natural about laissez-faire; free markets could never have come into being merely by allowing things to take their course. Just as cotton manufactures — the leading free trade industry — were created by the help of protective tariffs, export bounties, and indirect wage subsidies, laissez-faire itself was enforced by the State. The thirties and forties saw not only an outburst of legislation repealing restrictive regulations, but also an enormous increase in the administrative functions of the state, which was now being endowed with a central bureaucracy able to fulfil the tasks set by the adherents of liberalism. To the typical utilitarian, economic liberalism was a social project which should be put into effect for the greatest happiness of the greatest number; laissez-faire was not a method to achieve a thing, it was the thing to be achieved. [...] The road to the free market was opened and kept open by an enormous increase in continuous, centrally organized and controlled interventionism. To make Adam Smith's 'simple and natural liberty' compatible with the needs of a human society was a most complicated affair. [...] This paradox was topped by another. While laissez-faire economy was the product of deliberate State action, subsequent restrictions on laissez-faire started in a spontaneous way. Laissez-faire was planned; planning was not."

resultant effect of the totality of commercial trade. Moreover, Smith acknowledged the legitimacy of intervention situations for the sake of individual enterprises to serve the common good. However, this perspective would be subject to complete revision with the appearance of neoliberalism. Neoliberals contest the very idea of the common good. Friedrich von Hayek opposed any attempts at a holistic framing of society. Moreover, he believed that no institution or political authority has the right to impose anything upon the "spontaneous harmony". The function of the State is limited to ensuring individuals the opportunity for unfettered, rational commercial exchange, i.e., the State's role is to serve the market. Magdalena Prószyńska summates this position: "Individualist liberalism cannot construct any political idea, so it describes the State only in negative terms."[123] Alain de Benoist, in turn, remarks:

> In the end, the 'economy' and 'morality' seem to be inseparable in liberalism, not only because 'properly understood' morality guarantees free commerce, but also because the economy 'in and of itself' is seen as a 'moral activity'. Coinciding with (material) 'prosperity', commercial activity is regarded as 'naturally' aspiring for 'good' [...] The "good" that hitherto pertains to the individual's relation to 'things' (and not to interhuman relations) becomes one of the elements of contemporary hedonism.[124]

The ultimate effect of the secularisation of individualism is materialism. The individual's "striving for fortune" (without taking into account the common good) and strong orientation towards human-object relations makes the acquisition of material things the fundamental meaning of life (instead of "transcending oneself"). It is for this reason that liberalism constantly leads to economism. The primacy of economism is the

---

123 M. Prószyńska, "*Schmittiańskie pojęcie polityczności. Neutralizacja w ogniu krytyki*", *Teologia Polityczna* [https://teologiapolityczna.pl/magdalena-pruszynska-schmittianskie-pojecie-politycznosci-neutralizacja-w-ogniu-krytyki]

124 de Benoist, *Orientations pour des années*, 41.

foundation of the contemporary "market society".[125] As Karl Polanyi put it, incorporating society into the market mechanism subjugated the very essence of society to the laws of the market.[126]

Liberalism inherited individualism, egalitarianism, and universalism from Christianity.[127] On this basis, it holds a society that is an ordinary sum of individual atoms bound together by a "commercial pact". From the perspective of liberalism, peoples, nations, and cultures are a secondary issue; they are not bearers of intrinsic value, but rather are hindrances to the spread of quantitative logic and pure economic calculation.[128] Of all the modern versions of egalitarianism, the *Nouvelle Droite* sees liberalism as the most dangerous, as it most effectively causes social disintegration and the dilution of collective identities. Alain de Benoist summates: "The main enemy, for us, remains bourgeois liberalism and the Atlanticist-American 'West,' of which European social democracy is one of the most dangerous surrogates."[129]

3.2 Ethnopluralism and Differentialist Anti-Racism

Alain de Benoist and Charles Champetier write:

> In regard to universalist utopias and the withering of traditional identities, the French New Right affirms the primacy of differences, which are neither transitory features leading to some higher form of unity, nor incidental aspects of private life. Rather, these differences are the very substance of social life. They can be native (ethnic, linguistic), but also political. Citizenship implies belonging, allegiance and participation in public life at different levels. [...] By contrast, one cannot be a citizen of the world, for the 'world' is not a political category. [...] The French New Right upholds the cause of

---

125 Ibid., 42.
126 See Polanyi, *Great Transformation*.
127 de Benoist, *Orientations pour des années*, 38.
128 Ibid., 49.
129 Alain de Benoist, "*L'ennemi principal*", 39.

peoples [...]. The French New Right supports peoples struggling against Western imperialism.[130]

Thus, the *Nouvelle Droite* sees cultures as irreducible wholes which, all of them together, create the richness of the world. This richness is what needs to be preserved. Liberal-style globalisation entails universal deculturation. The dam to be set up against deculturation is "ethnopluralism", which is equipped with two fundamental postulates: "the right to difference" (*droit a la différence*) and the "cause of peoples" (*cause des peuples*). The first says that it would be better for humanity if cultural diversity is preserved and defended against the disintegrating impact of the world market. The second postulate demands that every community have the right to preserve its cultural particularity and unique identity.[131]

Alain de Benoist writes:

> What is the principal menace today? It is the progressive demise of the world's diversity. The levelling of people, the reduction of all cultures to a 'global *civilisation*' built on what is most *common*. Already, from one end of the planet to the other, we see the construction of the same kinds of buildings, the establishment of the same mental habits. From the Holiday Inn to Howard Johnson, we see the emerging contours of a universally grey world. I have travelled widely — over many continents. The *joy* that one experiences when travelling is to behold the varied modes of life still deeply-rooted, to see different peoples living according to their own rhythm, to see another skin-colour, another culture, another mentality — people who are proud of their *difference*. I believe that this diversity is the treasure of the world, and that egalitarianism is killing it. It is for this reason that it is important not merely to 'respect others' — half-heartedly — but to arouse everywhere the most legitimate desire possible: the desire to assert an identity that is unlike any other, to defend a heritage, to govern oneself according to that which one is. And this implies the struggle, head on, against a pseudo-antiracism

---

130 de Benoist and Champetier, "Manifesto", in Sunic, *Against Democracy and Equality*, 229.

131 Michael O'Meara, *Guillaume Faye and the Battle of Europe* (London: Arktos, 2013), 27.

that denies differences, and against a vicious racism which is also only the refusal of the Other — the denial of diversity.[132]

From the *Nouvelle Droite*'s perspective, racism is a theory that proclaims that (a) there are qualitative differences between races, and the existence of these differences allows for defining different races' place in a hierarchical order; (b) the value of an individual is entirely resultant of their belonging to a given race; (c) race is a decisive factor in the history of humanity. A racist is anyone who professes at least one of the above views. All three of these, however, are assessed by the *Nouvelle Droite* as false. They are false because, firstly, if there do exist significant differences between races according to one statistically isolated criterion, then there are no absolute qualitative differences between them. Secondly, there is no universal, para-human paradigm in a position to create a hierarchy of the different races. Thirdly, it is clear that one cannot evaluate an individual exclusively in terms of their belonging to a race. The *Nouvelle Droite* does not consider racism to be a pathological individual disease that is based on prejudices (thus suggesting the irrationality of racism), but rather a false doctrine whose origin lies in scientific positivism, according to which one can "scientifically" evaluate human communities, and in socio-cultural evolutionism, which frames the history of mankind as a whole as proceeding in a series of developmental stages tending towards progress (where some peoples are more "developed" than others).[133]

Through the *Nouvelle Droite*'s lens, one can adopt two basic positions against racism in principle. The first is "universalist anti-racism," the implications of which are identical to racism, i.e., rejecting the Other. This type of anti-racism is supposed to reduce, through the prospects of assimilation (ignoring cultural difference), the Other to One's Own, and thereby exhibits its own incapacity to affirm and

---

132 de Benoist, *View from the Right — Volume I*, 16.
133 de Benoist and Champetier, "Manifesto", in Sunic, *Against Democracy and Equality*, 230.

respect Otherness as such. In other words, Otherness simply isn't acknowledged. The opposite standpoint as postulated by the *Nouvelle Droite* is that of "differentialist anti-racism" ("ethno-differentialism", "differentialism"), which says that the irreducible pluralism of cultures is a value in and of itself. The first stance wants to erase culture difference. The second recognises this difference, but does not create a hierarchy of races. The first is heir to the Enlightenment, seeing human individuals as abstract beings. The second is heir to Romanticism (Johann Gottfried Herder) and argues that individuals are inseparably connected with collective identities which ought to be acknowledged in the public space. Universalist anti-racism wants a "united" humanity, whereas differentialist anti-racism regards the diversity of peoples and cultures as constituting the richness of humanity.[134] From the *Nouvelle Droite*'s perspective, racism is not opposed by negating the existence of races or by multiculturalism, but only by rejecting both exclusion and assimilation: "neither apartheid nor the melting pot; rather, acceptance of the other as Other through a dialogic perspective of mutual enrichment".[135]

However, one must be conscious that maintaining "authentic" diversity requires preserving relatively tight ethno-cultural borders. As Alain de Benoist argues, it is common knowledge in the social sciences that when two populations significantly different from each other in terms of mentality and culture live next to each other, then, once a certain threshold of migration is passed, social pathologies inevitably emerge from this state of affairs: discrimination, segregation, deculturation, and crime.[136] This, however, does not mean that immigrants themselves should be demonised. The phenomenon of immigration should be distinguished from the immigrants themselves. De Benoist considers the phenomenon of (mass) migration to be negative, because

---

134 de Benoist, *Racisme et xénophobie*, op. cit., 210.
135 de Benoist and Champetier, "Manifesto", in Sunic, *Against Democracy and Equality*, 231.
136 de Benoist, *Les Idées à l'endroit*, op. cit., 154.

it arises above all out of poverty and necessity. Accordingly, it needs to be rejected or considerably restricted. Moreover, it is obvious that the problems of the Third World cannot be solved by the mass relocation of entire populations to Western countries. It also bears emphasising that immigration, in de Benoist's view, is an effect, not the cause of these problems. It is not mass immigration that causes Western peoples to lose their clear identity (immigrants often preserve their traditions, while Europeans do not). Rather, the monolithic style of production and consumption, the cult of goods, the spread of the world market, Americanisation — in a word, global capitalism — are incomparably more responsible for causing the erosion of cultures than immigration. De Benoist writes: "Opening a 'fast food' site or a supermarket is significantly more harmful to our identity than the construction of a mosque".[137] The greatest threat to Europeans' identity is not the identity of the Other, but that which threatens all identities.[138] The right to difference, thus, means defending both "one's own" as well as "foreign" identities and particularities.

Besides ideological-doctrinal questions, there are also economic issues at stake. It's often hastily repeated that immigration is necessary for the economy. According to de Benoist, such a statement suggests that economic imperatives are more important than any others. This, however, can be contested — it is a matter of conscious choice. On the other hand, "the formulation 'necessary for the economy' actually means 'necessary for the profits of big companies'".[139] Thus, de Benoist connects the phenomenon of mass immigration with, above all, big business. It is big companies, ideologically assisted by the left, that are the ringleaders of mass immigration. De Benoist calls immigration the "reserve army of capital".[140] The majority of society, including immi-

---

137 de Benoist, *Racisme et xénophobie*, 212.

138 Ibid., 213.

139 de Benoist, *Les Idées à l'endroit*, 154.

140 Alain de Benoist, "*Imigracja — armia rezerwowa kapitału*", nacjonalista.pl [https://nacjonalista.pl/2011/08/25/alain-de-benoist-imigracja-armia-rezer-

grants, ultimately loses from such. Firstly, immigration halts innovation by encouraging the use of wage dumping. Immigrant workers, in turn, are treated like pariahs — disdained and exploited. Neither the right nor the left seems to understand the essence of the problem: the first erroneously associates unemployment and immigration and, drawing on this connection, wants to "kick out the Arabs". The second treats immigrants in an abstract manner as "people just like others" and doesn't see the need for any control of immigration.[141] De Benoist reproaches both sides of the debate: "Whoever criticises capitalism while simultaneously approving of immigration, whose first victim is one's own working class, should best shut up. Whoever criticises immigration while simultaneously being silent on the matter of capitalism should do the same".[142]

Moreover, de Benoist believes that the very idea of internally homogenous nation-states is an anachronism from the 19th century. He concludes that, regardless whether one likes it or not, the majority of Western societies are multicultural and will probably remain so.[143] Therefore, the question of integrating immigrants also remains. De Benoist thinks that the worst possible model for such is the Jacobin, where integration is taken to mean assimilation. In other words, immigrants are forced to cut themselves off from their own roots. Yet, dialogue with the Other is possible only if they remain Other and aren't

---

wowa-kapitalu] [accessed 05.05.2020].
141 de Benoist, *Les idées à l'endroit*, 155.
142 de Benoist, "*Imigracja — armia rezerwowa kapitału*".
143 de Benoist, *Racisme et xénophobie*, 213. Within GRECE itself, opinions on this matter differed. Guillaume Faye, when he still belonged to GRECE, wrote in 1983: "Between multi-racial society and civil war [...] there exists a third way: working with immigrants to organise their return to their ancestral lands, collaborating with destination countries, where we should help create jobs and rebuilt their nations that have been destroyed by neo-colonialism. On this condition, it may be said: 'Frenchmen and immigrants, the same struggle'!" Guillaume Faye, *La société multiraciale en question*, *Éléments pour la Civilisation Européenne* 48–49 (1983–1984), 76.

reduced to being moulded into one's Own. Human existence cannot be reduced to the biological level. Collective identities are partially consequential of ethnic origin, history, and culture.

In the era of economic, technological, and financial globalisation, national borders have become "porous". Therefore, Alain de Benoist deems it necessary to create conditions in which collective identities can be preserved. This should be done not from above, but from below — on the level of regions, cities, and neighbourhoods.[144] The model proposed by Alain de Benoist therefore calls into question the republican (French) model of assimilation as well as the liberal multicultural model.[145] The foundation of such would be a federation of ethnic groups in which each one has the right to cultivate its own particularity within the framework of a decentralised form of state.

3.3 Europe of a Hundred Flags: The Project for an Imperial Federal Europe

Alain de Benoist has christened the political project of a united Europe aligned with the *Nouvelle Droite*'s values "a Europe of a hundred flags".[146] This would be a federal and, in a certain sense (mainly symbolic-aesthetic), "imperial" Europe. It bears underscoring right away that the imperial principle should not be confused with "imperialism", i.e., military expansionism. De Benoist understands Empire as a certain political form that "has the most respect for the particularities of its diverse components".[147] Empire is a model which, in de Benoist's opinion, would enable the integration of European peoples (and ethnic groups) while simultaneously giving them relatively large autonomy on the local and regional level.

---

144 de Benoist, *Racisme et xénophobie*, 211.
145 A. Spektorowski, "The French New Right: Differentialism and the Idea of Ethnophilian Exclusionism", *Polity* 33(2) (2000), 302.
146 Alain de Benoist, *L'empire intérieur* (Cognac: 1995), 161.
147 Alain de Benoist, "*Imperium* — kwestionariusz", *Trygław* 16 (2015), 8.

The basis of such an empire is the autonomy of its particular parts, as was the case in the Roman Empire, which was characterised by religious freedom and the legal autonomy of its subjugated peoples. This is diametrically opposite to how things look in the case of the centralised nation-state, which, de Benoist argues, has proven to be destructive of local identities and cultural particularities.[148] From this standpoint, de Benoist advocates a decentralised, federal "imperial model" that would be the antithesis of the modern, centralised, "Jacobin" nation-state.

3.3.1 The Starting Point: The Primacy of Culture and Politics (Instead of the Economy and Commerce)

After the Second World War, the European integration model — in the guise of the European Community of Coal and Steel, which later gradually took on the form of the European Union — was based on (and is still based on) almost exclusively the economic level. According to de Benoist, this is an erroneous approach, as concentrating exclusively on the economic sphere (the free market, common currency, etc.) leads to neglect of the sphere of cultural and political identity. The Frenchman argues that this is not a proper foundation for European integration, for it leads to abandoning a political project *sensu stricto* or, in other words, a civilisational project. Instead of creating a Europe that is strong, autonomous, and politically sovereign, it creates a plutocratic "European market", an organism that is centralised, culturally homogenised, and hostilely predisposed towards the national question.[149]

From the *Nouvelle Droite*'s perspective, European integration should be based on different principles than hitherto. Integration is needed on the political and cultural levels as well, drawing on common history, tradition, and identity that would simultaneously foster local particularities. This is what is supposed to characterise the "imperial" model. The *Nouvelle Droite* by no means neglects the economic

---

148 Ibid.
149 O'Meara, *New Culture, New Right*, 232.

question, but it emphasises that the economy should be subordinated to long-term political and civilisational goals.[150] Instead of the current neoliberal model, the *Nouvelle Droite* is for a decentralised, federal model and relative economic protectionism in the form of a semi-autarkic, continental economic zone.[151] De Benoist writes:

> For us, the people is not a secondary entity after the economy. Economic activity should be subordinated to the needs of the people […]. The economy is a political 'means', and not vice versa. This equally means that, among other things, economic activity should support 'national independence', and not — as is the case today — threaten national independence by […] the politics of free trade.[152]

And further:

> Economic life cannot be reduced to free trade or business and market values. The economy must take social reality into account, and it cannot be entirely free from political leadership. It is by all means possible to implement an economy that is based on social solidarism, with private and public sectors, and free associations like cooperatives and workers' collectives. The dictatorship of financial markets must be destroyed, and the economy must be based on real production, not speculation.[153]

3.3.2 Organic Democracy

Alain de Benoist states:

> According to its original meaning, democracy means 'the power of the people'. Yet, this power can be interpreted in very different ways. The most reasonable approach, then, appears to be the historical one, which begins with the premise that 'genuine' democracy is first of all the political system

---

150 Ibid., 233.
151 Ibid., 233–234.
152 de Benoist, *Orientations pour des années*, 50.
153 de Benoist, "*Nowoczesność jako wróg tożsamości*", 10.

established in Antiquity by those who invented both the thing itself and the word that describes it.[154]

Therefore, in de Benoist's opinion, in order to properly investigate what democracy is in essence, it is necessary to turn to Greek democracy, not to the system that the modern world calls "democracy".[155]

The concept of "democracy" has to a large extent been subject to distortion — virtually all contemporary states present themselves as democracies, even the Democratic Republic of the Congo and the Democratic People's Republic of Korea. When Alain de Benoist speaks of democracy, he has in mind its original, ancient Greek version, not its liberal simulacrum — liberal democracy — with its emphasis on the rule of law. In the Athenian model of democracy, all political decisions were established with citizens in a direct manner, and citizenship was connected to belonging to the *polis*, i.e., to the political community based on common culture, religion, and kinship,[156] rather than inalienable rights of the abstract individual.

Essential here is the question of the notion of "freedom". For the ancient Greeks, freedom was not understood as emancipation, but as belonging — as the right and political ability to participate in the life of the community. Freedom was not associated with secession, but with being tied to the *polis*: "This was not *liberty as autonomy*, but *liberty as participation*. It was not meant to extend beyond the community, but was practised solely within the framework of the *polis*. Liberty

---

154 Alain de Benoist, *The Problem of Democracy*, trans. Sergio Knipe (London: Arktos, 2011), 19.

155 Ibid., 21.

156 Ibid., 23-24: "To some extent, *demos* and *ethnos* coincide: democracy is conceived here in relation not to the individual, but to the *polis*, which is to say the city as an *organised community*. [...] To be a citizen meant, in the fullest sense of the word, to belong to a homeland — that is, to a homeland and a past. One is born an Athenian — one does not become it (rare exceptions notwithstanding). [...] Political equality, established by law, derived from a common origin [...]. Democracy was rooted in a notion of *autochthonous* citizenship."

implied belonging."¹⁵⁷ Immediately striking here is that de Benoist draws on Benjamin Constant's distinction between ancient and modern liberties.¹⁵⁸

Organic democracy, thus, is based on a concrete ethno-cultural community, not on being a citizen in a formal-legal sense. According to de Benoist, authentic democracy is possible only where there exists a real feeling of the common good and common destiny. And this happens only when a community is fused together by culture, heritage, and historical memory, and not merely by the right to vote. De Benoist writes:

---

157 Ibid., 25.

158 Henri-Benjamin Constant de Rebecque (1767–1830), whom Émile Faguet deemed "the inventor of liberalism", was one of the first individuals to define himself as a "liberal". He drew a distinction between Athenian democracy, which he described as direct-participatory, and modern democracy, which is taken to be based on law, freedom from state intervention, and a representative system (which is due to the significantly greater population size of modern societies compared to ancient ones). See J. Trybusiewicz, "*Idea wolności w myśli Benjamina Constant*", *Archiwum historii filozofii i myśli społecznej* 13 (1967), 23: "Constant makes a distinction between the modern and ancient understandings of freedom. The freedom of the ancients was based on the collective and direct execution of authority as a whole [...]. Such a freedom — which is based on every citizen being an authentic and direct sovereign — went hand-in-hand with a complete subordination of the individual to the authority of the collective [...]. Such a freedom is impossible today. [...] Firstly, ancient states were small states, whereas today — in the whole of Europe — the participation [of the individual] in authority is so little that it even becomes a proper abstraction. The second reason that the ancient type of freedom is an anachronism today is the development of commerce, which has everywhere replaced war as the means of gaining goods [...]. This fact influences modern nations' social life in an essential way. Commerce does not leave individuals free time — to engage in politics, for example — as war once did: it demands unceasing hustle and bustle. Hence the necessity of delegating power and transferring it into the hands of representatives. Commerce also does not tolerate any intervention in its own affairs: such would mean its annihilation. In this way, commerce inclines people towards a 'keen desire for independence'. Thus, commerce is in a certain sense the father of modern freedom."

Democracy must be founded not on the alleged inalienable rights of rootless individuals, but on citizenship, which sanctions one's belonging to a given folk — that is, a culture, history and destiny — and to the political structure within which it has developed. Liberty results from one's identity as a member of a folk: the liberty of the folk commands all other liberties. In genuine democracies, citizens only possess equal political rights as members of the same national and folk community. [...] A democracy based not on the idea of rootless individuals or 'humanity' but on the *folk* as a collective organism and privileged historical agent might be termed an *organic democracy*. It would represent the logical evolution of Greek democracy [...].[159]

3.3.3. Federalism, Subsidiarity, Decentralisation

Europe should be a federal structure that integrates all of its component parts while simultaneously recognising their autonomy. The *sine qua non* condition of a renaissance of European civilisation is this affirmation and fostering of historical cultures. Of key significance here is the principle of subsidiarity.[160]

In de Benoist's perspective, the imperial model is a structure that is strongly decentralised and consists of self-governing communities. Federalism is the proper means of integrating these communities into an empire that would enable them to preserve their relative autonomy. The essential point of reference here is Johannes Althusius,[161] whom de Benoist puts on par with Thomas Hobbes, Niccolo Machiavelli, Jean Rodin, and Jean-Jacques Rousseau.[162] According to Althusius, the individual is not a self-sufficient entity. Rather, Althusius discerns human existence to be based on belonging to a community or to many

---

159 de Benoist, *The Problem of Democracy*, 98.
160 de Benoist and Champetier, "Manifesto", in Sunic, *Against Democracy and Equality*, 235.
161 Johannes Althusius (1563–1638) was a German Calvinist philosopher and theorist of the State and law. He is known for raising the topic of federalism and subsidiarity. His main work is *Politica Methodice Digesta, Atque Exemplis Sacris et Profanis Illustrata* (1603).
162 de Benoist, "Johannes Althusius (1557–1638)" in *Critiques — Théoriques*, 283.

interdependent communities. Althusius drew on Aristotle, for whom man is a "social animal" who by nature strives for mutual solidarity.[163] What is essential is that this German philosopher rejected the concept of natural law, which holds that basic social rights can be derived from the individual in separation from concrete political belonging.[164] The starting point of Althusius' political considerations is the idea of a "symbiotic community" (*consociato symbiotica*), which is defined as "an organic group composed of social beings". Althusius argued, like Cicero, that community life arises out of the social nature of man. Society is primary to the individual. Society is, firstly, a relationship between members of a group; secondly, a set of social and political agreements constituted from the bottom up and established by autonomous groups ("consociations"), ranging from families and households to guilds, corporations, cities, provinces, etc. These "consociations" create a certain whole, grouping together from the smallest to the largest, and on each of these levels individuals create a network of mutual social relations. In turn, the State is seen as the aggregate of symbiotic communities constituted on the basis of subsidiarity. For Althusius, political science is the methodological description of the conditions of social life, which he calls "symbiosis".[165]

The federalist vision finds de Benoist's favor inasmuch as it is free from "Jacobinist" perversions (centralisation from above, forced unification, lack of respect for local particularities, etc.). Decentralisation, federalism, and subsidiarity, or, in other words, "building from the bottom up", enable a relatively large degree of autonomy for smaller political communities which, thanks to this structure, can preserve their regional specificity and relative sovereignty. At the same time,

---

163 Alain de Benoist, "What is Sovereignty?", *New European Conservative* [https://neweuropeanconservative.files.wordpress.com/2012/11/what-is-sovereignty.pdf].

164 Ibid.

165 Ibid.

the whole is preserved by the multi-levered network of cooperation and political authority.[166]

3.3.4 Continental Geopolitics: Sovereign Europe vs. *Pax Americana*

The *Nouvelle Droite* is critical of the concept of the "West" since, in their opinion, it is mistakenly treated as a synonym for Europe — whereas, in reality, this concept is a symptom of the alienation of Europeans. The term "Americanosphere"[167] would be one of their own approximate expressions for such. From the *Nouvelle Droite*'s perspective, the United States is an "anti-Europe", as in some sense it took shape as a counter to Europe.[168] The first immigrants to find themselves on the American continent wanted to sever themselves from Europe culturally, not create a better version of it. For them, the biblical Israel was the symbol of a new, potentially better society. In other words, American identity is foreign to European identity.

One of the most important elements of the project for a "European Empire" is what could be termed a "continental" geopolitics. This geopolitics is presented as an alternative to the Euroatlantic orientation that dominates today. Attention should be paid first and foremost to the fact that the *Nouvelle Droite* does not see Europe as solely a geographical concept. Europe is not only a continent, but a civilisation shaped by Greek philosophy and Roman law, a civilisation that is, in its own way, a synthesis of related peoples mainly of Indo-European origin. All of this shaped a particular heritage: identity, mentality, social institutions, and moral norms.[169]

"World history is the history of the wars waged by maritime powers against land or continental powers and by land powers against sea

---

166 O'Meara, *New Culture, New Right*, 231.
167 Ibid., 219.
168 Ibid., 176.
169 Ibid., 235.

or maritime powers", states Carl Schmitt.[170] In all likelihood, the archetypal example of the clash between thallassocracy and tellurocracy would be the Punic Wars, or the war between Carthage and Rome. In the modern era, the place of Carthage has been taken — in the *Nouvelle Droite*'s eyes — by the Anglo-Saxons: first the English, later the Americans. As for the role of Rome, first the Germans tried to take it upon themselves, and later the Russians.[171] What is essential is that the rivalry between Land and Sea takes on the rank of a symbol in the *Nouvelle Droite*'s perspective, wherein thallassocracy is seen as "maritime nomadism" that is hostile to the "rooted" cultures and peoples settled on land.[172] The strategic goal of "modern Carthage" (the US) is to dominate "Rome" (Europe) through cultural colonisation, economic dependence, and the deployment of military bases.

Up until the collapse of the Soviet Union, the *Nouvelle Droite* held the position of "Neither West nor East". In that time, Europe was divided between two camps: liberal and communist. The collapse of the USSR meant the ultimate triumph of liberalism in Europe and, as follows, the complete hegemony of the US. Euroatlanticism, NATO, and the current form of the European Union are seen as keeping Europe in a status of dependency. One way to break *Pax Americana* would be to ally with Russia and the Third World (against the US).[173] Only by breaking American hegemony on the Old Continent can Europe regain real sovereignty.

---

[170] Carl Schmitt, "Land & Sea, Part I" [https://counter-currents.com/2011/03/carl-schmitts-land-sea-part-1/].

[171] Appeals to the heritage of ancient Rome were made before the modern era by the German "Holy Roman Empire" and the Russian concept of the "Third Rome".

[172] O'Meara, *New Culture, New Right*, 237.

[173] Ibid., 219, 238.

3.4 An Alliance of Europe and the Third World: Right-Wing Third-Worldism

From the *Nouvelle Droite*'s perspective, Europe finds itself in a state of economic and cultural dependence on the United States. Of course, this is not a desired state of affairs. The *Nouvelle Droite*'s atypical attitude towards the Third World (atypical for a movement associated with the right) is a result of this.

First, we need to start with specifying the term "Third World". Until 1989, this term was used for states that belonged neither to the Western-capitalist bloc nor to the Eastern-communist bloc. The differences between these particular countries were already significant, but only with the collapse of the Eastern bloc did the validity of the term come to be questioned. The term "developing countries" is more often used in current political science and international relations.[174] However, this concept is equally to be treated with certain reservations. Alain de Benoist emphasises that the very term "developing country" is ideologically loaded inasmuch as it posts the conviction, dominant in the contemporary Western world, that the "development" of a country is conceived solely in its economic aspect. The economy is thus seen as a factor that determines national existence. In line with the perspective of economism, everything is evaluated through the prism of economic efficiency and the order of quantity — other aspects of life are devalued.[175]

However, if one looks at the world from the point of view of, for example, the strength of social ties, living tradition, or spiritual life, then one could claim that it is actually the West that is "behind". De Benoist draws attention to the fact that cultural and geographical context has an enormous influence on economic and consumer behaviour — in traditional societies, most motivations are of a non-economic nature.[176]

---

174 W. Giełżyński, *Trzeci Świat — dwie trzecie świata* (Warsaw: 1984), 11.
175 de Benoist, *Europe, Tiers Monde, même combat*, 102–103.
176 Ibid., 118.

Moreover, there are significant differences between people from the Western cultural circle and people from the Third World. Among the latter, wealth is often understood not only on the material dimension, but also on the social and cultural dimensions.[177] The model of development that the West "proposes" to Third World countries is based on a linear, gradual concept of social development which is presented as having no alternative: over the course of gradual convergence, all societies are driven towards the singular recognised form of "developed" society, one that emerges "on the ruins of traditional society, the erosion of differences and collective particularities, and the spread of social anomie".[178]

De Benoist describes this vision of universalistic development as a "hypertrophied ethnocentrism" who takes its own "swelling" to be universal truth.[179] This is the case because this model of unipolar development causes the gradual disintegration of traditional social structures and, in effect, the destruction of the diversity of socio-political systems.[180] In other words, Western "support" for the modernisation of Third World countries is their de facto deculturation, i.e., economic and cultural dependence.

Consequently, the promotion of the Western capitalist model in the Third World countries that are unfit and unprepared for such disturbs their traditional modus operandi, in effect yielding, among other phenomena, the loss of markets for local artisans, the mass exodus of the rural population, turbulent proletarianisation, etc. In summary, what was supposed to be modernisation tuns out to be really a second colonisation. Such has nothing in common with authentic development. In this way, as Alain de Benoist maintains, the countries of the Third World will never get out of the state of "underdevelopment".[181]

---

177 Ibid., 129–130.
178 Ibid., 105.
179 Ibid., 84.
180 Ibid., 86.
181 Ibid., 138–139.

In connection with this, it is necessary to revise the concept of "development". What the Western cultural circle understands with this term is the result of an ideological choice. De Benoist sees no reason why all of the world's cultures would put forth qualitative growth as their main goal. In his opinion, attention needs to be paid to ceasing to see "development" in exclusively economic terms. Instead of the strictly quantitative, de Benoist proposes a qualitative notion of development which can be defined as "balance". To quote the French thinker: "Understood in purely economic categories, growth has nothing in common with balance; it is nothing more than a synonym for the primitive increase of production which in no case whatsoever is necessarily bound up with improving the life of the majority [of citizens — P. B.]. [...] In other words, growth cannot be separated from extra-economic factors."[182]

As for a good example of a well-conceived strategy of development, de Benoist cites Japan, which based its modernisation on two fundamental premises: (1) not importing products that are dispensable when it comes to the growth of local industry, and (2) not importing products which either are or can be produced locally, even if at higher cost.[183] This example is essential: Japanese products were once associated with being of poor quality, but thanks to responsible economic policy, Japan eventually managed to become an economic power while preserving the strong position of its national tradition and culture.[184] The French thinker holds the position that the Third World should not strive to copy Western solutions and should rid itself in general of seeing the global economy as a homogenous market space. Instead, he proposes applying the concept of endogenous development within

---

182 Ibid., 128–129. A similar view was taken by the English economist Edward Mishan. See E. Mishan, *Spór o wzrost gospodarczy* (Warsaw: 1986)

183 Alain de Benoist, "*Pour le Tiers monde, quelles solutions?*", *Éléments pour la Civilisation Européenne* (1983–1984), 45.

184 de Benoist, *Europe, Tiers Monde, même combat*, 204.

autarchic great spaces.¹⁸⁵ In de Benoist's opinion, only such a strategy can enable the countries of the Third World to modernise in a way that would also preserve their political independence.

Colonisation, de Benoist argues, was not beneficial for European states at all. He points to the fact that the countries that first started colonising America (Spain and Portugal) achieved a high degree of economic development later than northern states. In turn, France and England in the 19th century saw relatively small growth compared to Germany. It is precisely in this that de Benoist sees Germany's path to economic might: in his opinion, it is not that Germany succeeded despite not possessing colonies, but rather only thanks to not having them.¹⁸⁶

The *Nouvelle Droite*'s anti-colonialism arises from its anti-universalist as well as its anti-Christian position. After all, carrying the Word of God was a strongly present motivation among the conquerors of the New World.¹⁸⁷ Moreover, de Benoist treats racism as a modern form of biblically originated universalism, presenting his own position as "against all racisms". This concerns not only the very fact of the conquest of the New World, but above all the declaration of the indigenous

---

185 de Benoist, "*Pour le Tiers monde, quelles solutions?*", 39.

186 de Benoist, *Europe, Tiers Monde, même combat*, 25. A similar opinion has been expressed by Piotr Kownacki, *Trzeci Świat a polityczny aspekt globalizacji gospodarczej* (Warsaw: 2006), 28: "The relatively insignificant extent of German involvement in the colonisation of the world cannot be regarded as coincidental. It was strictly connected with the prioritisation of internal reforms, to which colonial engagement was not conducive. The leaning towards and encouragement of colonisation manifested by Chancellor Bismarck was directed towards other European states with the calculation that such would weaken them by drawing them into colonial battles and lower their capacity to counteract the German economic challenge."

187 See Howard Zinn, *A People's History of the United States* (New York: 2015). It is also worth mentioning the fact that the Catholic Church "legalised" the colonial division of South America between Spain and Portugal in 1494 through the Treaty of Tordesillas. See Kownacki, *Trzeci Świat a polityczny aspekt globalizacji gospodarczej*, 24–25.

population through forced conversion.[188] Such Christian conceptual clichés still have an impact on politics — the "universal mission of democracy" (US foreign policy) is taken to be a manifestation of such.

Summary and Clarifications

Adequately classifying the *Nouvelle Droite* is no easy task. This current is just as rich as it is variegated and multi-dimensional, which lends to many misunderstandings.

First and foremost, it should be highlighted that the *Nouvelle Droite* is not a political movement.[189] The *Nouvelle Droite* is a cultural and intellectual movement, a school of thought. In this respect, any attempts at situating and classifying it "by force" necessarily lead to distortions or reductions that in no way help one understand or explain the movement. As mentioned in the introduction, the very term "New Right" is a label pinned by the movement's opponents — it was not coined by the movement's own representatives. Of course, the *Nouvelle Droite* does have a significant political component, but his is only one element of the movement — in no case does it constitute it as a whole. The *Nouvelle Droite*'s ideational legacy encompasses vast and variegated subject matter involving works from, among others, the fields of epistemology, theoretical physics, polemology, linguistics, economics, religious studies, law, and ecology.[190] Attempts at describing the *Nouvelle Droite* as a strictly political current, passing over its philosophical and even theological level, seem to be a matter of intellectual dishonesty or a sign of a lack of credibility. Unfortunately, this is often the case among researchers, especially in the case of English-language works.[191]

---

188 Alain de Benoist, "*Les métamorphoses du colonialisme*", *Éléments pour la Civilisation Européenne* 48–49 (1983–1984), 6.

189 de Benoist, "Alain de Benoist answers Tamir Bar-On", 143; Sunic, *Against Democracy and Equality*, 11.

190 de Benoist, "Alain de Benoist answers Tamir Bar-On", 145.

191 Alain de Benoist addresses exactly this accusation to Tamir Bar-On in ibid., 144.

Classifying the "New Right" simply as a right-wing political current on the basis of the name is just as sensical as attempting to describe a book with the same title. One can, however, have the impression that this sometimes happens to be the case. The title of Jarosław Tomasiewicz's article from 1993 is "Against Equality and Democracy: The New Right in France". Tamir Bar-On claims in turn — allegedly following Tomislav Sunic, although without citing any source — that the thinkers of the *Nouvelle Droite* reject equality and democracy in principle.[192] Taking into consideration the fact that one of the most well-known works of the *Nouvelle Droite* by Tomislav Sunic is titled *Against Democracy and Equality: The European New Right* (1990), there rather can't be any talk of a complete coincidence here.[193] It bears dwelling on this briefly. Despite its appearance, the very expression "against equality and democracy" does not at all communicate the ideational content of the *Nouvelle Droite*. This "catchy" expression used by Sunic plays the role of an intellectual provocation,[194] on which point Alain de Benoist himself points out:

> The English edition of Tomislav Sunic's book carries the title *Against Democracy and Equality: The European New Right*. I suspect the author chose this title out of sheer provocation — a title that I have always considered inappropriate! It must be emphasised that the ENR has never held positions hostile to equality and democracy. It has been critical of egalitarianism and has highlighted the limits of liberal democracy — which is quite a different

---

192 Tamir Bar-On, "The French New Right: Neither Right, nor Left?", *Journal for the Study of Radicalism* 8:1 (2014), 12.

193 Tomasiewicz, "*Przeciwko równości i demokracji*" in idem, *Między faszyzmem i anarchizmem*, 25–28.

194 Sunic, *Against Democracy and Equality*, 13: "Someone may strongly object to my usage of the title *Against Democracy and Equality* — as if I am hell-bent on offering a recipe for destroying democracy. Things would have been much easier if I had instead employed the terms 'mobocracy', 'plutocracy', 'mafiocracy', 'kleptocracy', or 'democratism' in order to denounce the ex-Communist and the present liberal democratic system — both systems which have never tired, to be sure, of posing as 'the only true democracy'."

matter. Between equality and egalitarianism there is roughly the same difference as between liberty and liberalism, between the universal and universalism, or between the common good and Communism. Egalitarianism aims at introducing equality where there is no place for it and where it does not match with reality, as for instance when somebody argues that all individuals have the same skills and the same gifts. But egalitarianism also aims at apprehending equality as a synonym for 'sameness', i.e., the opposite of diversity. Equality of men and women, for example, does not obliterate the reality of the differences between the two sexes. Similarly, equal political rights in democracy do not presuppose that all citizens must be identical or have the same talents; rather they must have the same rights based on their belonging equally to the same polity of citizens.[195]

The above-mentioned article by Tomasiewicz claims, among other things, that: (1) according to the *Nouvelle Droite*, man is an animal just like all others;[196] (2) in connection with this, the *Nouvelle Droite* affirms social Darwinism; (3) the *Nouvelle Droite* rejects the idea of equality as "contradicting nature"; and (4) according to the *Nouvelle Droite*, democracy is an unrealistic system, for the law of nature is inequality.[197] Firstly, however, one of the cardinal traits of the *Nouvelle Droite* is anti-reductionism — man is not considered to be an "animal just like all others", as we have discussed in this chapter. Secondly, the *Nouvelle Droite* current does not profess a "cult of nature" (in any form[198]), nor does it support social Darwinism. The last claim is completely bizarre, especially if we take into account that de Benoist

---

195 Alain de Benoist, "The New Right: Forty Years After" in Sunic, *Against Democracy and Equality*, 18–19.

196 Tomasiewicz refers to a quotation of Konrad Lorenz, who was essentially one of the inspirations for the *Nouvelle Droite*, but having an inspiration does not mean that one adopts every particular statement uncritically.

197 Tomasiewicz, "Przeciwko równości i demokracji" in idem, *Między faszyzmem i anarchizmem*, 27.

198 "Paganism" or "neo-paganism" is sometimes identified with a cult of nature of social-Darwinist provenance. Although social-Darwinist ideologies sometimes cite "pagan" sources on the symbolico-axiological level (often superficially understood Nietzscheanism), this is by no means the general rule. Alain de

devoted an entire book, *Démocratie: le problème* (1985), to defending democracy[199] (Tomasiewicz's article appeared seven years after the first edition of this book).

The *Nouvelle Droite* is often described as "elitist".[200] This is a source of many misunderstandings. With all certainty, the *Nouvelle Droite* is not elitist in the capitalistic-economic-materialist sense, nor in the natural-social-Darwinistic sense. One should firstly ponder what it means to speak of "elitism" at all. Tomasiewicz also uses the term "aristocratism", which is somewhat better but still doesn't fully capture or exhaust the matter. De Benoist himself rejects describing the *Nouvelle Droite* as "elitist" or "hierarchical":[201]

> The New Right [...] does not defend 'aristocratic' values but the values of any traditional society, i.e., any society not yet conquered by modernity. From the traditional point of view, aristocratic and popular values are about the same. These are all the values inherent in an ethics of honor. In opposition to economic and commercial values, they are also the values of disinterestedness and generosity, as expressed in the system of the gift and the counter-gift.[202]

And elsewhere:

Benoist himself has repeatedly emphasised that "paganism" cannot be reduced to worshipping nature. See de Benoist, "*Wywiad z Alainem de Benoist*", 31.

199 de Benoist, "*Imperium — kwestionariusz*", 6: "Today, political legitimisation can be based solely on the sovereignty of the people, i.e., it can only be democratic. The critique of democracy 'from the right' is very unconvincing to me. One great merit of democracy is that it is the only system that enables the participation of all citizens in public affairs."

200 Bar-On, "The French New Right: Neither Right, nor Left?", 33; idem, *Rethinking the French New Right*, 57, *passim*; Tomasiewicz, "*Przeciwko równości i demokracji*" in idem, *Między faszyzmem i anarchizmem*, 28; Bartyzel, "*Metapolityka*".

201 de Benoist, "Alain de Benoist answers Tamir Bar-On", 157.

202 Bryan Sylvain, "Interview with Alain de Benoist" in Greg Johnson (ed.), *North American New Right* (San Francisco: Counter-Currents, 2012), 70–71.

I am deeply convinced that aristocratic values and folk values are fundamentally identical or mutually complementary. Both stand in opposition to *bourgeois* values. When speaking of aristocratic values, I have in mind: a sense of honor, courage, fidelity to one's word, challenging oneself, unselfishness, a sense of dedication and gratitude. Folk values, which are also connected to land, largely overlap with the latter, to which I would add what George Orwell encapsulated in the beautiful expression 'common decency'.[203]

Extolling the free market, economic liberalism, and global capitalism, the liberal right is based on the bourgeois, entrepreneurial ethos. On this point, the *Nouvelle Droite* is found at the opposite pole: for it, the aristocratic ethos of honour is central. On the symbolic level, the bourgeois is the enemy of the aristocrat — these are two completely differing systems of values. The *Nouvelle Droite*'s ethos is the ethos of nobility, glory, and dedication as opposed to interests, enterprise, and accumulating capital.[204] What is essential is harmony, not growth, and order, not competition. In other words, the modern capitalist "market society" is not a point of reference when it comes to designating the criteria of what it means to be elite, as this society itself is the negation

---

203 de Benoist, *Mémoire vive*, 12–13. My italics.

204 Sunic, "*Wywiad z Tomislavem Suniciem*" 47: "We need to reconsider our values, we need to resurrect our values [...] and these values are: Tradition — not only tradition from the Middle Ages, but also the tradition of Homer; Friendship, Honour, Dedication, and, of course, rejecting materialism. Here we have many points in common with the old Catholic Church. [...] Not judging someone through the lens of their cars or homes, but according to their knowledge, books, and the languages they know. That's how we should judge people. If we were to succeed in creating an elite, and we might succeed — it's not too difficult — then we would be able to convey new values [...]. What do we have now? We have, as Nietzsche said 150 years ago, a total transvaluation of all values. Now the model for young Poles is not Sienkiewicz, but a conman, a bank manager — and that's unfortunate. As long as the models will be conmen [...], small gangsters who speculate on money, as long as this will be the model for the young generation, then we won't succeed. We need to violate, change, and replace those values. Nobility of the soul, friendship, and dedication — that must be our driving force for action."

of elitism (from the "aristocratic" point of view). There is no place consecrated for hierarchy, honour, or higher values in the market — all that matters is who owns more. The bourgeois does not take "imponderables" into account, for if something cannot be counted, weighed, bought, or sold, then it has no meaning.

If we were to speak of any (symbolic) elitism in the *Nouvelle Droite*, then such would arise from the adoption of the Dumézilian trifunctional model[205] as a point of reference in which the economic function (the third) is at the very bottom of the hierarchy, whereas it has become normative in modern society. This means that, from the *Nouvelle Droite*'s perspective, the traditional (Indo-)European social order has been inverted. Therefore, any hierarchy created within the framework of a market society is implicitly taken to be unimportant or, in the best case scenario, void of greater meaning. An "elite" whose "legitimacy" comes from the possession of capital is of no moral or cultural value. The New-Right "elitism" or "aristocratism" has decisively more in common with a feeling of mission, obligation, and solidarity towards those "situated lower" than with arrogance, haughtiness, and social Darwinism — and this is precisely what is supposed to testify to "aristocratism". It is only in this sense that we can speak of any "elitism" in the *Nouvelle Droite*,[206] although a decidedly more accurate description would be — no matter how paradoxical such might sound — "(anti-bourgeois) aristocratic populism".[207]

---

205 See Georges Dumézil, *Mitra-Varuna: An Essay on Two Indo-European Representations of Sovereignty* (New York: 1988); idem, *Na tropie Indoeuropejczyków. Mity i epopeje. Z Georges'em Dumézilem rozmawia Didier Eribon* (Warsaw: 1996).

206 Of course, this refers to elitism within the *Nouvelle Droite*'s doctrine. The question of the hierarchical organisational structure of GRECE is an entirely separate matter.

207 Inspiration for this very characteristic approach can be discerned in the thought of Arthur Moeller van den Bruck, who postulated an alliance between Conservatives and Revolutionaries (Socialists) in order to fight their common enemy: Liberals. See Paweł Bielawski, "*Arthura Moellera van den Brucka*

Is the *Nouvelle Droite* "Fascism"?

One can encounter the *Nouvelle Droite* being described, especially in English-language studies, as a movement that is "anti-democratic" or simply outright "fascist".[208] The argumentation for this is the allegation that elements defined as fascist have been retained or reformulated by the *Nouvelle Droite* with the aim of giving them a new guise.

The standard most often adopted in the majority of English-language studies[209] is Roger Griffin's definition, which describes the essence of fascism as consisting of two main components: (a) populist ultra-nationalism and (b) palingenetic myth. Discussing this definition, Griffin acknowledges that it "is a highly flexible concept which embraces a wide range of organic and hence anti-individualistic, anti-rational, anti-liberal, and above all, anti-egalitarian and anti-universalist concepts of the nation-state or the ethnic community".[210] The second element, "palingenetic myth", is supposed to mean a "the

---

konserwatywno-rewolucyjna krytyka liberalizmu", *Pro Fide Rege et Lege* 2(80) (2018), 193.

208 Alain de Benoist has repeatedly disavowed fascism, understood in any way whatsoever, and always protests when someone tries to pin fascism on him. For example, see his polemic with Tamir Bar-On: "If Bar-On wants to connect the ND with the Right, it is because he then hopes to be able to connect the Right with the extreme right, the extreme right with fascism, and so on. For this, he is prepared to take every shortcut, to make every simplification, and to disregard everything that contradicts his thesis. There one recognizes the fundamentally polemical character of his process." — de Benoist, "Alain de Benoist answers Tamir Bar-On", 146.

209 See Tamir Bar-On, "Fascism to the *Nouvelle Droite*: The Dream of Pan-European Empire", *Journal of Contemporary European Studies* 16(3) (2008), 327–245; idem, *Where have all the Fascists Gone?*; Roger Griffin, "Between metapolitics and apoliteia : The *Nouvelle Droite*'s strategy for conserving the fascist vision in the 'interregnum'", *Modern and Contemporary France* 8(1) (2010), 35–53; Alberto Spektorowski, "The New Right: Ethno-regionalism, ethno-pluralism, and the emergence of a neo-fascist 'Third Way'", *Journal of Political Ideologies* 8(1) (2003), 110–130.

210 Griffin, "Between metapolitics and apoliteia", 37.

vision of a process of rebirth or regeneration destined to put an end to a process of decline, decadence, or dissolution".[211] In Griffin's understanding, "fascism" is more of an archetype than a description of a definitive doctrine. A. Spektorowski presents the almost identical definition of Stanley Payne, who defines fascism as "a form of ultranationalism that seeks national rebirth".[212]

Without a doubt, the above-presented definition is extraordinarily broad and very elastic. For comparison, Tomasiewicz has adopted a narrower understanding of the term. He believes that fascism, firstly, was characterised by its own "style" featuring a cult of vitality, youth, dynamism, and force. Secondly, fascism's most original contribution to political thought was the concept of the totalitarian state. Thirdly, on the level of culture, there was also the postulate of the brith of a "New Man". Fourthly, fascism, declaring itself to be against modernity, de facto carried out modernisation. Fifthly, fascism is characterised by "uniformisation", that is the desire for total cultural homogenisation through political centralisation and the militarisation of society. Describing the difference between fascism and conservatism (or "reactionism"), Tomasiewicz puts forth that conservatives — unlike fascists — are for decentralisation, e.g., for the autonomy of provinces and respecting their identities. In summary, according to Tomasiewicz, the necessary condition for the existence of fascism is the joint figuring of two elements: a certain programmatic vision and the apparatus for its implementation. To quote Tomasiewicz himself: "The very idea of 'homogenous cultural communities' is not fascism, but only a retrospective utopia that is present even in tendencies that are far removed from fascism (such as bioregionalism, agrarianism, our Proudhonist anarchism). We can speak of fascism only once this goal is to be imposed by a totalitarian state."[213] At the same time,

---

[211] Ibid.

[212] Spektorowski, "The New Right", 114.

[213] J. Tomasiewicz, "*W poszukiwaniu istoty faszyzmu*", *Historia i Polityka* 2–3(9–10) (2009–2010), 136.

Tomasiewicz indicates that the trouble with adequately defining the term "fascism" stems from, among other things, the fact that this term has been annexed by various writers and often functions as an epithet intended to discredit opponents.[214]

The impression can therefore be gleaned that the popular, journalistic use of the term "fascism" is, unfortunately, present in scholarship. As things seem to stand, Griffin's definition is linguistic overuse, and the motives that prompt its supporters and Griffin himself to apply it are of a political character. This interpretation is suggested by the fact that in many of the above (English-language) studies, the term "fascism" is repeated *ad nauseam* (and in a manner obviously intended with highly negative connotations) and entails the adoption of its broader definition. This might arouse suspicion over writing with a thesis adopted in advance, which would lead scholarship — rightly or wrongly — to political agitation. Scholarship, however, has the task of getting down to the facts in the most objective and impartial way.

The absence of totalitarian and imperialist drives, the absence of militaristic aesthetics, opposition to social uniformisation, a more reflexive rather than revolutionary attitude, the absence of authoritarianism, populist demagoguery and anti-Semitism, support for democracy, advocacy of decentralisation, regional autonomy, and the principle of subsidiariness — all of these aspects lend to recognising that the *Nouvelle Droite* is significantly closer to conservatism than to fascism.

Positioning the *Nouvelle Droite* on the Left-Right Axis

Besides its ambiguities, can the *Nouvelle Droite* be classified in any way? Can this current be situated within a definite category, especially as it has obviously evolved over the decades of its existence?

---

214 Ibid., 122.

In his article "An Attempt at Theorising the Concept of the 'Right'", Jacek Bartyzel undertakes to systematise the concept of the "right" and introduces variations of it:

1) The traditionalist "extreme right of the right" (e.g., ultra-Montanism, Carlism, Catholic traditionalism, integral Traditionalism);

2) The authoritarian (reactionary) "right of the right' (e.g., the young National Democracy in Poland, Francoism, Salazarism, decisionism, American paleoconservatism, the New Right);

3) The moderate (conservative or national) "center right" (e.g., British Toryism, conservative aristocratic liberalism, Italian neo-Guelphism, Cracowian conservatism);

4) The democratic-plebiscitary "left of the right" (e.g., Bonapartism, classical liberalism, neo-liberalism, the early Polish National Democracy [Endecja], the social-Christian right);

5) The national-radical and social "extreme left of the right" (e.g., National Bolshevism, Third Positionism, Belgian *Rex*, Spanish Falangism, Brazilian integralism).[215]

The current of interest to us here was thus classified as part of the "authoritarian, reactionary right of the right". Although attributing the *Nouvelle Droite* to this category in the movement's early phase might not arouse any particular reservations, counting the *Nouvelle Droite* in this category in its later phase can very much be called into doubt. This concerns economic questions, relations with the Third World, as well as the attitude towards democracy, which, as mentioned before, is decisively positive. Moreover, especially interesting is the fact that, in another article on on the same topic, entitled "The Right", Bartyzel places the *Nouvelle Droite* in the last category, that is, the "extreme left

---

215 J. Bartyzel, *"Próba teoretyzacji pojęcia 'prawica'"* in R. Łętocha (ed.), *Religia, Polityka, Naród* (Kraków: 2010), 62–63.

of the right".²¹⁶ This is by all means telling as an exhibit of the difficulty of unambiguously classifying a current which, *nota bene*, never had the ambition of fitting into extant, worn-out typologies.

It is worth paying attention to how the *Nouvelle Droite*'s own perspective looks on this matter. Initially, the current defined itself as right-wing, where "right" was taken to mean anti-egalitarianism. However, over the course of its evolution, the *Nouvelle Droite* increasingly positioned itself beyond the left-right division. Alain de Benoist himself, at least from the mid-1980s,²¹⁷ has distanced himself from the label of the "right"²¹⁸ and argued that this division has become an anachronism that in no way refers to the reality of contemporary politics. In de Benoist's words:

> On the global level, the main opposition is no longer between right and left, liberalism and socialism, fascism and communism, 'totalitarianism' and 'democracy'. It is between those who want a one-dimensional world and those who advocate a pluralistic world founded on the diversity of cultures, between those who defend the rights of an abstract 'human' and those who defend the rights of peoples as well as the rights and obligations of the citizens who compose them.²¹⁹

One decent exemplification of this perspective is de Benoist's view on the topic of mass immigration. Whereas the mainstream right stands for capitalism and is usually against immigration, and the left approves

---

216 J. Bartyzel, "*Prawica*" [http://www.legitymizm.org/ebp-prawica].

217 In Stéphane François, de Benoist's rejection of being associated with the right *stricte* was already noticeable in the 1970s. See François, *Les paganismes de la Nouvelle Droite (1980–2004)*, 158.

218 De Benoist, "*Intelektualna pustka starej prawicy*": "Personally, for already more than a quarter of a century I haven't regarded myself as a member of any branch of the right or held any solidarity with them [...]. I should add that I do not consider myself to be a representative of the contemporary left, which itself makes me not want to have even the smallest desire of being counted in their ranks. I can be described as a 'left-wing right-winger', a person of left ideas and right values."

219 de Benoist, *Europe, Tiers Monde, même combat*, 17.

immigration while being skeptical of capitalism, this French thinker is against both capitalism and mass immigration, which he sees as mutually conditioned, i.e., as a joint vessel. In this respect, any attempts at fitting into a camp, whether right or left, are void of any sense.

It is further of interest that the above-presented position to a large extent coincides with the alternative political division proposed by Michał Kuź: instead of left and right, there is globalism and localism.[220] The term "localism" seems to be more apt than "right-wing" in conveying the direction in which the *Nouvelle Droite* has ultimately traversed as well as, above all, the way the movement sees itself.

---

220 "The division between traditional left and right has become much less essential for real politics. The new division into globalists and localists seems to organize nearly all of the most important political processes today [...]. Globalists are [...] those who advocate unfettered markets and a largely ritualistic democracy and who are against political sovereignty, which affords weaker members of society real protection from economic turmoil. Localists are those who choose sovereignty within the framework of traditional political entities and support halting economic globalization. Western localists are further distinguished by the fact that, for most of them, sovereignty means sovereignty of the people, not only the State, and so they appeal to the idea of democracy against enlightened technocratism. On the dimension of religion and customs, globalists, in order to win, must undermine all differences and cultural 'inequalities'. This includes those that concern language, religion, history, and even — in the longer term — gender. For localists, it is the opposite: in order to have a basis to build sovereignty, they must defend the distinctiveness and peculiarities proper to their political peoples." M. Kuź, "*Globaliści vs. Lokaliści*", *Nowa Konfederacja*, 3(57) (2015), 4.

CHAPTER III

PAGANISM: THE "RELIGION OF EUROPE"

According to the Polish *Lexicon of Religious Studies* from 1998, "neo-paganism" (in the sense of the Polish term *neopogaństwo*) should be understood as "one current among new religious movements that does not represent a monolithic confessional trend; it possesses numerous, diverse forms. It most often appears under the guise of reviving ancient ethnic religions (e.g., Celtic, Germanic, Lithuanian) which refer to ancient, indigenous mythologies and associated ritual-magical practices in relation to a spirituality formed on their basis"..[1]. In turn, a second variation of "neo-paganism" (in the sense of the Polish term *neopoganizm*) is defined as "a religio-social phenomenon characterised by a negation of Christian orthodoxy, or Christianity in general, in favor of returning to the pagan religions (which are not necessarily interpreted consistently) that were once predominant on a given territory... before the adoption of Christianity"..[2] As has already been mentioned, the *Nouvelle Droite* is a school of thought, an ideational current. Therefore, while it might be associated with *neopoganizm*, it is not a form of *neopogaństwo*, i.e., it is not religious movement *sensu stricto* engaged in conducting rituals or organising the life of a religious

---

1 Z. Stachowski (ed.), *Leksykon religioznawczy*, Przegląd Religioznawczy 3–4/189–190 (1998), 71.
2 Ibid., 70.

community. That being said, it is arguable that the *Nouvelle Droite* is engaged in something which might be called "pagan theology".[3]

When Alain de Benoist speaks of "paganism", he does not have in mind the religious tradition of a single (Indo-)European people. Instead, "paganism" for him is a rather conventional term that in a more collective sense means the religions that had emerged and developed in Europe before the appearance of Christianity. In his opinion, they constituted the spiritual root of Europe.[4] In other words, Alain de Benoist's "paganism" is a kind of comparativistic, intellectual construct or worldview paradigm that generalises the traits of the pre-Christian, (Indo-)European polytheistic religions. The common denominator connecting all of the European "pagan" traditions is supposed to be the trifunctional ideology described by Georges Dumézil. This idea occupies an essential place in the *Nouvelle Droite*'s thought, as it is not only understood as scientifically researched fact, but is treated as a certain axiom. It is a model whose structure is present in the Indo-European religions as well as in the societies built around these religions. The opposition to egalitarianism at work in the *Nouvelle Droite*'s thought is therefore justified "religiously", i.e., by this hierarchical model, which is *ex definitione* anti-egalitarian. In positing that a community's identity is to a predominating extent defined by religion, the *Nouvelle Droite* arrives at the conclusion that the trifunctional model is the indigenous European structure of thought (that was later gradually displaced by Christian egalitarianism).

However, it bears recalling that de Benoist's understanding of "paganism" has undergone a certain evolution over the years (as has the entirety of the *Nouvelle Droite*'s ideas). Two basic periods should be noted: the Nietzschean (1968–1985) and Heideggerian-Eliadean (1986-present). The first period can be described as succinctly as

---

[3] Collin Cleary puts forth this thesis in "Paganism Without Gods: Alain de Benoist's *On Being a Pagan*" in idem, *Summoning the Gods: Essays on Paganism in a God-Forsaken World* (San Francisco: 2011), 62.

[4] de Benoist, "*Wywiad z Alainem de Benoist*", 31.

possible as quasi-atheistic and humanistic. Its culmination was most likely de Benoist's most well-known work on the topic of religion, namely, *Comment peut-on être païen?*[5] (1981). The notion of "paganism" expressed in this work is explicitly Nietzschean. Collin Cleary argues that anyone adverse to Alain de Benoist could glean from this work the impression that the "paganism" which de Benoist expresses is "Nietzschean humanism masquerading as paganism".[6] According to Cleary, the two characteristic traits of this notion of paganism are: (1) anthropocentrism and (2) the thesis that the gods and mythical creatures were thought up by man.[7] In this respect, the French thinker treats faith instrumentally and pragmatically. At the center of attention is not as much faith, religion, and cult as ancient pagan values:

> There is no need to 'believe' in Jupiter or Wotan — something that is no more ridiculous than believing in Yahweh however — to be a pagan. Contemporary paganism does not consist of erecting altars to Apollo or reviving the worship of Odin. Instead it implies looking behind religion [...] seeking for the 'mental equipment' that produced it, the *inner world* it

---

5 "How Can One Be Pagan?"

6 Cleary, *Summoning the Gods*, 64.

7 Ibid., 65. Very important in this context is de Benoist's quoting of a fragment from Nietzsche's *Gay Science* entitled "The greatest advantage of polytheism": "There was only one norm; *man* and every people thought that it possessed this one ultimate norm. But above and outside, in some distant overworld, one was permitted to behold a plurality of norms; one god was not considered a denial of another god nor blasphemy against him. It was here that the luxury of individuals was first permitted; it was here that one first honored the rights of individuals. The invention of gods, heroes, and super-humans of all kinds, as well as near-humans and sub-humans, dwarfs, fairies, centaurs, satyrs, demons, and devils was the inestimable preliminary exercise for the justification of the egoism and sovereignty of the individual: the freedom that one conceded to a god in his relation to other gods — one eventually also granted to oneself in relation to laws, customs, and neighbors. Monotheism on the other hand, this rigid consequence of the doctrine of one human type — the faith in one normal god beside whom there are only pseudo-gods — was perhaps the greatest danger that has yet confronted humanity." De Benoist, *On Being a Pagan*, 114.

reflects, and how the world it depicts is apprehended. In short, it consists of view ing the gods as 'centers of values' [...] and the beliefs they generate as value systems: gods and beliefs may pass away, but the *values* remain.[8]

De Benoist therefore underscores the axiological dimension of "paganism", passing over religiosity as such. His intention is to revive values, not belief in the gods, which, in his opinion, is not his important task. According to the French thinker, the moral imperative for *Homo paganus* is to "transcend oneself", to "go beyond oneself" (Nietzsche), which thus reaches far beyond the worship of deities. The decisively greater emphasis is put on "comportment" or "attitude" rather than belief *sensu proprio*.

In the mid-1980s, de Benoist significantly changed his perception of paganism. This second period, the start of which can be seen in the publication of *Éclipse du sacré*[9] (1986), is marked by a certain distancing from the Nietzschean approach[10] and by adopting a perspective that is to a greater extent based on the thought of Martin Heidegger and Mircea Eliade. This is bound up with leaving behind anthropocentrism, quasi-atheism,[11] and the thesis that the gods are human inventions. Even the language itself has changed: instead of "transcending

---

8   de Benoist, *On Being a Pagan*, 15–16.

9   "Eclipse of the Sacred"

10 Fifteen years after *Comment peut-on être païen?* was written, de Benoist admitted that today he would undoubtedly have written certain parts of the book in a somewhat less Nietzschean perspective. In this respect, the work *L'éclipse du sacré* better conveys his current views. See de Benoist, *Jésus et ses frères*, 268. If we compare *Comment peut-on être païen?* to *Éclipse du sacré*, then the former at times appears to be a strictly philosophical work, while the latter is more of a work in philosophical religious studies. For example, instead of discussing concepts themselves, the latter book refers to the concrete beliefs of Indo-European peoples.

11 de Benoist, *Jésus et ses frères*, 203: "Getting rid of any religiosity, as is the case in the contemporary Western world, is in my eyes a sign of losing humanity. I am not an atheist."

oneself", terms like "being" and "sacred" increasingly come into usage. This can be seen in the following quote:

> The sacred [...] is transcendent in relation to the human condition, but at the same time it is not transcendent in relation to the cosmos. This is very important. Among the Greeks, divinehood is not as much an attribute of God as it is — 'in the light of the sacred' — the basis of the existence of gods. The world is not an 'object' of the gods. Rather, the gods are its emanation. The existence of the world is the condition of the existence of the gods, just as the sacred exists within the world. [...] The conviction was widespread in antiquity that human existence depends upon faith in the gods as well as in forces above the gods. Analogously, in the case of the Germanic religion, it is fate that governs the gods. The cosmic catastrophe of *Ragnarök*, the "twilight of the gods", illustrates the assertion of the end of the cycle: the gods themselves can die.[12]

In this second period, the French thinker revised Nietzschean thought under the influence of Heidegger. Symptomatic of this is the abandonment of "Promethean" inclinations,[13] the manifestation of which is, among other things, the conviction that man is capable of being his own master and ruler. Man is no longer the main reference point of "pagan" reflection; instead, the cosmos is. Anthropocentrism is taken to be one of the distinctive traits of Western Modernity (which is a secularised form of Christianity). Paganism, in turn, is a pre-modern entity. And just as "the sacred is the opposite of the profane", so is the man of paganism the opposite of modern man. Whereas modern man, who functions within a desacralised reality, measures, weighs, counts, and wants to "have", "religious man deeply desires *to be,* to participate in *reality,* to be saturated with power", "for the man of all premodern societies, the *sacred* is equivalent to a *power,* and, in the last analysis, to

---

12 Alain de Benoist and Thomas Molnar, *L'éclipse du sacré* (Paris: 1986), 100.
13 It is worth mentioning that in 1970 de Benoist still had a decidedly positive attitude towards the figure of Prometheus. See Alain de Benoist and Jean-Luc Marion, *Avec ou sans Dieu — L'avenir des valeurs chrétiennes* (Paris: 1970), 64–66, quoted in Taguieff, *Sur la Nouvelle Droite,* 188–189.

reality".[14] Here the essential shift from the first period is that "paganism" is not reduced to adopting an ancient system of values, but rather is a way (implicitly more "authentic") of being-in-the-world.

De Benoist does not hold back on word of criticism of contemporary neo-pagans who think that they can simply revive ancient faith. Moreover, someone who loves and worships "nature" in the modern (scientific-materialist) sense of the word is not an authentic pagan. A positive relation to "paganism" is impossible without a deep fore-understanding of how ancient people understood the world and nature.

The ensuing reconstruction of Alain de Benoist's views on paganism is based on taking the second period as the most representative.

What Paganism Is Not

In *Jésus et ses frères*, de Benoist outlines a "Dumézilian" analysis of contemporary neo-paganism. The first function corresponds to the spiritual and intellectual approach, which is founded on a welcoming affirmation of the legacy and system of values bequeathed to us by the "great cultures and religions of antiquity". De Benoist situates himself within this function. The second function corresponds to "brutal, intolerant, ethnocentric neo-paganisms" that are based on a cult of violence and are essentially a caricature of the old religiosity. The third function corresponds to "foolish" neo-paganisms of the New Age type and "naturalist neo-pietism".[15] De Benoist strongly underscores that the pre-Christian European religions' conception of the world did not at all boil down to worshiping nature, and the pagan gods were no mere personifications of the forces of nature. However, some contemporary neo-pagan groups, as de Benoist notes, seem to believe that "paganism" can be reduced to "taking communion with nature". He evaluates this view as naive, and on this point he refers to the works of Dumézil,

---

14 Mircea Eliade, *The Sacred and the Profane: The Nature of Religion*, trans. Willard R. Trask (New York: Harvest, 1987), 12, 13.

15 de Benoist, *Jésus et ses frères*, 298.

who indicated that the religious beliefs of the Indo-Europeans were constituted in alignment with their trifunctional ideology.¹⁶

On the question of critiquing contemporary neo-paganism, de Benoist directly cites Julius Evola, who reproached contemporary neo-paganism for deifying nature, a biological-naturalist philosophical anthropology, and belief in a "golden era of pagan innocence", etc. Evola pointed out that such an understanding of "paganism" is of Christian origin.¹⁷ To quote Evola himself:

---

16   de Benoist, "*Wywiad z Alainem de Benoist*", 31.
17   In Evola's opinion, his neo-pagan contemporaries often interpreted neo-paganism as a negation of Christianity, as a counter-religion, and they excessively drew orientations from the writings of Christian apologists who largely distorted "paganism". See Julius Evola, "Against the Neo-Pagans: The Misunderstandings of the New 'Paganism'", *Counter-Currents* [https://counter-currents.com/2011/11/against-the-neo-pagans/]: "What are the main traits of today's pagan outlook, as its own apologists believe and declare them to be? The primary one is the imprisonment in Nature. All transcendence is totally unknown to the pagan view of life: it remains stuck in a mixture of Spirit and Nature, in an ambiguous unity of Body and Soul. There is nothing to its religion but a superstitious deification of natural phenomena, or of tribal energies promoted to the status of minor gods. Out of this there arises first of all a blood- and soil-bound particularism. Next comes a rejection of the values of personality and freedom, and a condition of innocence that is merely that of the natural man, as yet unawakened to any truly supra-natural calling. Beyond this innocence there is only lack of inhibition, 'sin,' and the pleasure of sinning. In other domains there is nothing but superstition, or a purely profane culture of materialism and fatalism. It is as though only the arrival of Christianity [...] allowed the world of supra-natural freedom to break through, letting in grace and personality, in contrast to the fatalistic and nature-bound beliefs ascribed to 'paganism,' bringing with it a catholic ideal (in the etymological sense of universality) and a healthy dualism, which made it possible to subjugate Nature to a higher law, and for the 'Spirit' to triumph over the law of flesh, blood, and the false gods. These are the main traits of the dominant understanding of paganism [...] Anyone who possesses any direct acquaintance with cultural and religious history, however elementary, can see how incorrect and one-sided this attitude is." In Polish: "Przeciwko neo-poganom" in Julius Evola, Na antypodach modernizmu (Biała Podlaska, 2014), 206–207.

> Many of these neo-pagans seem to have fallen into a trap deliberately set for them, often ending up by advocating and defending ideas that more or less correspond to that invented, nature-bound, particularistic pagandom, lacking light and transcendence, which was the polemical creation of a Christian misunderstanding of the pre-Christian world.[18]

Instead, Alain de Benoist emphasises that "nature" (in the purely physical sense) is only one aspect of the world, whereas pagan theology is a "theology of the world," not a "theology of nature".[19] Therefore, defining "paganism" as a "cult of nature" is erroneous. De Benoist underscores that such a position is indefensible in the wake of the works of Dumézil and Eliade. "But we cannot say, as Hegel did, that primitive man is 'buried in nature,' that he has not yet found himself as distinct from nature, as himself".[20] De Benoist argues that paganism "was never pure naturalism", even if the theme of nature was of considerable weight.[21] Nor was it ever a pantheism, for such would be incompatible with the distinction between *sacrum* and *profanum*. "Among some 'neo-pagans', pantheism is nothing other than a pretext to plant man in the place of God, as in the best tradition of modernity!"[22]

Moreover, de Benoist points out that one cannot pretend that hundreds of years of Christian indoctrination have not left their mark on the interpretation of nature in European thought. In connection with this, many neo-pagans perceive nature in an opposite manner to the Christian one, but still one which by no means corresponds to the original, ancient pagan *Weltanschauung*. This is the case because, for many neo-pagans, the basic point of reference is (anti-)Christianity. But this is not the point. The point of "paganism" today is not to stubbornly and recklessly negate Christianity, but to "regain the conceptual

---

18   Evola, "Against the Neo-Pagans".
19   de Benoist, *On Being a Pagan*, 155.
20   Eliade, *Sacred and Profane*, 166.
21   de Benoist, *Jésus et ses frères*, 298.
22   Ibid., 291.

apparatus" connected to original European religiosity. Only this can be the real basis for a new, positive relation[23] to the old spiritual heritage of Europe.

It is also worth recalling that contemporary neo-pagans often cite folk customs with the aim of attaining to the old spirituality. This harbors a potential danger, because "these festivals and customs probably only give us a fairly distorted echo of what they were originally — and, most importantly, in the best of cases they only reflect the lower forms of belief and worship".[24] In other words, they represent a paganism of the "third function" in the Dumézilian sense. This leads to paganism today being exhibited as a phenomenon that is almost entirely provincial-peasant in character. In the times of Christianisation, de Benoist argues, the "great gods" (paganism of the "first function") were most fiercely opposed by missionaries, whereas the "little goods" were seen as "less dangerous" and were ultimately Christianised to the point that "they became local saints or characters of folklore".[25] The "paganism of the first function" or "sovereign paganism", de Benoist writes, therefore became "the least preserved for the very reason that it was quite often the established 'elites' who betrayed it soonest or most deeply".[26] But it is this "first function" paganism that is of the most fundamental significance. In times when fewer people live in the countryside, it would be a paradox, in de Benoist's opinion, to appeal to an Indo-European religiosity exclusively bound up with the "peasant rhythm" of nature. This is supposed to be yet another argument for maintaining a certain distance towards naturalistic tendencies in contemporary paganism.

What, then, is "authentic" paganism?

---

23   That is, rather than a literal 1:1 "return" to ancient cults.
24   de Benoist, *On Being a Pagan*, 165.
25   Ibid.
26   Ibid.

Cosmocentric-Polytheistic Monism

Alain de Benoist compellingly emphasises that the difference between paganism and Christianity cannot be reduced to the question of the number of gods in a given system of beliefs. The fundamental difference is on the ontological level. De Benoist writes:

> When it comes to specifying the values particular to paganism, people have generally listed features such as these: an eminently aristocratic conception of the human individual; an ethics founded on honor ('shame' rather than 'sin'); an heroic attitude toward life's challenges; the exaltation and sacralisation of the world, beauty, the body, strength, health, the rejection of any 'worlds beyond'; the inseparability of morality and aesthetics, and so on… However, while all this appears to be accurate, the fundamental feature in my opinion is something else entirely. It lies in the denial of dualism.[27]

The world is a value in and of itself, as the divine is already contained within it. There is no radical separation between the *sacrum* and the world. The gods are of this world, not from beyond it. According to de Benoist, the transcendental unity of the cosmos and in the indivisibility of God (or the gods) and the world is one of the fundamental motifs of pagan thought.[28] He writes: "God is not separate from the world. And yet he is not commingled with it. God is the *depth* of the world: he is above all but beyond nothing."[29] From the pagan perspective, it is impossible to understand God as separate from the world. The gods always function within the world, not outside of it. "Fundamentally, the god of paganism is 'not-other.'"[30] Theogony is thus identical with cosmogony.[31] The gods do not create the world, but rather appear along with the world. There is no distinction between created and

---

27 de Benoist, *On Being a Pagan*, 21. See also idem, "La religion de l'Europe", *Éléments pour la civilisation européenne* 36 (1980), 8.

28 de Benoist, *On Being a Pagan*, 172.

29 Ibid., 174.

30 de Benoist, "La religion de l'Europe", 9.

31 Ibid.

uncreated beings, for there is no idea of an absolute, first creation. The soul is a particle of the divine substance, and the divine substance is identical with the substance of the world. The universe is one being, uncreated and eternal. Thus, paganism is ontologically monistic.

In connection with the above, the cosmos is seen and treated subjectively as something that emerged "by the power of its ember".[32] It is not an object that was created by someone with a certain aim. The cosmos is not subject to the gods, the gods are subject to the Cosmos.[33] "The Gods [...] are not the last word of paganism, because paganism places the gods themselves under the horizon of being."[34] In other words, the gods are not above the cosmos — they are a part of it. "They represent an invisible dimension of the world while always being a part of the world; on the Earth, the gods are 'at home.'"[35] De Benoist underscores that "in ancient Europe the sacred was not conceived as opposed to the profane but rather encompassed the profane and gave it meaning".[36] The *sacrum* connects earth and heaven, people and gods.[37] Of course, the ancient Greeks clearly distinguished between the sphere of the *sacrum* (the Gods) and the *profanum* (themselves), but, in their optic, there was no radical, ontological difference between these spheres; rather, they were integrally interconnected. De Benoist states: "Far from desacralizing the world, it [paganism] *sacralizes* it in

---

32 F. Michalski (trans./ed.), *Hymny Rigwedy* (Warsaw, 1971), 126.

33 W. Lengauer, *Religijność starożytnych Greków* (Warsaw, 1994), 156: "[I]t is not the gods who created the world, for the world itself arose without their involvement. Rather, the gods are a product of the cosmogonic process — an element of the world that appears only in a certain moment along with the transformation of Chaos into Cosmos."

34 de Benoist, *Jésus et ses frères*, 298.

35 de Benoist, *L'empire intérieur*, 20.

36 de Benoist, *On Being a Pagan*, 17.

37 de Benoist and Molnar, *Éclipse du sacré*, 109.

the literal sense of the word; it regards the world as sacred — and this is precisely [...] the core of paganism".[38]

Conceiving and understanding divinity in such a way is conditioned by an already existing type of connection with the world and a sensitivity to it. Different peoples can perceive the *sacrum* in different ways.[39] In European religiosity, the divine is not identical with sacrality (*sacrum*). Experiencing the *sacrum* or having contact with the gods is possible in paganism thanks to the position of "being open to the world". Eliade calls this stance "open existence"[40] and writes: "Religious man lives in an open cosmos and [...] he is open to the world. This means (a) that he is in communication with the gods; (b) that he shares in the sanctity of the world. [...] religious man can live only in an open world".[41]

Using Heideggerian terminology, de Benoist states that the pagan gods "are not identical to being".[42] They are not more primordial than being as such. In his "Letter on Humanism", Heidegger wrote: "Only from the truth of being can the essence of the holy be thought. Only from the essence of the holy is the essence of divinity to be thought. Only in the light of the essence of divinity can it be thought or said

---

38 de Benoist, *On Being and Pagan*, 16. This perspective clearly exhibits ideational affiliations with Eliade's understanding of the relation between the world and the sacred. Mircea Eliade, *Patterns in Comparative Religion*, trans. Rosemary Sheed (Lincoln: University of Nebraska Press, 1996), 459: "The *real* in archaic ontology is primarily identified with a 'force', a 'life', a fertility, an abundance, but also with all that is strange or singular — in other words with everything that exists most fully or displays an exceptional mode of existence. Sacredness is, above all, *real*." Idem, *Sacred and Profane*, 117: "The cosmic rhythms manifest order, harmony, permanence, fecundity. The cosmos as a whole is an organism at once real, living, and sacred."

39 de Benoist and Molnar, *Éclipse du sacré*, 102.

40 Eliade, *Sacred and Profane*, 166.

41 Ibid., 172.

42 Alain de Benoist, "*Un mot en quatre lettres*", *Éléments pour la civilisation européenne* 95 (1999), 18.

what the word 'God' is to signify."⁴³ De Benoist affirms in turn: "The fundamental sense of the *sacrum* in Indo-European thought is: the affirmation of the Cosmos, the fundamental structure of things as it really exists... In Indo-European thought, the *sacrum* is the certain, fundamental ground of existence".⁴⁴ Alternatively formulated, the cosmos is not the gods' object; rather, the gods are an emanation of the cosmos, its (deep) dimension. The cosmos is the condition of the existence of the gods as well as the condition of the existence of the *sacrum*.⁴⁵

In de Benoist's opinion, European paganism draws on an "antagonistic pluralism of values". Polytheism is an expression of this. What is important is that this antagonism does not lead to any insurmountable contradictions or radical dualism. According to de Benoist: "The pagan gods fight amongst themselves, and yet this struggle never provides a challenge to the tripartite structure that emerged from the foundational war."⁴⁶ Whatever conflict there might be between the gods, everything always leads to the harmony of the whole. The Dumézilian trifunctional structure presents the archetype of Indo-European social pluralism: the roles differ and at times can even be antagonistic, but the structure itself is ultimately maintained in a more or less balanced state. The very fact of the existence of conflicts is not seen as something bad, for conflict itself is the essence of all life, "and its extinction implies entropy and death".⁴⁷

The example comes from above, *ergo*, the same applies on the human level. The "enemy" is not equivalent to evil itself, for it is always

---

43 Martin Heidegger, "Letter on 'Humanism'", trans. Frank A. Capuzzi, in Heidegger, *Pathmarks*, ed. William McNeill (Cambridge: Cambridge University Press, 1998), 267.

44 de Benoist and Molnar, *Éclipse du sacré*, 105.

45 Ibid, 100.

46 de Benoist, *On Being a Pagan*, 144.

47 Ibid.

a relative adversary.[48] Nothing prevents enemies from showing each other respect. An enemy is simply someone on the other side of the barricades. In this respect, there is no need to punish him, to deprive him of his dignity, to dehumanise him, or to force him to convert. An enemy might even be astonished at the bravery and courage that one displays. "Pagan thought puts conflict and confrontation beyond good and evil."[49] In this sense, European paganism is a "political"[50] religion, i.e., conflict does not fall under moral interpretation, since an enemy does not represent "evil". If hostility towards the Other is relative, then the Other might be an enemy as well as a friend. Other does not mean evil, worse, or immoral.[51] Analogously, the Other's religion is not necessarily something worse or hierarchically lower. The world of the pagan mentality excludes something in the likes of religious war (understood as a war between different belief systems).[52] Every religious system is irreducible, and the Other is not negated *ipso facto*.[53] As de Benoist argues, "only paganism can accept that different cities have different gods".[54] Such diversity is not perceived as something bad. Polytheism, itself being a "sublimated form of pluralism",[55] logically leads to recognising the Other and his right to exist. As de Benoist puts it, paganism is tolerant by nature not only because it is polytheistic, but because it is not dualistic, as it opposes any fundamental lack of

---

48   Ibid. That is, *hostis* as opposed to *inimicus*.

49   Ibid., 145.

50   "Political" in the sense imparted to the term by Carl Schmitt. Jean Haudry also uses this term in his discussion of the Indo-European worldview. See Jean Haudry, *The Indo-Europeans* (Lyon: 1994), 14.

51   de Benoist, *On Being a Pagan*, 147.

52   Ibid.,145.

53   Ibid.

54   Ibid., 148.

55   Ibid., 110.

continuity between God and the world.⁵⁶ In this sense, it can be said that paganism as such is "tolerant".

World-Affirming Ethnic Religion

The Indo-European pagan worldview is based on a positive attitude towards the manifest world and is always connected to a particular people — it is an ethnic religion or "folk religion". Therefore, proselytism has no *raison d'être*, and this fits with the above-mentioned kind of "tolerance" towards other worldviews and religions. The pre-Christian European religions had a communal character.⁵⁷ The weight of the community was expressed by rituals that *de facto* promoted group solidarity and fused the community's relationship with the gods.⁵⁸ The world is taken as it is, accepted without the desire for "salvation" from it in some better, "other world".⁵⁹

In contrast to biblical monotheism, paganism is characterised by an inherent tolerance. As de Benoist points out, in ancient religions a cult was inseparable from a given society or community.⁶⁰ For the latter, the cult represented the "infrastructure" rather than a

---

56 Ibid.
57 Alain de Benoist, "*Christianisme et paganisme*" in *C'est-à-dire. Entretiens — Témoignages — Explications*, vol. 2, 330.
58 de Benoist, *Jésus et ses frères*, 296.
59 Ibid., 240. Idem, *L'empire intérieur*, 22.
60 Ibid., 331. See also idem, "*Un mot en quatre lettres*", 20: "The notion that one can isolate a system of beliefs from their anthropo-social specificity is a common mistake. When torn out of its cultural matrix, a 'religion' becomes a group of abstract symbols, myths, and rituals, and one loses the context of meaning of those who experience the religion in their concrete existences. This, indeed, is the concept of 'conversion.' It is based on the conviction that one can revere (or force one to revere) a faith without living on the land that gave birth to this faith. In reality, 'religion' is inseparable from the *modus vivendi* and worldview of a given culture. The diversity of 'religions' is a reflection of the diversity of cultures."

"superstructure". Religion was the "cement" of collective structures.[61] De Benoist explains: "Sacrifice did not have the aim solely of worshiping the gods [...] it also had the aim of the harmonious coexistence of people and the gods, so that the order of the world might be based on this coexistence. [...] The maintenance of this cosmic order is based on the possibility of open communication through the *sacrum*."[62]

Offering sacrifices to the gods was not only a religious deed, but also a civic duty.[63] The cult sanctioned a common existence in which religious confession, citizenship, and ethnos were harmoniously intertwined.[64] In the ancient understanding, there was no such thing as a person without an identity belonging to a community.[65] Community was the fundamental point of reference for pagan religiosity and — as follows — for identity as such. For the ancients, there was no such thing as a human being understood in a purely abstract way, that is, a person torn from a network of overlapping socio-cultural relations.[66] It is for this reason that the concept of converting the Other to one's faith is, from the point of view of the ancient pagan mentality, something

---

61 de Benoist, *On Being a Pagan*, 151.

62 de Benoist and Molnar, *Éclipse du sacré*, 111.

63 de Benoist, "*Christianisme et paganisme*" in *C'est-à-dire. Entretiens — Témoignages — Explications*, vol. 2, 331.

64 de Benoist, *View from the Right*, vol. 2, 169: "Indo-European peoples were [...], in fact, profoundly religious peoples for whom participation in communal acts of worship was closely tied to civic life (one was thus born into a religion in the same manner that one is born into a community, and it is for this very reason that the ancient Romans considered Christian universalism to be profane)."

65 de Benoist, *On Being a Pagan*, 123: "Pagan thought, which is fundamentally attached to roots and to place as the preferred center around which identity can crystallize, can only reject all religious and philosophical forms of universalism. [...] For the Ancients, 'man' did not exist. There were only men: Greeks, Romans, barbarians, Syrians, and so forth."

66 Alain de Benoist, *Beyond Human Rights: Defending Freedoms*, trans. Alexander Jacob (London: Arktos, 2011), 61.

completely senseless.⁶⁷ The Indo-European religions were organically bound to the particular peoples professing them. As James Russell argues, folk religions, unlike universalist religions, define themselves first and foremost on the ethnocultural dimension rather than the dogmatic level.⁶⁸ In some sense, for the Indo-Europeans religion was not an end in and of itself,⁶⁹ as it constituted an inseparable part of the life of the broader community (fulfilling the role of "cultural infrastructure) and constituted their vision of the world: it constituted the ground of their *Weltanschauung*. Rather, it was the community that was an end in an of itself, i.e., man as an individual found realisation within the framework of his community in this world. The emphasis was on existing within this world.

The Indo-European religions did not concentrate on the question of the afterlife,⁷⁰ for "immortality" (understood as "immortal glory"⁷¹) was achieved in this world through heroic deeds. The *heros* was the

---

67 Eliade, *Sacred and Profane*, 32: "For in the view of archaic societies everything that is not 'our world' is not yet a world." Idem, *Patterns in Comparative Religion*, 381: "The labyrinth could be defending a city [...] but, in every case, it was defending some magico-religious space [...] The military function of the labyrinth was simply a variant on its essential work of defending against 'evil', hostile spirits and death. [...] Religiously, it barred the way to the city for spirits from without, for the demons of the desert, for death. The 'center' here includes the whole of the city which is made, as we have seen, to reproduce the universe itself."

68 James C. Russell, *The Germanization of Early Medieval Christianity: A Sociohistorical Approach to Religious Transformation* (Oxford: Oxford University Press, 1994), 48.

69 de Benoist, *On Being a Pagan*, 115: "The Indo-European peoples, before their conversion to Semitic ideas, never regarded their religion as an absolute truth. Rather they viewed it as a kind of family or caste heritage, and for this reason intolerance and proselytizing remained foreign to them. This is why we find among these peoples a freedom of thought, a spirit of critical inquiry, and individual research".

70 Russell, *The Germanization of Early Medieval Christianity*, 162.

71 Haudry, *Indo-Europeans*, 14.

human ideal. Accordingly, the warrior was a central point of the Indo-European social system.[72] Character was seen as a person's most essential trait, and a person's most important aim was eternal glory. The hero's dream was for the poet to sing of his deeds and bravery long after his death. Death could be overcome in this way: through a life worth remembering, in this world, and within one's own community.

In this respect, pagans did not feel the need to "flee" from this world, to be "saved" from the world, or attain "salvation", for the meaning of their existence was realised in this world. The world was not an "illusion" or "veil of tears", or a collection of resources that need to be "subjugated". The world was a subject—the Cosmos, an order in its own right that was full of the divine. The *sacrum* was within the world, not outside it. Man was not separate and different from this world, but was an elementary part of it. To quote de Benoist: "If man is God's kin and partner, he is not himself an object placed in the world but is himself partially connected with the world."[73]

The Hierophany of Nature

Alain de Benoist writes:

> In my opinion, there has been far too much depiction of paganism as a 'nature religion' that disregards all transcendence and is limited in some sense to only sacralising natural determinisms... Furthermore, this interpretation was systematised by Christian propaganda in order to have an easy means of opposing with the prerogative of the 'spirit', which this new faith claims as its monopoly, the naturalistic cloddishness of those 'who worshiped stones and imaginary things'.[74]

The ancient Greeks understood the world and nature differently from Christians and moderns. Heidegger, whom de Benoist cites directly,[75]

72　Russell, *The Germanization of Early Medieval Christianity*, 117.
73　de Benoist, *On Being a Pagan*, 177.
74　Ibid., 154.
75　de Benoist and Molnar, *Éclipse du sacré*, 117.

discusses this question in detail in his *Introduction to Metaphysics*. The modern concept of "nature" is derived from Latin *natura* (interpret through the prism of Christianity, and later positivism), and means "that which is born". In other words, "nature" means a collection of material things, e.g., trees, rocks, animals, understood as objects. Yet the fundamental ancient Greek notion of *physis*[76] defined nature as "the totality of what exists, beings as such as a whole".[77] What is the difference here? In contrast to *natura*, *physis* is not a reductionist framing in materialistic terms, but rather is holistic and subjectifying. In other words, reducing *physis* to natural phenomena is a simplification, hence the Latin *natura* distorts its original meaning. The term *physis* does not delimit the physical from the spiritual, nor does it lay down a border between the field of nature and the sphere of human activity.[78] *Physis* defines the nature-world as something living, animated, dynamic, and simultaneously containing "divine" potential which might "manifest" in given circumstances.[79] In paganism, after all, the divine "manifests

---

76 Martin Heidegger, *Introduction to Metaphysics*, 2nd ed., trans. Gregory Fried and Richard Polt (New Haven: Yale University Press, 2014), 16: "*Phusis* as emergence can be experienced everywhere: for example, in processes in the heavens (the rising of the sun), in the surging of the sea, in the growth of plants, in the coming forth of animals and human beings from the womb. But *phusis*, the emerging sway, is not synonymous with these processes, which still today we count as part of 'nature.' This emerging and standing-out-in-itself-from-itself may not be taken as just one process among others that we observe in beings. […] It was not in natural processes that the Greeks first experienced what *phusis* is, but the other way around: on the basis of a fundamental experience of Being in poetry and thought, what they had to call *phusis* disclosed itself to them."

77 B. Dembiński, *Zagadnienie skończoności w ontologii fundamentalnej Martina Heideggera* (Katowice: 1990), 18.

78 L. Kula, "Pojęcie φύσις w interpretacji Martina Heideggera", *Kwartalnik Filozoficzny* XL (2012), 42.

79 A very similar perspective can be found in Eliade, *Sacred and Profane*, 121: "There is no question of naturism here. The celestial god is not identified with the sky […]. But he lives in the sky and is manifested in meteorological phenomena — thunder, lightning, storm, meteors, and so on. This means that certain privileged structures of the cosmos — the sky, the atmosphere — constitute

itself" (in the world, in nature) rather than "reveals" itself (through a book or prophet). The world is "transparent" for the divine.

"Nature" as *natura* (since the Christian era) presents the nature-world in a static, mechanical, objectified, descralised way as a collection of things that someone once created with a definite end. In other words, *natura* is not a value in and of itself — it is something for "mastering" instead of something for "astonishing". It is not something that arouses fear and fascination, but merely something that needs to be "subjugated".[80] As Heidegger pointed out, the nature studied by modern physics is not the same nature that ancient Greek thought perceived. The ancient Greek *physis* defined being as such, as a whole (with all of its aspects), not merely the material dimension. For the pagan Greek, a tree, river, or stream were not simply physical objects (understood in a purely instrumental way), but were part of a living world full of power, mystery, and the divine. *Physis* is that which "emerges from itself", an "unconcealing unfolding that emerges into unconcealment".[81] Heidegger defined *physis* as "emerging-abiding sway" (*das aufgehend-verweilende Walten*).[82] In Heidegger's words, "*Phusis* is Being itself, by virtue of which beings first become and remain observable".[83] It is through this notion of *physis* that the idea of

---

favorite epiphanies of the supreme being; he reveals his presence by what is specifically and peculiarly his — the majesty (*majestas*) of the celestial immensity, the terror (*tremendum*) of the storm."

80 J. Galarowicz, *Martin Heidegger — genialny myśliciel czy szaman?* (Kraków: 2014), 108: "Our metaphysical approach to the world has expressed and perpetuated a will to objectify everything, a desire to take possession of reality and manipulate it. Metaphysical and scientific cognition of beings have at bottom one aim: to rule over beings, to become master of the universe. All of reality is — as we take it to be — in our possession and for us. […] There is no sacrality, nothing that would demand our reverence and adoration."

81 Dembiński, *Zagadnienie skończoności w ontologii fundamentalnej Martina Heideggera*, 18.

82 Heidegger, *Introduction to Metaphysics*, 16.

83 Ibid.

"nature" should, in de Benoist's opinion, be reinterpreted today.[84] De Benoist writes:

> This bond of man to 'nature,' let's say right off, should not be interpreted as flat naturalism — the 'return of Nature' dear to Rousseau's disciples, ecologists, and volkish sects — but as an active participation of man in all that exists, based on his clear awareness of what exists. In this perspective, God can be in all things, not in the sense of a *logos* that contrives tangible reality from within, but as a *dimension* of this reality, its *depth* dimension. The mist on the mountain, the song of a bird, the flickering path of an insect can bear its mark. God can spread out toward man in the movement of the waves, the seeding grass, the blossoming flower.[85]

God and Man: Ontic Closeness

Paul Veyne once wrote:

> Nothing could have been more different from, on the one hand, the relationship between the pagans and their gods and, on the other, that between the Christians and their God: a pagan was content with his gods if he had elicited their help by means of his prayers and vows; a Christian instead endeavoured to make his God content with him. Augustus did not serve Apollo; he simply turned to him for help […] In contrast, throughout the twenty-five years that followed, Constantine repeatedly declared that he was simply the servant of Christ, who had admitted him to his service […][86]

In de Benoist's opinion, in European paganism there is no radical distance between god and man in the likes of that in Christianity. Both god and man are elements of the cosmos — they are contained "within" it. Pagan thought maintains that man is an integral part of the world; therefore, there can be no talk of an insurmountable distance between man and God. Man participates in the sacrality of the world along with

---

84   de Benoist, *Jésus et ses frères*, 291.
85   de Benoist, *On Being a Pagan*, 151.
86   Paul Veyne, *When Our World Became Christian*, trans. Janet Lloyd (Cambridge: Polity, 2010), 6.

the gods. "Because paganism does not view the world as something apart from God, both are equal in perfection. God is as 'imperfect' as the world."[87] The idea that man could achieve a semi-divine status after death was, de Benoist argues, widespread in antiquity[88] (hence heroes were seen as such demi-gods[89]). The moral aim of the pagan man of antiquity was to become more than he is. In other words, man is supposed to achieve his full potential by going beyond himself.[90] In this way, by elevating himself to measure up to God, rather than prostrating before him, pagan man "can attain the divine":[91] "By honoring his gods, man honors his ability to live in symbiosis with them, [...] he honors his own capacity, by means of a free will to power, to become equal to the models he has chosen."[92]

This does not mean, however, that pagan man believed that he could replace God. De Benoist underscores that paganism should not be associated with a Promethean attitude. To the contrary, de Benoist sees Prometheus as as a negative figure in that he rebelled against the cosmic order. For him, paganism is synonymous with rejecting the "titanic hubris" that drives man to displace the gods from their rightful place out of the vain hope that he might replace them.[93] "Man should not have the ambition to become God, but to become *like the gods*."[94]

Pagans worshiped their gods differently than Christians. The latter have a servile, obsequious relation to God — in the face of God, man is nothing. In paganism, man's relation to God is based on a mutual exchange: "The gods give unto me, and I give unto them. Sacrifice is not a demonstration of subordination, but a way to contribute to and

---

87   de Benoist, *On Being a Pagan*, 32.
88   Ibid., 179.
89   Ibid., 33.
90   Ibid., 178.
91   Ibid.,179.
92   Ibid.,109.
93   de Benoist, *Jésus et ses frères*, 296.
94   de Benoist, *On Being a Pagan*, 178.

uphold the cosmic order."⁹⁵ Zeus and Odin are more "sovereigns" than "despots".⁹⁶ They are neither creators nor redeemers of the world. They expect honour and recognition, but not unconditional, blind subordination; they do not impose dogma or holy books. "They do not proclaim commandments, but offer luminous ideals. They do not issue commands with the threat of 'punishment', but through their very presence are cause for joy."⁹⁷ Through their very existence, the gods uphold the order of the world. Being both the guarantors and the guardians of the cosmic order, they need people just as people need them.⁹⁸

Another characteristic of "polytheistic religions" like Indo-European paganism is that man faces the divine not as an individual, but as a member of a community.⁹⁹ In paganism, a person is understood to be inseparable from their lineage. In ancient Scandinavia, family was seen as one of the fundamentals of human existence alongside destiny and honour.¹⁰⁰ In ancient Greece, the *oikos* was a religious unit.¹⁰¹ To quote de Benoist:

> In paganism, religion tends to primarily govern situations of collective interest; it gives a large role to the person (rather than the individual), but taking into consideration those groups the person belongs to which are indispensable toward the grasp of his or her identity. 'It is not as an individual," notes Jean-Pierre Vernant, "that the Greek man respects or fears a god, but as the head of the family, the member of a *genos*, a *phratry*, a *demos*, a city.'¹⁰²

---

95   de Benoist, *Jésus et ses frères*, 296.
96   de Benoist, *On Being a Pagan*, 151.
97   de Benoist, *Jésus et ses frères*, 243.
98   Ibid., 243-244.
99   de Benoist, *On Being a Pagan*, 153; Haudry, *Indo-Europeans*, 68.
100 de Benoist, *On Being a Pagan*, 153.
101 L.B. Zaidman, *Grecy i ich bogowie* (Warsaw: 2008), 22.
102 de Benoist, *On Being a Pagan*, 153.

In such societies, man is seen above all as a member of a particular organic community, not as an abstract individual free from any socio-historical context, as is the formula of modern Western individualism.

De Benoist warns against equating paganism with atheism,[103] an accusation which has repeatedly been raised by Christians. For the ancient mentality, the concept of atheism — in today's understanding — is senseless. As already mentioned, in paganism the gods are not "outside" the world, are not separate from it, but are an integral part of it, "intertwined" with it. Moreover, de Benoist emphasises, the gods themselves are not the *ultima ratio* of paganism. Atheism itself could only emerge as a concept after Christianity: "Christian atheism is… a modern phenomenon which implies Christian theism as the antithesis, without which it wouldn't exist."[104]

De Benoist does not treat the very question of the existence of the gods with any priority. It is unimportant whether the gods "exist" or not, for the point is man's "opening up" to their presence. One way for paganism today to be "revived" is to renew this position and sensitivity towards the world, one which makes it possible for the gods to "reveal" or "manifest" themselves to man. In other words, what is needed is a "non-closed" posture of being opened and turned anew to the world (*physis*). This is the *sine qua non* of "authentic" paganism.

De Benoist summarises: "The point is not whether 'God' exists or not, but whether the divine is coming closer or moving further away. 'God', *sensu stricto*, means nothing to me. The gods mean the possibility of presence."[105]

---

103 de Benoist, *Jésus et ses frères*, 296: "I believe that paganism is incompatible with atheism if we understand the latter as radically negating any form of divinity or the absolute."

104 Ibid.

105 de Benoist, "*Un mot en quatre lettres*", 22.

How to Be a Pagan (Today)

De Benoist argues that despite the "death of God", Europe still doesn't want to get rid of his corpse,[106] i.e., Europe does not want to take to heart that God has left the world of values. The French thinker proposes that we reject Christian metaphysics (creation *ex nihilo*) as well as modern metaphysics (what Heidegger called the "metaphysics of subjectivity") and establish a new system of values. This is bound up with creating a neo-paganism that would make the realisation of "authentic existence" possible.[107]

According to de Benoist, paganism is fundamentally anti-modern. Whereas for the man of modernity God is an invention, and a stone is simple a stone, "for those who have a religious experience all nature is capable of revealing itself as cosmic sacrality".[108] For modern man, myth is an artificially devised tale. "Pagan" man, like Alain de Benoist for his part, "is committed to the truth of myth."[109] A "pagan", therefore, is *Homo religiosus*, whose being-in-the-world comes close to Eliade's "archaic man": "Religious man *wants to be other* than he finds himself on the 'natural' level and undertakes to *make himself* in accordance with the ideal image revealed to him by myths."[110] In other words, paganism, as in de Benoist's understanding, is bound up with rejecting the worldview of modernity, in which "for the non-religious men of the modern age, the cosmos has become opaque, inert, mute".[111] But on what, actually, is this rejection to be based?

It bears explicitly stressing that Christianity and modernity are, from the "pagan" point of view, two sides of the same coin. Both are based on the biblical imperative of "ruling over the earth". Decisively

---

106 de Benoist, *On Being a Pagan*, 196.
107 Ibid., 200–201.
108 Eliade, *Sacred and Profane*, 12.
109 de Benoist, *Jesus et ses frères*, 203.
110 Eliade, *Sacred and Profane*, 187.
111 Ibid., 178.

rejecting this imperative is one of the most important elements of the "pagan" *Weltanschauung*. Another key element is rejecting the language of Judeo-Christian egalitarianism[112] (the dogma of the equality of souls) which in today's realities translates into, among other things, the ideology of human rights. The next noteworthy direction is rejecting the bourgeois (materialist-capitalist) ethos in favour of the ethos of honour. "Pagan" life is heroic life. *Homo paganus* is the antithesis to *Homo oeconomicus*. As Eliade wrote:

> More than any other humanistic discipline [...], history of religions can open the way to a philosophical anthropology. For the sacred is a universal dimension and, as we shall see later, the beginnings of culture are rooted in religious experiences and beliefs. [...] Thus, the historian of religions is in a position to grasp the permanence of what has been called man's specific existential situation of 'being in the world,' for the experience of the sacred is its correlate.[113]

Here lies the meaning of the positive appeal to "paganism" in the *Nouvelle Droite*'s ideas. The point is not so much about resurrecting past forms of cult as it is regaining the sensitivity and comportment towards the surrounding world that were intrinsic to ancient man. In other words, the point is to grasp "pagan being-in-the-world". Regaining this way of being is something that would enable European culture to overcome the current crisis and undergo a renaissance.

From the *Nouvelle Droite*'s perspective, what makes the pagan mentality "better" than the Christian-modern mentality is the fact that the pagan mentality is inherently anti-totalitarian. One practical consequence of polytheistic structures of thought is a natural tendency towards tolerance of diversity on the principle that every city has the right to worship its own gods. History seems to confirm this. The conquests accomplished by the Romans, among others, did not entail the

---

112 de Benoist, *On Being a Pagan*, 201.
113 Mircea Eliade, *The Quest: History and Meaning in Religion* (Chicago: University of Chicago Press, 1969), 9.

systematic extermination of entire peoples or ethnic groups, were not bound up with any forced destruction of the existing religious forms they encountered, nor did they demand conversion. The moment that Christianity entered the arena of European history, this situation changed entirely.

CHAPTER IV

CHRISTIANITY: THE "BOLSHEVISM OF ANTIQUITY"

OSWALD SPENGLER WROTE: "All Communist systems in the West are in fact derived from Christian theological thought [...]. Christian theology is the grandmother of Bolshevism."[1] From the *Nouvelle Droite*'s perspective, the West is constituted by a constant tension between two opposite sources which have caused an ongoing crisis of identity.[2] Thus, the *Nouvelle Droite* views Christianity in a decidedly negative way. However, it is noteworthy that there is virtually no anti-clericalism in the *Nouvelle Droite*'s thought — the institutional Church and its possible misdoings are not the object of critique, or of any interest for that matter. Instead, the critique is aimed above all at the monotheism and universalism that are characteristic of Christianity,[3] and also at what is often deemed to be the latter's "intolerance" (or even "proto-totalitarianism"), which is seen as entailing an inclination towards persecution on religious grounds. In other words, the *Nouvelle Droite*'s critique of Christianity is first and foremost conducted on the philosophical level.

Although calling Christianity the "Bolshevism of antiquity" might at first glance seem to be shocking, it is worth recalling that the *Nouvelle Droite*'s perspective on this matter is not entirely new. For

---

1   Spengler, *The Hour of Decision*, 97
2   Moos, *Les intellectuels de la Nouvelle Droite et la religion*, 75.
3   Ibid., 43.

example, Oswald Spengler and Mircea Eliade seem to present convergent views on this topic, and the concepts of both are indeed an important inspiration and reference point in the thought of the *Nouvelle Droite*. However, Alain de Benoist goes decisively further and does not restrict himself to singular slogans. He presents a deep-running critique of Christianity as such. The position from which this critique is made could, for lack of a better term, be deemed "historical-pagan". Bracketing the philosophical critique for a brief moment, we can begin with pointing out that Alain de Benoist treats Christianity as the *bête noire* in the history of European civilisation, while he himself identifies with the other side, i.e., the "pagan" Greeks and Romans. In other words, the latter (along with other European peoples, of course) are regarded as the proto-layers of today's Europe, whereas Christianity is seen as a destructive force that distorted and destroyed the "authentic" roots of European civilisation by way of progressive ideational undermining.[4] Of importance in the present context is de Benoist's remark that "the first Church in Rome had nothing Latin about it".[5] The Christian message was a negation of everything Roman.[6] In the end, Christianity was a religion that originated out of an entirely different cultural circle.

---

4   de Benoist, *Les idées à l'endroit*, 168. A similar thesis was put forth by the historian Edward Gibbon, whom de Benoist cites. See Gibbon's *History of the Decline and Fall of the Roman Empire*. See also P. Komorowski, "Koncepcja historii Edwarda Gibbona", *Analecta* 7/2(14) (1998), 71–106.

5   de Benoist, *Les idées à l'endroit*, 171.

6   Ibid., 175: "Christian doctrine implied a 'social revolution'. What it affirmed for the first time was not that the soul exists [...] but that 'everyone' possesses the same soul. The people of ancient culture, being born into a given religion on account of being born in their 'ancestral land', instead had the tendency to think in categories of self-discipline and self-overcoming, and they were convinced of the necessity of hammering-out their own soul, although this was obviously reserved for the 'best' among them. The idea that 'all people' can be equally gifted by the very fact of their existence was shocking. Christianity proclaimed [...] that everyone is born with a soul, which was equivalent to claiming that all people are 'equal' before God."

In addition, one rather often encounters in the *Nouvelle Droite*'s discourse the term "Judeo-Christian" (as in "Judeo-Christianity", "Judeo-Christian tradition", etc.),[7] which in essence and *de facto* is a blade of critique pointed at Christianity. The use of the prefix "Judeo-" is not intended to critique Judaism or the Jewish people, but rather to underscore the non-European, i.e., Middle-Eastern roots of the Christian religion and thus its implicit foreignness to the European spirit.

Following Ernest Renan and Emil Gilabert, de Benoist points out that none of the ancient religions exhibited such a degree of intolerance as the religion of the Hebrew people (which is supposed to be a logical consequence of its monotheism). Of course, de Benoist is not thereby suggesting that such cruelty only figures among the Semitic peoples. Above all, the point is that one would seek in vain any religious or moral justifications for killing on a mass scale in "pagan" writings, whether religious or secular.[8] In the Bible, however, as de Benoist argues, one can find many passages in which genocide is justified for religio-moral reasons (e.g., Deuteronomy 12:29, 20:16; 1 Samuel 27:9; Numbers 31:7; Joshua 11:10–11, 20–21): "For the perpetrators of these crimes, good consciousness continues to rule, not despite these massacres, but entirely for the sake of the massacres."[9]

Yet, it is precisely in Christian monotheism, not Jewish monotheism, that the germs of totalitarianism are encapsulated. Monotheism is seen as taking on a totalitarian nature as soon as it went beyond the framework of nationality (Jewish), that is, as soon as it turned from an

---

7   De Benoist points out that, for the sake of precision of expression, the term "Judeo-Christianity" can be used in basically two meanings: first, in the historical sense, to distinguish the first Christians of Jewish origin led by John from the Helleno-Christians led by Paul; secondly, in the ideological sense, to highlight the common theological roots of Judaism and Christianity. See de Benoist, *On Being a Pagan*, 19.

8   See Alain de Benoist, "Monotheism vs. Polytheism" in Sunic, *Postmortem Report: Cultural Examinations from Postmodernity*, 25.

9   Ibid.

ethnic religion into a universalist religion.[10] In other words, universalism "awakened" the totalitarian potential in biblical monotheism.[11]

This intolerance accompanied Christianity from its very beginning — towards Jews, pagans, heretics, and all other "infidels", who were "subhumans in the eyes of the apostles".[12] For St. Peter, such ilk were "unreasoning animals, creatures of instinct, born only to be caught and destroyed" (2 Peter 2:12), and for St. Paul they "deserve death" (Romans 1:32).[13] Christianity therefore took up the task of "exterminating all aspects of ancient culture" by means of, among other things, banning pagan cults and the Olympic games, destroying sculptures and temples, and, in 389 CE, burning the Serapeum in Alexandria (along with 700,000 manuscripts) on the suggestion of Bishop Theophilus. In a later era, the next steps would be forced conversion, condemning science, persecutions, and burning at the stake.[14]

De Benoist argues that the Jews were among the first to suffer at the hands of Christian monotheism. Christian anti-Judaism, whose

---

10   Moos, *Les intellectuels de la Nouvelle Droite et la religion*, 44.

11   The idea of the specificity of Christian monotheism is drawn from Louis Rougier, who argued that the fanaticism contained in the Bible was "internationalised" by Christianity. See Louis Rougier, *Le conflit du christianisme primitif et de la civilisation antique* (Paris: 1977), 58–59: "Yahweh, the one and only God of the Sinai, the cruel God of the deserts of Arabia, was an authoritarian, exclusive, and jealous God who saw all other gods as false and called upon his faithful to stone their sons and brothers guilty of idolatry. However, this fanaticism for a long time did not go beyond the [Jewish] race. Yahweh is, of course, a universal god [...], yet the people of Israel made him into their own on the basis of the Covenant with him and made him bound to contract with the Jewish people alone. As soon as the Kingdom of God was opened to *goyim* as well as Jews, to Barbarians as well as Hellenes, Christianity took up the mission of converting the whole world regardless of racial and national differences [...]. The intolerance contained within it spread to the whole world."

12   de Benoist, *Les idées à l'endroit*, 172.

13   Ibid.

14   de Benoist, "Monotheism vs. Polytheism" in Sunic, *Postmortem Report*, 24.

genesis was contained in the Gospel of St. John,[15] came out of the very proximity between Jewish and Christian faith. From the very first centuries, Christianity was seen by its believers as the "rightful successor" to Judaism. De Benoist writes:

> For Christians, 'salvation is of the Jews' (John 4:22), but it is only Christianity that can be *verus Israel*. Saint Paul was the first to formulate this distinction. With his replacement of the Law by Grace, Paul distinguished between the 'Israel of God' and the 'Israel after the flesh' (1 Corinthians 10:18), which also led him to oppose circumcision: 'For he is not a Jew, which is one outwardly; neither is that circumcision, which is outward in the flesh: But he is a Jew, which is one inwardly; and circumcision is that of the heart, in the spirit, and not in the letter; whose praise is not of men, but of God' (Romans 2:28–29). Conclusion: 'For we are the circumcision' (Philippians 3:3).[16]

In abolishing the hitherto Law, Jesus Christ thereby annulled the importance of the distinction between Jew and *goy* (Galatians 3:28). Henceforth, de Benoist argues, Christianity took on the role of the "true Israel."[17] The consequence was persecuting anyone who refused to convert, who did not recognise Christianity to be the *verus Israel*. In other words, from the *Nouvelle Droite*'s perspective, Christianity's assumption of the role of Israel (in the spiritual sense) denied the Jews being Isreal, for Christianity became the true Israel that the Jews did not acknowledge. Citing Shmuel Trigano, de Benoist argues that if Christianity laid the foundations for the West, then the real place of Israel is the West.[18]

---

15 The discernment of Christian anti-Semitism or anti-Judaism in the Gospel of St. John is a matter of controversy. See A. Kuśmirek, "Żydzi w Ewangelii Jana", *Studia Theologica Varsaviensia* 30/2 (1992), 121–135; M. Wróbel, *Antyjudaizm a Ewangelia według św. Jana. Nowe spojrzenie na relację czwartej Ewangelii do judaizmu* (Lublin: 2005).

16 de Benoist, "Monotheism vs. Polytheism" in Sunic, *Postmortem Report*, 26–27.

17 Ibid.

18 Ibid., 26.

In connection with this, de Benoist describes Christian anti-Semitism as a neurosis. On account of being alienated from its original identity, the West becomes incapable of self-fulfilment and discovering itself:

> By replacing its original myth with the myth of biblical monotheism, the West has turned Hebraism into its own superego. As an inevitable consequence, the West had to turn itself against the Jewish people by accusing them of not pursuing the 'conversion' in terms of the 'logical' evolution proceeding from Sinai to Christianity. In addition, the West also accused the Jewish people of attempting, in an apparent 'deicide', to obstruct this evolution. [...] The Church ordered Jews to choose between exclusion (or physical death) or self-denial (spiritual and historical death). Only through conversion could they become 'Christians, as others'.[19]

Hence, according to de Benoist, it is not difficult to notice where the sources of modern totalitarianism lie.[20] The sources of the secular totalitarian systems do not lie in the thoughts of Louis de Saint-Just, Hegel, Fichte, or Stalin, for the latter are only the aftermath of "Middle Eastern mentality" crystallised by Christianity. In other words, totalitarianism never would have taken shape in Europe if Christianity had never sown its seeds in European minds. For the *Nouvelle Droite*, the core of any totalitarianism is the negation of the right to difference, and this is precisely what characterises the Christian religion. If one were to acknowledge (as is proper for "paganism") tolerant pluralism as a typical trait of the European (pre-Christian) mentality, then totalitarianism in turn is a typical trait of monotheism, which is universalist as "de-territorialised" (going beyond the boundaries of one particular ethnos or culture).

De Benoist's approach to Christianity was formed largely under the influence of three thinkers. As de Benoist himself says, in his early years he was fascinated with Nietzsche, whose works he assessed as "joyful

---

19 Ibid., 28.
20 Ibid., 27.

and liberating". In the early 1960s, de Benoist became acquainted with Louis Rougier, who held conservative-liberal views on the one hand, but on the other hand was an admirer of the Greco-Roman heritage and was critical of Christianity. Our French thinker's views changed in the early 1970s, when he began to view liberalism in ever more critical terms. This entailed a rejection of Enlightenment philosophy as well as positivism and scientism, of which Rougier was a supporter. In his later years, de Benoist's reading of Heidegger compelled him to re-evaluate Nietzsche's thought.

Taguieff describes de Benoist's anti-Christianity as an "anti-Biblism", and more generally as "anti-monotheism". In his view, Christianity is subjected to a double critique: first, on the level of identity, it is described as an offshoot of a mentality that is foreign to European peoples; second, the Christian religion is subjected to a philosophical critique — both Nietzschean as well as positivistic-logical, i.e., anti-metaphysical.[21] Thus, Taguieff categorises three phases of de Benoist's anti-Christianity in terms of his main inspiration at each stage: (1) Rougier, 1963–1973; (2) Nietzsche, 1974–1978; (3) Heidegger, 1979–1982 to present.[22] In the 1960s, de Benoist went through a brief fascination with "militant" logical positivism, then passed to rediscovering Nietzsche, during which time he distanced himself from Rougier's rationalism and scientism, and the finale of this evolution came with the adoption of the "post-metaphysical" perspective of Heidegger.[23] Thus, de Benoist's ideational evolution led him from the idea of defending the West (as the creator of scientific and technological rationalism) to "returning to the Greeks" as the source culture of European thought.[24]

Yet, a certain inconsistency can be noticed here: on the one hand, the *Nouvelle Droite* is against monotheism in general; on the other

---

21   Taguieff, *Sur la Nouvelle Droite*, 188.
22   Ibid., 187.
23   Ibid., 188.
24   Ibid., 187.

hand, a certain expiation is made for Judaism. Taguieff believes that this is a tactical manoeuvre with the aim of avoiding accusations of anti-Semitism, a position which has been unacceptable since 1945, at any cost.[25] At the same time, the fact may be recalled that de Benoist has denied that the non-European roots of Christianity influenced his critical position towards this religion — rather, he emphasises that he is sympathetic towards some non-European religions (e.g., Shinto and Zen) at the same time as he is critical of more than one ideology born in Europe.[26] Nonetheless, it is difficult to deny that the issue of Christianity's foreign origin is rather explicitly accentuated in the *Nouvelle Droite*'s narrative on the topic of religion.

Theocentric-Monotheistic Dualism

According to Alain de Benoist, the most essential trait of the biblical religion is not, contrary to the widespread opinion, the idea of one God, but rather its "irreversible ontological separation",[27] that is, the complete separation of God and the world.[28] De Benoist writes: "The fundamental trait of Christianity is not monotheism, but the ideology of a rupture (of being and the world, of the world and man, of immanence and transcendence, of soul and body, of the earthly and the spiritual, of being and becoming, etc.) with God, whose existence is inextricably bound to the universal issue of salvation."[29]

Placing the divine at the origins of the world's existence is not something unheard-of in religions. However, de Benoist stresses, there is a radical ontological separation planted in Christianity in the

---

25 Ibid., 89.
26 Sylvain, "Interview with Alain de Benoist" in *North American New Right*, 72.
27 Alain de Benoist, "*Sacré païen et desacralisation judéo-chrétienne du monde*" in D. Théiraios (ed.), *Quelle religion pour l'Europe?* (Geneva: 1990), 30.
28 de Benoist, *On Being a Pagan*, 29.
29 Alain de Benoist, "*Un mot en quatre lettres*", 18–19.

distinction between created and uncreated being.[30] The perfection of uncreated being (God) is contrasted to the imperfection of created being (the world). God is not an emanation of the world, but rather its one and only creator, and the very creation of the world does not add anything to his perfection. God is omnipotent, almighty, and simultaneously transcendent and immanent, eternal and infinite. The world is dependent upon him and — more importantly — is separate from him. The Yahweh of the Bible is the only god not merely in the sense of being the only holder of power. He is the one and only god in the sense of complete otherness. He is the "only one of his kind", which means that he is "Completely Other" to the world. De Benoist describes this "revolutionary", radical ontological separation of the world and the divine as the "inaugural dissociation",[31] as the objectification of the world through the rupture of its direct connectedness with the divine principle. In de Benoist's opinion, this "inaugural dissociation" constituted the first and most decisive stage in the revolutionary change of Europeans' worldview-mentality over the course of history.[32] Thus, in de Benoist's words, "the beginning of desacralisation was the assertion that the cosmos is something separate from God".[33]

The "inaugural dissociation" of Christianity "tossed out" the foundation of reality "outside here" to somewhere "outside the world".[34] Consequently, the world is no longer seen as a place of truth, for truth is understood as meaning compliance with the divine rules that lie "outside" the world, a world which, according to Christianity, has nothing sacred in and of itself. *Physis* was thus subjected to disintegration and became an ordinary object. Where, then, is the source of values and truth? The source is Yahweh alone, the one and only God.

---

30   de Benoist, *On Being a Pagan*, 29.
31   de Benoist and Molnar, *Éclipse du sacré*, 131.
32   de Benoist, *Sacré païen*, 31.
33   de Benoist and Molnar, *Éclipse du sacré*, 130.
34   de Benoist, *Sacré païen*, 31.

Indo-European polytheism and Judeo-Christian monotheism differ on more questions than the number of gods. In both belief systems, an entirely different content lurks behind the term "god". As de Benoist puts it:

> The supreme being of which the Bible speaks is decisively different from the gods of the Indo-European space. It is a moral 'God', a creator 'God', a 'God' who reveals himself historically and whose relation to the world implies an absolute beginning and end of this world. Classical Christian theology defined him as a personal being of infinite imperfection that created everything that exists out of nothing [...] and which calls man to salvation and to respect his commandments. All of these traits are foreign to the gods of paganism.[35]

Furthermore:

> Yahweh is neither the fallen father nor the culmination or survivor of 'mythic gods'. Furthermore, the term God, which emerged from European Paganism, is an imperfect label; it was the Septuagint which, in order to be understood by Greeks and Hellenized Jews, gave the deity of Sinai, YHWH (Yahweh) Elohim, the name *theos/dues*, which up to that time strictly speaking designated only the gods of paganism.[36]

As de Benoist underscores here, the use of the term "God" (*theos*) for the biblical deity (devoid of feminine gender and always written with a capital letter) was a purely arbitrary move, as such a translation emptied the word "god" of its primordial meaning and imparted it with an entirely different sense.[37] The Indo-European languages did not use any term that would fully convey the sense of the biblical supreme being. The gods of paganism are not self-sufficient beings or the source of all things; rather, their significance comes from their mutual relations

---

35 de Benoist, "*Un mot en quatre lettres*", 18.
36 de Benoist, *On Being a Pagan*, 99–100.
37 de Benoist, "*Un mot en quatre lettres*", 18: "Wherever we read 'The Lord your God' (Deuteronomy 18:15), we should read, in accordance with the original Hebrew: '*Yahweh Adonai, ton Elohim.*'"

and their relationship with the world. Moreover, Indo-European religiosity knew gods as well as goddesses, which is absolutely inconceivable from the Hebrew perspective.[38] The Bible does not know a single "god" in the above sense of the word, for Yahweh is not so much a "god" (in the sense of *theos*) as he is the supreme being and central point of the Christian religion: "Christianity has made us accustomed to thinking that there is not religion without a Saviour-God and that the only basis of morality is faith in this God."[39] Hence, "the illusion is created that all religions have 'God' and differ only in their way of naming him, which conceals the fact that this very same word is being used to describe realities that completely differ from each other".[40] Thus, de Benoist emphasises that this ambiguity cannot be passed over in considerations on the question of deities and the divine.

The gods of paganism were born along with the world and they function within a constantly renewing cosmic cycle. Mythical time is repeatable and "transhistoric".[41] In other words, secular-historical time and sacred-liturgical time are not identical. The world is eternal, while the gods and men are not.

In the Judeo-Christian world, God is eternal: He created the world and thus gave time its beginning — Creation is identical with the beginning of time. In the Judeo-Christian vision, history has an absolute beginning and an absolute end.[42] Moreover, God reveals himself in historical time.[43] Christianity carried out a revolution by definitively

---

38 de Benoist, "*La Condition Féminine*", 110.
39 de Benoist, "*Un mot en quattre lettres*", 19.
40 Ibid., 18.
41 Eliade, *Patterns in Comparative Religion*, 395.
42 de Benoist, *On Being a Pagan*, 80.
43 Eliade, *Sacred and Profane*, 72: "Christianity radically changed the experience and the concept of liturgical time, and this is due to the fact that Christianity affirms the historicity of the person of Christ. The Christian liturgy unfolds in a historical time sanctified by the incarnation of the Son of God. The sacred time periodically reactualized in pre-Christian religions (especially in the archaic

breaking with the cyclical concept of time. As St. Augustine proclaimed, since time is God's matter, this means that time itself is the bearer of God's revelation in Creation and through Creation — time is a reality of an historical character. Hence, time has an inherent, theological sense as well as a direction and aim. God reveals himself in time. Time "heads towards" its eschatological fulfilment, from Creation to the *Parousia*. As Jan Edling summates: "With its entire essence consisting in constant change and linear directedness towards eternity, [time] becomes, unlike the Greek cyclical concept, a kind of sign or *vestigium* of the unchangingness of God. He creates history through present, past, and future. God reveals himself therein and thus fulfils his praeternal plan of salvation."[44]

A World-Rejecting Universalist Religion

The Judeo-Christian worldview is universalist and, at the same time, has a negative attitude towards this world — an attitude which is oriented towards soteriology and eschatology. For Christianity as a universalist religion, the issue of community is secondary. In this sense, it is an "apolitical" religion. And it is this Christianity, de Benoist maintains, that introduced individualism into the space of the European mentality.[45] Christianity is above all a religion of the salvation of the individual soul. This "spiritual individualism" goes hand-in-hand with monotheism, universalism, and, in effect, proselytism and the acculturation of all peoples.[46]

The Bible presents a relation between the universal and particular that differs entirely from that found in paganism. In ancient Greek thought, "the conceptualization of the universal is based on the

---

religions) is a mythical time, that is, a primordial time, not to be found in the historical past, an original time [...]"

44 J. Edling, "*Czas i historia epifanem Boga w ujęciu św. Augustyna*", Warszawskie Studia Teologiczne IX (1996), 94.

45 Alain de Benoist, "*Christianisme et paganisme*" in *C'est-à-dire*, vol. 2, 331.

46 Ibid., 330.

abstraction and successive generalization of a plurality of concrete particulars".[47] Pagan thought, on the other hand, attributes importance to roots and one's ancestral land, to place, for a particular place in the world is the centre around which identity crystallises. In this regard, there is no place for the dogmatic universalism of monotheistic provenance.[48] The biblical approach proceeds from the universal to the particular, i.e., it is "based on *deduction* from a *revealed absolute* and not by induction based on lived experience".[49] From one God one comes to one truth. The one truth logically leads to the argument that *tertium non datur:*[50] "Whoever is not with me is against me" (Luke 11:23). Either one lives in truth and virtue, or one is living in sin. There is no place for a multiplicity of truths or interpretations. While pagan peoples respect foreign gods and other cultures, Christianity rejects them *en bloc*.

With the entry of Christianity into the fold of European culture, the concept of "man in general" appeared for the first time as Christianity proclaimed the value of every individual person (every soul). Every person possesses a soul and therefore finds himself in a direct relation to God. Thus, man becomes a carrier of an absolute value. Moreover, every person is equal before God, for all people share the same genesis: creation by (one and the same) God in his likeness. In connection with this, ethnic belonging becomes something secondary.[51] Therefore, in de Benoist's opinion, Christianity effected an "anthropological revolution": the "ontological anchor" of man in his ancestral land and concrete social existence was pulled up and the focal point of gravity was shifted onto the soul. "From Yahweh's viewpoint, the differences between men and between peoples are transitory, secondary, and in

---

47   de Benoist, *On Being a Pagan*, 95.
48   Ibid., 123.
49   Ibid., 95.
50   Ibid., 111.
51   Galatians 3:28 "There is neither Jew nor Hellene, neither slave nor free, nor is there male and female, for you are all one in Christ Jesus."

a word, superficial."[52] This new, revolutionary anthropology opened the way for proselytism and intolerance (the dogmatic rejection of the Other[53]), which consequently led to the spread of the egalitarian mass society and to the emergence of totalitarianism.[54] In de Benoist's opinion, totalitarianism is derived from the desire to accomplish social unity by way of reducing individual and group diversity to a single model.[55]

Paganism naturally legitimises politics as such, whereas Christianity abolishes it.[56] Politics as such is negated in Christianity already on the anthropological level ("monohumanism"). Paganism acknowledges differences between peoples and cultures as being normal and natural, whereas Christianity's intention is to "go and make disciples of all nations, baptising them in the name of the Father and of the Son and of the Holy Spirit, and teaching them to obey everything I have commanded you" (Matthew 28:19–20). The universalist goal of Christianity is the removal of differences: ultimately, the aim is for each and every culture and people to be baptised. From this point, according to de Benoist, arises the religious intolerance that emerged in world history alongside the birth of monotheism.[57] [58] The concept of conversion is

---

52 de Benoist, *On Being a Pagan*, 112.

53 Ibid.: "Yahweh is the *god who refuses the Other*, the god who started by setting himself up as superior to the other gods, then later declared that he regarded them as *non-existent*. For the other god does not exist. He is depicted as only an 'idol,' an appearance of god, *a god lacking the value of a god*."

54 Sunic, *Against Democracy and Equality*, 111.

55 de Benoist, *On Being a Pagan*, 121.

56 Ibid., 148.

57 de Benoist, *Jésus et ses frères*, 116.

58 A similar perspective seems to be presented by Mircea Eliade: "The intolerance and fanaticism that are characteristic of the prophets and missionaries of the three monotheisms have their model and their justification in Yahweh's example." Mircea Eliade, *A History of Religious Ideas — Volume I: From the Stone Age to the Eleusinian Mysteries*, trans. Willard R. Trask (Chicago: University of Chicago Press, 1978), 181.

key to Christianity. Christianity is identified with Good and Truth; therefore, what does not align with it is taken to be Falsehood and Evil. "In the eschatological perspective", de Benoist argues, "the coexistence of Good and Evil, Truth and Falsehood is impossible. Only Good has the theological right to exist."[59] Hence, in the Christian perspective, the non-Christian cannot be moral or good, for he is "wandering astray", "erring"; he must abandon idolatry in favour of the one and only true faith. For, after all, Christianity is absolute Good and Truth. De Benoist summates: "The only God is by nature jealous and does not tolerate the existence of another God; in contrast to this, polytheists are by nature tolerance — they live and let live."[60]

While the ancient Greeks saw human creativity as only an imperfect imitation of Nature, Judeo-Christian monotheism puts man above the world. Just as there is an ontological chasm between God and man, so is there an ontological chasm between man and the world of nature.[61] The gods of pagans are conjoined together with the world as a whole as well as with a particular earth, a concrete land revered by the people inhabiting it. De Benoist points out that nature is not an important aspect of Semitic religiosity. The Covenant was concluded by Yahweh with a nomadic people who did not have a homeland and who only later received the Promised Land from him.[62] Yahweh chose Abel, not Cain — the former lived the live of a rootless, nomadic herder, whereas Cain, by contrast, was connected to the land by tilling it.[63]

Pagan man has his own place in the world — his homeland, with which he is connected by birth and ancestors. The people of Israel are not "sons of the earth", but children of Yahweh.[64] The myth of Odysseus returning to Ithaca is contrasted by the history of Abraham

---

59   de Benoist, *Jésus et ses frères*, 118.
60   Ibid., 119.
61   Ibid., 234.
62   de Benoist, *On Being a Pagan*, 150.
63   Ibid., 50.
64   Ibid., 82.

who forever leaves his lands. As de Benoist puts it, "In the Bible, one must never go *back*; one must *leave*...and go toward the Promised Land."⁶⁵ In paganism, space makes the world. Judeo-Christian monotheism does not assign any importance to the world and space, only to time and history.⁶⁶ In paganism, the world is eternal, while the gods and mean are not. In monotheism, God is eternal, while the world awaits its end.⁶⁷ It is not the world but God that is the source of any and all values. Judeo-Christian monotheism imposes upon the world its codex, the source of which lies outside the world.⁶⁸

Totalitarian Egalitarianism

Alain de Benoist has deemed Christianity the "Bolshevism of antiquity"⁶⁹ because, among other reasons, it is dogmatically egalitarian and totalitarian like communism. In fact, Christianity shares many other traits with communism, to which we shall now turn.

De Benoist writes:

> Every egalitarian or universalist ideology is 'necessarily' totalitarian in that it aims at a 'reduction' of the whole of social and spiritual reality in accordance with a single model. Monotheism implies an idea which proclaims the existence of only one truth, one God, one model of man that is pleasing to God. The Bible exhibits 'one Lord our God' (Deuteronomy 6:4) who is also a 'jealous God' (Deuteronomy 6:15). Jesus says: 'Whoever is not with me is against me.'⁷⁰ In other words, to be against God is to be a supporter of Evil. And everything is permitted against Evil: genocide, torture, the Inquisition. Of course, cruelty existed in the ancient world, yet it was

---

65 Ibid., 81.
66 Ibid., 79.
67 Ibid., 80.
68 Ibid., 62.
69 Before de Benoist, this very same term was used by Louis Rougier. See Rougier, *Le conflit du christianisme primitif et de la civilisation antique*, 89.
70 de Benoist describes this phrase as the "keyword of any totalitarianism" — see de Benoist, *Les idées à l'endroit*, 172.

never justified by an Absolute. Only starting with the emergence of Judeo-Christianity in history did totalitarianism reveal itself—from the moment Yahweh made massacring infidels into the highest virtue (Deuteronomy 13:9), from the moment he announced to his people: 'You must destroy all the peoples the Lord your God gives over to you' (Deuteronomy 7:16). This intolerance makes Christianity a subversive ideology.[71]

In Indo-European polytheism, the gods are diverse and of unequal significances and meanings, and this diversity found reflection in society and among people in different social layers with differing origins and different vocations. In monotheism, everything is brought to one level. As already mentioned, according to the Bible, man has one source, one origin, and this forms the foundation of philosophical universalism.[72] Although Christianity does not deny the "phenomenal" differentiation of individuals, it regards such differences as fundamentally unessential.[73] In the final analysis, all people are equal before God, the one, only, and same God for all of humanity. There exists only one possible model of Good, and the whole world must be converted to this one possible and rightful model of the absolute Good—regardless of the consequences and costs that such might entail.

In the context of ancient civilisation, Christianity was a factor of disintegration. Proclaiming that all people come from one couple, that all people can be saved through Jesus, rehabilitating physical labor, proclaiming that slaves are equally children of God, promising a better world in the afterlife, and proclaiming that even God himself voluntarily took on a position of humility and martyrdom—all of this was a complete inversion of values, a revolution *par excellence*.[74] As de Benoist puts it:

---

[71] Alain de Benoist, "*L'Église, l'Europe et le Sacré*" in Pierre Vial (ed.), *Pour une renaissance culturelle* (Paris: 1979), 204.

[72] de Benoist, *Jésus et ses frères*, 118; idem, *On Being a Pagan*, 128.

[73] de Benoist, "*L'Église, l'Europe et le Sacré*", 203.

[74] Rougier, *Le conflit du christianisme primitif et de la civilisation antique*, 71.

Jesus's preaching was situated within the framework of resistance against occupation: the struggle of Judea against Rome [...]. Where armed revolts failed, Jesus shaped a somewhat more subtle form of revenge: spiritual revenge by way of disintegrating the overpowering myth, by way of condemning the *goyim* and completely inverting values. Messianism, belief in a meaning of history and historical finitude, the idea of mercy above the idea of justice, favouring the 'oppressed', devaluing the world, etc. — all of these elements made up the 'revolutionary quality' of Christianity.[75]

Of course, later times saw Christianity as legitimising authority, as was the case in mediaeval Europe, or even earlier in the Eastern Roman Empire. However, such was already a different Christianity — not the revolutionary one, but the "conservative" one in an arrangement with power. De Benoist does not maintain that Christianity is a monolithic entity that hasn't changed over time. Rather; he distinguishes between, roughly speaking,[76] early Christianity (the early centuries of "egalitarian and subversive" Christianity) and later Christianity ("relatively constructive" Christianity of the Middle Ages "strongly colored by pagan organicism")[77] or, in other words, between "the Christianity of opposition" and "triumphant Christianity".[78] As long as Christianity was in opposition and did not possess cultural hegemony, it undermined the institutions of family, tribe (cf. Luke 14:26; Matthew 10:35), nation, and service of the fatherland. It was an instrument of total revolution. "The Constantinian compromise", de Benoist argues,[79] "inaugurated

---

75 de Benoist, "*L'Église, l'Europe et le Sacré*", 206–207.
76 Of course, de Benoist also discerns other, later changes in Christianity (such as in the Counter-Reformation period, the contemporary period, etc.). This simplification is due to focusing on the question of the Westernisation of Christianity. See Sylvain, "Interview with Alain de Benoist" in *North American New Right*, 73–74; de Benoist, "*Entretien avec 'Zinnober'*" in de Benoist, *C'est-à-dire*, vol. 1, 169.
77 de Benoist, *On Being a Pagan*, 20.
78 de Benoist, "*L'Église, l'Europe et le Sacré*", 208.
79 de Benoist seems to be drawing this perspective directly from Rougier, who distinguished between the Church and the Gospel. See Rougier, *Le conflit du*

an alliance between the throne and the altar, and thereby changed the character of Christianity from revolutionary to 'conservative'."[80] It is in the latter moment in history that one might discern the origin of the entity that came to be called the "Christian West".

Western Christianity: The Result of Syncretism

According to James Russell, "there may exist at least a sub-conscious reluctance by Western Christians to accept the notion that their mainstream religious tradition is itself the result of a syncretic development which eventually became normative"; however, Russel explains, "such reluctance among Christians may be somewhat ironic, since, were it not for its Germanisation, Christianity might never have spread throughout Northern and Central Europe".[81]

---

christianisme primitif et de la civilisation antique, 68–69: "If Jesus had returned in the late 4th century, he would have been perplexed by what was being done in his name [...]. The Church is not the Gospel. The Gospel proclaims the 'inevitable nearness' of the Kingdom of God, thus creating a morality of waiting that demands caring about tomorrow, and proclaims that one should not be bound to the goods of this world, in which one should practice in solitude, in a desert or in the shadows of a monastery, far away from the commotion of the world—'imitating Jesus Christ'. The Church, however, lives an earthly life. It needs to be strong. It strives to get along with the powers-that-be of this world. It proclaims that 'authority comes from God' and, in connection with this, 'whoever does not respect authority rebels against the order established by God' [...]. The Gospel is revolutionary and will be a source of inspiration for all of the popular movements of the Middle Ages. The Church is conservative, politically and socially conformist. Christianity never managed to smooth over this constant contradiction. There will always be a triumphant Church and a Church of the poor, a dogmatic Church and a Church of the ministry."

80   Taking the above into consideration, it bears highlighting de Benoist's words: "The egalitarian message of Christianity remained, even if only partially perceived and expressed, and even if somewhat tamed by institutions, at the centre of the ideological infrastructure of the system." — "*L'Église, l'Europe et le Sacré*", 213.

81   Russell, *The Germanization of Early Medieval Christianity*, 39–40.

If, as de Benoist maintains, Christianity is so alien to the European mentality, then how did it come to be adopted in Europe and how has it survived for so long? The French thinker argues that there are a number of reasons for this. First, in the case of Mediterranean Europe, Christianity took advantage of the obvious crisis of the ancient Roman world. Secondly, evangelisation across Northern Europe did not in the least proceed unproblematically; rather, it took hold through monarchical intrigues, ruse, as well as extermination.[82] De Benoist arbitrarily declares: "The number of paganism's martyrs is incomparable greater than the Christians who gave their lives for their faith."[83] Thirdly, wherever pre-Christian practices couldn't be weeded out, Christian missionaries consciously reinterpreted countless elements of pagan beliefs in a Christian spirit,[84] in effect creating a highly syncretic religious entity.[85] The old cultic sites were "baptised" by overlaying them

---

82 As examples, we can cite the Saxons' extermination by Charlemagne and the Northern crusades. See Alain de Benoist, "*Le massacre des Saxons païens de Verden*", *Krisis* 47 (2017), 70–102; Eric Christiansen, *The Northern Crusades* (New York: Penguin, 1997).

83 de Benoist, "*L'Église, l'Europe et le Sacré*", 211.

84 Sylvain, "Interview with Alain de Benoist" in Johnson (ed.), *North American New Right*, 71.

85 See Russell, *The Germanization of Early Medieval Christianity*, 23, 39, 43: "Anglo-Saxon missionaries did not emphasize the central soteriological and eschatological aspects of Christianity. Instead, seeking to appeal to the Germanic regard for power, they tended to emphasize the omnipotence of the Christian God and the temporal rewards he would bestow upon those who accepted him through baptism and through conformity to the discipline of his Church. [...] Germanic peoples did not bother to object to individual dogmas, because dogmatic orthodoxy was not central to their notion of religion. [...] Rather, [the acceptability of Christianity to the Germanic peoples] was primarily a consequence of the deliberate inculturation of Germanic religiocultural attitudes within Christianity [...]. This process of accommodation resulted in the essential transformation of Christianity from a universal salvation religion to a Germanic, and eventually European, folk religion. The sociopsychological response of the Germanic peoples to this inculturated form of Christianity included the acceptance of those traditionally Christian elements which coincided with Germanic religiosity and

with churches or chapels, local deities were changed into saints, pagan priests were killed, the traces of the old beliefs were erased, and pagan holidays were swapped out with Christian ones — even the birthdate of Christ was arbitrarily set as 25 December in order to cover the Winter Solstice holiday. Christianity itself was gradually subjected to a process of "de-Judaisation" and "Hellenisation" (which also reached the point of the schism into the Eastern and Western Churches).[86]

The European mentality, as de Benoist maintains, to a certain extent adjusted Christianity to fit itself just as Christianity in a certain manner influenced the European mentality. Initially promoting iconoclasm,[87] the Church later began to support the plastic arts (on the condition that such engendered a Christian art). Initially glorifying the "underdogs", the Church later leaned hard on the strong and became a great political power. At first condemning violence, the Church itself began to use and support violence in the struggle against "pagans", "heretics", and "infidels". At first supporting pacifism and prohibiting its faithful from military service, the Church later began to consecrate weapons, organise crusades, and create knightly orders. At first glorifying celibacy as a state most pleasing to God, the Church later began to praise marriage (in the Christian manner).[88] On the political level, there emerged the concept that obedience is owed to the king insofar as his authority is a result of God's will. De Benoist concludes: "The *institution* of Christianity could only survive at the price of a compromise between its constituent principles and an elementary political realism

---

    the resolution of dissonant elements by reinterpreting them in accordance with the Germanic ethos and world-view. [...] A noteworthy example of such accommodation was the portrayal of Christ as a victorious Germanic warlord."

86 de Benoist, "*L'Église, l'Europe et le Sacré*", 212.
87 de Benoist and Molnar, *Éclipse du sacré*, 233.
88 de Benoist, "*L'Église, l'Europe et le Sacré*", 212.

of primarily Roman origin."[89] Briefly speaking, Christianity "in the Western version" significantly departed from its "original".[90]

---

[89] de Benoist, *On Being a Pagan*, 136.

[90] Exactly the same opinion was expressed by Julius Evola, whom de Benoist cites. See Julius Evola, *Revolt Against the Modern World*, trans. Guido Stucco (Rochester: Inner Traditions, 1995), 287: "Although the new faith was successful in overthrowing the ancient civilization, it nevertheless was not able to conquer the Western world as pure Christianity; wherever it achieved some greatness it did so only thanks to Roman and classical pre-Christian elements borrowed from the previous tradition, and not because of the Christian element in its original form. For all practical purposes, Christianity 'converted' Western man only superficially; it constituted his 'faith' in the most abstract sense [...]. In theory, the Western world accepted Christianity but for all practical purposes it remained pagan [...]. Thus, the outcome was some sort of hybridism. Even in its attenuated and Romanized Catholic version, the Christian faith represented an obstacle that deprived Western man of the possibility of integrating his authentic and irrepressible way of being through a concept and in a relationship with the Sacred that was most congenial to him. In turn, this way of being prevented Christianity from definitely shaping the West into a tradition of the opposite kind, that is, into a priestly and religious one conformed to the ideals of the ecclesia of the origins, the evangelical pathos [...]." Idem, *Men Among the Ruins: Post-War Reflections of a Radical Traditionalist*, trans. Guido Stucco (Rochester: Inner Traditions, 2002), 186: "We should not try to dissimulate the antithesis existing between, on the one hand, the pure Christian morality of love, submission, humility, and mystical humanism and, on the other hand, ethical-political values such as justice, honor, difference, and a spirituality that is not the opposite of power, but of which power is a normal attribute. The Christian precept of returning good for evil is opposed by the principle of striking the unjust, of forgiving and generosity, but only to a vanquished foe, and not to an enemy who still stands strong in his injustice. In a virile institution [...], there is little or no room for love (conceived as the need to communicate, to embrace others, to lower oneself, and to take care of those who may not even ask for it or be worthy of it). Again, in such an institution there can be relationships among equals, but without a communitarian-social and brotherly tint, established on the basis of loyalty, mutual acknowledgment and respect, as everyone retains his own dignity and a healthy love for distance. I will not discuss here what consequences would ensue on the political plane if we were to take literally the evangelical parables concerning the lilies of the field and the birds of the air, as

Taking into account the above-outlined context, it is worth citing at length the following passages from Oswald Spengler's *Decline of the West*, which was one of de Benoist's most significant inspirations:

> It is quite wrong to bind up Christianity with the moral imperative. It was not Christianity that transformed Faustian man, but Faustian man who transformed Christianity — and he not only made it a new religion but also gave it a new moral direction. [...] And in virtue of it the Gothic springtime proceeded to a profound — and never yet appreciated — *inward transformation* of the morale of Jesus. A quiet spiritual morale welling from Magian feeling — a morale or conduct recommended as potent for salvation, a morale the knowledge of which was communicated as a special act of grace — was recast as a *morale of imperative command*. [...][91]
>
> The father-godhead men felt as Force itself, eternal, grand, and ever-present activity, sacred causality, which could scarcely assume any form comprehensible by human eyes. But the whole longing of the young breed, the whole desire of this strongly coursing blood, to bow itself in humility before the *meaning of the blood* found its expression in the figure of the Virgin and Mother Mary, whose crowning in the heavens was one of the earliest motives of the Gothic art. [...] She is the guardian of the Church's store of Grace, the Great Intercessor. [...] But this world of purity, light, and utter beauty of soul would have been unimaginable without the counter-idea, inseparable from it, an idea that constitutes one of the maxima of Gothic, one of its unfathomable creations — one that the present day forgets, and *deliberately* forgets. While she there sits enthroned, smiling in her beauty and tenderness, there lies in the background another world that throughout nature and throughout mankind weaves and breeds ill, pierces, destroys, seduces — namely, the realm of the Devil. [...] All around is an army of goblins, night-spirits, witches, werewolves, all in human shape. [...] An appalling fear, such as is perhaps only paralleled in the early spring of Egypt, weighs upon man. Every moment he may stumble into the abyss. [...] It is the two together, light and night, which fill Gothic art with its indescribable inwardness [...]. It was not only the love-glowing hymns to well as all the other nihilist teachings that are built on the overthrow of earthly values and on the idea of the imminent advent of the *Regnum*."

[91] Oswald Spengler, *The Decline of the West*, vol. 1, 451

Mary, but the cries of countless pyres as well that rose up to heaven. Hard by the Cathedral were the gallows and the wheel. Every man lived in those days in the consciousness of an immense danger, and it was hell, not the hangman, that he feared. [...] Inquisitors, in tears and compassion for the fallen wretches, doomed them to the rack in order to save their souls. That is the Gothic myth, out of which came the cathedral, the crusader, the deep and spiritual painting, the mysticism.[92]

Thus, de Benoist deems the consequence of the implementation of Christianity in Europe to be "the schizophrenia of the West"[93] — such is the duress of a life spent in a split of worldview-axiology, at once within two different spiritual universes. Yet, such has not been left without defensive reactions. Initially, there was open, armed defense put up by those loyal to their native faith, later there was reaction latent in the form of schisms, heresies (Arianism, Catharism, etc.), as well as in Protestantism. Allusions to paganism have remained persistently present in European culture and art from the Renaissance to our days.

Summary

Alain de Benoist writes: "Faustian energy and the Christian spirit are in the middle of a divorce at the end of a union that was never truly consummated [...]."[94] This quote is essentially the *clou* to the *Nouvelle Droite*'s current approach to Christianity. De Benoist draws a picture of the relationship of Europe and Christianity as one of attempting to mix water and oil — they ultimately always end up separating themselves from each other. This French thinker cautions against treating the terms "Christianity" and the "West" as synonyms.[95] The point is

---

92 Oswald Spengler, *The Decline of the West — Volume II: Perspectives of World-History* (Legend Books, 2024), 363–366.
93 de Benoist, "*L'Église, l'Europe et le Sacré*", 214.
94 de Benoist, *On Being a Pagan*, 137.
95 According to de Benoist, the "Christian West" is only a "period in which the history of the West to a certain extent merged with the history of Christianity". — de Benoist, "*L'Église, l'Europe et le Sacré*", 208.

that "Western" (or "European") Christianity is not Christianity *tout court*. It is not Christianity in its original, essential form. Rather, it is a "warp" of Christianity, a highly synthetic entity that emerged out of connecting Christianity *sensu proprio* with pre-Christian, Indo-European religiosity. Ever since Christianity entered Europe, the old beliefs and mentality have not disappeared, but have only become pushed aside in one way or another. One could advance the argument that Europeans have never stopped believing in "paganism"; instead, they have only in a certain sense "changed the sides of the barricade". With the onset of the new religion, the pre-Christian demonic beings did not disappear from people's consciousness — they only "reinforced the army" of God's opponent, Satan. Pagan spirituality has remained constantly alive, and only after a long time was it pushed into the collective unconscious.

When it comes to the question of assessing the weight of Christianity's contribution to European culture, de Benoist proposes the method of studying the development of Christianity outside of Europe on the one hand, and the history of the non-Christian on the other, so as to then compare them. Such a comparison, de Benoist thinks, promises revelatory insight. His comparative conclusions are the following: (a) (Indo-)European civilisation has existed for around 2,000 years; (b) before Christianity, (Indo-)European civilisation had rich achievements in the fields of culture and art; (c) before Christianity, Europeans were already constructing magnificent temples. Upon the rise of Christianity, cathedrals took the place of temples, of course, but the forms of construction changed while "the creative spirit, artistic sense, and constructive dynamism remained the same".[96] In non-Western Christian countries, one would search in vain for similar civilisational and artistic achievements. In this French thinker's opinion, ascribing the achievements of mediaeval sacred architecture to Christianity is just as nonsensical as ascribing

---

96 Ibid., 208–209.

the construction of the Eiffel Tower to democracy. "The period of the 'Christian West'", he writes, "was not great because it was Christian, but only because, above all, it was Western."[97] In other words, "what is good in Christianity isn't new, and what is new in it isn't good".[98] Furthermore, de Benoist argues that in the present time the Church seems to be striving to liberate itself from its own history for the sake of returning to its roots. For 2,000 years, it has tried to fit in with the European mentality by restricting the literalness of the Gospel. Today, however, de Benoist argues, Christianity is clearly de-Europeanising and is returning to its root ideas: egalitarianism and universalism.[99] As this French thinker states, the Church "wants to bracket the European episode" and return to the "subversive Christianity of the catacombs". One evident expression of this would be the Second Vatican Council.[100] In other words, Christianity is ceasing to be any kind of carrier of European identity whatsoever.

It is not commonplace to encounter analyses and interpretations of the Christian religion (and biblical monotheism in general) as profound and critical as Alain de Benoist's. Hence, it is exceptionally interesting that a very similar perspective seems to be represented in contemporary scholarship by the German Egyptologist Jan Assmann,[101] according to whom the emergence of monotheism represents one of the most important shifts in the history of mankind.[102] This German scholar regards biblical monotheism to be essentially constituted by

---

97 Ibid., 209.
98 Sylvain, "Interview with Alain de Benoist" in Johnson (ed.), *North American New Right*, 74.
99 de Benoist, *Les idées à l'endroit*, 184.
100 Moos, *Les intellectuels de la Nouvelle Droite et la religion*, 68.
101 See Jan Assmann, *Moses the Egyptian: The Memory of Egypt in Western Monotheism* (London: 1998), idem, *the Price of Monotheism* (Stanford: 2010); idem, *Of God and Gods: Egypt, Israel, and the Rise of Monotheism* (Wisconsin: 2008).
102 Assmann, *The Price of Monotheism*, 1.

what he calls the "Mosaic distinction", or the distinction between true and false religion. Assmann decisively underscores that this distinction did not begin with the emergence of religion in general, but arose with biblical monotheism. Compared to polytheism, what is most revolutionary in monotheism is not its belief in one God, but its claim to be the only one and absolute truth revealed to mankind once and for all.[103] Assmann calls the biblical religions "counter-religions" in that they radically and uncompromisingly reject and condemn whatever preceded them. This leads to the creation of successive distinctions: Jews and *goyim*, Christians and pagans, Christians and Jews, Muslims and infidels, true believers and heretics, etc. The ensuing consequence is "countless acts of violence and bloodshed. A number of highly significant and central passages of the old Testament already tell of such violence and bloodshed."[104] Like de Benoist, Assmann discerns a subtle difference between Judaism on the one hand and Christianity and Islam on the other. In the case of the Jewish religion, the Mosaic distinction is turned inwards,[105] i.e., what the *goyim* believe in is of no significance to Jews themselves. In the case of Christianity and Islam, the Mosaic distinction is turned outwards, as these religions do not recognise ethnic barriers, the inevitably effect being excluding the Other, "and they have therefore lashed out in violence again and again throughout their history".[106]

---

103 Ibid., 3.
104 Ibid., 11.
105 Ibid., 17: "The law erects a high wall around the chosen people, a cordon sanitaire that prevents any contamination by, or assimilation of, the ideas and customs of the environment. [...] The massacres recounted in the biblical texts — that of the worshippers of the golden calf, or that of the priests of Baal at the command of Elijah and Joshua — are an internal affair of the Jewish people."
106 Ibid., 18: "In choosing Israel to be his people, God marks it out from all other peoples and forbids it to adopt the customs of the environment. By commanding Christians and Muslims to spread the truth to all four corners of the earth, God ensures that those who close their minds to this truth will be shut out. Only

In contrast to "intolerant" monotheism, polytheism is characterised by a "tolerant" attitude. As Assmann puts it, intolerance comes from an inability or lack of will to tolerate different convictions and the practices that arise therefrom. This presupposes not only a distinction between what is one's own and what is foreign, but also their incompatibility by virtue of the distinction between true and false. "I 'tolerate' something, in the strict sense of the word, that runs counter to my own views, yet which i can afford to tolerate because I am powerful or generous enough not to have to treat it as a threat."[107] In Assmann's opinion, according to this definition, the term "tolerance" cannot be used with respect to ancient polytheism, because the criterion of incompatibility is inapplicable here: "As far as other peoples' religion is concerned, there is nothing that would need to be 'tolerated.'"[108] Thus, "translatability" is taken to be a better term.[109] On this point, Assmann is referring to the practice, extant since the time of the Sumerians, of translating the names of deities from one language into another and from one religion into another. In this sense, the religion of one people could be "compatible" with another. In other words, polytheistic religions do not lend any grounds for (religious) intolerance. Of course, this does not mean that pre-Christian times did not know violence or cruelty. Rather, this means simply that political violence could not be justified theologically, whereas in the case of the Mosaic distinction, conversion by fire and sword was religiously motivated.[110]

---

in this form does monotheism's inherent potential for exclusion explode into violence."

107 Ibid.

108 Ibid.

109 Ibid.

110 A similar framing of the problem seems to be presented by Pierre Crépon: "The Christian Church supported virtually all military ventures that had purely political goals, and its intolerance awakened fanaticism that yielded cruelty unknown to Greco-Roman antiquity. Many factors compacted together to form this state of affairs. Some of them were not rooted in Christian doctrine as such, but rather arose out of the conditions of its development [...]. Others

As we can see, Assmann's perspective is almost deceptively similar to de Benoist's, but the obvious and most important difference between them is that Assmann's judgements are only descriptive, while de Benoist's are normative. Nevertheless, it is worth pointing out here that although de Benoist's theses are undoubtedly ideological in nature, they seem not to be entirely unfounded, as this case shows that they find a certain substantiation in contemporary scholarly literature.

Monotheism as the Germ of Secular Totalitarianism

One of Alain de Benoist's most iconoclastic theses claims that both of the 20th-century's secular totalitarian systems, Communism and National Socialism, have their genesis in the monotheistic worldview. This thesis is especially controversial in the case of National Socialism, as it is widely known that this ideology, besides its open anti-Christianity, is often associated with neo-paganism (and this charge is indeed raised from the Christian side). However, de Benoist presents an entirely different point of view on the matter.

De Benoist argues that modern totalitarian systems are secular religions based on secularised theological concepts.[111] The explicitly "religious" traits of these systems are: (a) a dualistic vision of the world, (b) messianism (anticipating a new era), (c) boundless will to create an unprecedented society.[112] Dualism is evident in how these ideologies create a categorical division into us (absolute good) and them (absolute evil). In communism's case, this is the proletariat and the bourgeoisie; in Nazism, this is the Aryan race and Jews. In de Benoist's opinion, this is "an obvious borrowing [of the division

---

were already encapsulated in the very sources of Christian religion and only needed favourable conditions for the most negative aspect of this religion to develop — a religion which recognised power over this world for itself." Pierre Crépon, *Religie a wojna* (Gdańsk: 1994), 86–87.

111 Alain de Benoist, *Communisme et nazisme. 25 réflexions sur le totalitarisme au XX siècle (1917–1989)* (Paris: 1998), 99.

112 Ibid., 101.

between] Christ and Antichrist".[113] Moreover, both totalitarian systems intended to bring history to a final solution, to a moment upon which all conflicts and wars would finally end — this is the progressive, linear vision of history[114] ("lion will graze alongside the lamb"). To this end, the world must be purified of hostile elements — people who are not adversaries or rivals but "ontological enemies", incarnated Absolute Evil.[115] Monotheism, after all, "'morally' justifies the elimination of the Other".[116]

De Benoist argues that this perspective is completely foreign to "paganism". History knows no case in which a European people of pre-Christian times persecuted another solely for belonging to another people.[117] In "paganism", to the contrary, the diversity of gods found reflection in the diversity of peoples. This multiplicity is acknowledged and "consecrated": "Different peoples, different gods. One does not exclude the other."[118]

In de Benoist's eyes, National Socialism has significantly more in common with the Catholic Church than with paganism. He enumerates the following features as characteristic of Nazism: the institutionalisation of a single party, the dictatorship of universal salvation, centralisation, the mobilisation of the masses, intentional and targeted terror, the conviction of a new era and creation of a "new man". The slogan of the Third Reich — *ein Volk, ein Reich, ein Führer* — is an obvious exemplification of "political monotheism". In this respect, National Socialism resembles a secularised Catholic Church. It has its infallible pope in the Führer, its clergy in the party, and its Jesuits in the SS. Like the Church, National Socialism proclaims its dogmas and excommunicates and persecutes "heretics". The NSDAP itself arose in Bavaria,

---

113 Ibid., 102.
114 Ibid., 106.
115 Ibid., 111.
116 de Benoist, *Les idées à l'endroit*, 188.
117 Moos, *Les intellectuels de la Nouvelle Droite et la religion*, 53.
118 de Benoist, *Les idées à l'endroit*, 187.

a Catholic land *par excellence*. For de Benoist, National Socialism is a secular millenarian religion which aims to "implement the promise of universal salvation, which is possible thanks to the total transformation life, absolute dominance over the Earth, and the inauguration of a thousand-year 'kingdom'",[119] in which the German people plays the role of the "chosen nation".

When it comes to the relation between Christianity and Communism, then matters are rather clear. Like Rougier, de Benoist sees Communism as a "state religion of the messianistic type".[120] Marxism itself is simply one secularised form of Judeo-Christian egalitarianism. As in the case of early Christianity, Marxism's aim is an egalitarian revolution. The New Right's critique of Communism is nothing other than a reflection of its critique of Christianity, and Communism itself is supposed to represent the last phase of the "egalitarian cycle" (first the equality of souls before God, then legal equality, and finally economic equality). In de Benoist's opinion, Marxism took the Christian egalitarian ideas that have been present in Europe for 2,000 years to their extreme consequences. It is, therefore, nothing qualitatively new, but merely an old idea in a new, secular packaging. The French thinker sees the historical conflict between Communism and Christianity as superficial, as they are altogether similar on the axiological level.[121] In both cases, the leitmotif is a revolution that begins with the proclamation that all people are equal (the equality of souls) and with calling into doubt the substantive relation between faith and homeland (universalism).[122] Both are complete negations of the convictions widespread among the people of antiquity. According to de Benoist, nothing was more repulsive to early Christians than the idea of homeland. Loyalty to the state, kin, or tradition of one's

---

119 Alain de Benoist, "*Comment peut-on être païen?*", *Éléments pour la civilisation européenne* 89 (1997), 21.

120 Moos, *Les intellectuels de la Nouvelle Droite et la religion*, 57.

121 Ibid., 59.

122 Ibid., 60.

ancestral land does not count — the only thing of importance is paying homage to universalist dogma.[123] In other words, Christianity, just like Communism, undermines social order and harmony and precipitates collapse.

Alain de Benoist's intention is to underscore that authentic, historical, pre-Christian paganism never operated with categories in the likes of absolute Good and Evil, absolute Truth and Falsehood, chosen nations, the End of History, the total transformation of social life, the creation of a new man, messianism, final salvation, the end of all conflicts, etc. Thinking in these categories (as was the case in the totalitarianisms of the 20th century) is, in de Benoist's opinion, the aftermath of Christianity, and more concretely, the result of the Christian conceptual clichés that have held on in European minds. For ancient European peoples, the above-mentioned categories simply didn't exist. They appeared only with the onset of Christianity. This is the reason why the *Nouvelle Droite* calls monotheism "the greatest catastrophe that has befallen European peoples". In a word, if it were not of the emergence of monotheism, there would be no totalitarianism.

Of course, the influence of Christianity is not limited to totalitarian systems alone. From the *Nouvelle Droite*'s perspective, secularised Christian dogmas also underlie the whole of Western modernity, and they continue to shape it to this day.

---

123 Ibid.

CHAPTER V

THE *NOUVELLE DROITE*'S POLITICAL THEOLOGY

POLITICAL THEOLOGY CAN be understood as the process of transferring concepts from the sphere of theology into the domain of the State and law. The term first appeared in 1922, when it was introduced by Carl Schmitt, a German jurist and expert in constitutional law, in a work entitled *Politische Theologie*. The idea of political theology arose out of the need to underscore that if reflection on politics is not to remain superficial, then it must reach deeper to the metaphysical, religious, and theological sphere. Today, such an idea might not seem to be too revolutionary, but it bears remembering that at the time, the dominant conviction among specialists in statehood and law was that politics is basically a purely technical question, i.e., it boils down to managing and organising material and human resources.[1] Schmitt challenged this modern, technological view, where the central point is man as an autonomous individual, with an entirely different perspective which can be summarised with the first sentence of the third chapter of his *Political Theology*: "All significant concepts of the modern theory of the state are secularized theological concepts [...]."[2] This German jurist exposed the small extent to which Western thought on

---

1   Z. Stawrowski, "*Czym jest teologia polityczna?*", *Chrześcijaństwo — Świat — Polityka* 22 (2018), 190.
2   Carl Schmitt, *Political Theology: Four Chapters on the Concept of Sovereignty*, trans. George Schwab (Chicago: University of Chicago Press, 2005), 36.

the State and law has managed to be independent of theology, in connection with which it bears recognising that political science cannot be completely detached from religious and theological questions.

The field of political theology was analysed and systematised by another German jurist and political thinker, Ernst-Wolfgang Böckenförde, who distinguished three kinds of political theology: institutional, appellative, and juridical (legal).[3] The first is of normative character and de facto constitutes the legitimisation of the existing religio-political order along with its corresponding relations between church and political authorities. Appellative political theology is postulative in character and is oriented towards action and change, i.e., bringing the socio-political order to a state that would embody a defined ideal (implied in the Christian sense). It creates the ideological basis for definite actions and political initiatives. Juridical political theology is the sociology of legal concepts (as Carl Schmitt engaged in deliberating).

The *Nouvelle Droite*'s approach to political theology is principally one of adopting and developing the method of juridical political theology. Following Schmitt's trail, Alain de Benoist deconstructs the political dimension of modernity, whose sources are seen as rooted in Christianity. The political forms of Western modernity (human rights, individualist liberalism, the idea of progress, etc.) are interpreted by this French thinker as being crystallisations of political monotheism[4] *par excellence*, and for this reason the *Nouvelle Droite* maintains a negative assessment of them. According to de Benoist, the entirety of Western political thinking is the result of the secularisation of Christian theological concepts. In turn, he proposes something that could be called "political polytheism", which can be briefly defined as acknowledging the right of every people to worship its own gods and to resist any

---

3   E. W. Böckenförde, "*Teoria polityki a teologia polityczna. Uwagi na temat ich wzajemnego stosunku*", *Teologia Polityczna* 3 (2005–2006), 304.

4   In this context, de Benoist uses the term "the ideology of the Same" (*l'idéologie du Même*).

religion, ideology, or political tendency of a uniformising-convergent character. The right to differentiation (which translates into a political pluriverse instead of a universe of a monolithic, global political form) is one example of political polytheism, where the plurality of political forms is a reflection of the idea of polytheism, which de Benoist treats as normative.

The present chapter aims to meticulously trace the ways in which, in de Benoist's opinion, Christian theological concepts translate into modern political ideas.

Desacralisation, Rationalisation, Secularisation

For the first time in the history of Europe, Christianity introduced the notion that man is an abstract individual set apart from socio-political context. This was a consequence of the belief that (one type of) man was created by God in his likeness, i.e., the human species consists of God's children equal among each other ("monohumanism"). According to de Benoist, one consequence of such a perspective is that considerations of an optimal system and set of rights for a given state ignore the particularity of any specific social, cultural, political, and ethnic context. Instead of citizenship without universalism, there appears universalism without citizenship, as Christianity proclaims the moral oneness of the entire human race and the irreducibility of the individual to the political community to which he belongs. An entirely different situation existed in ancient Athens, where man was conceived as first and foremost a member of a political community. Christianity removed the "ontological anchorage" of man in social existence (and, as follows, religious existence), and shifted the weight onto the individual soul. In effect, man ceased to be conceived as a particular entity shaped by specific socio-cultural conditions, and began to be seen as an abstract entity stripped of any social, cultural, and religious context.

This inaugural dissociation, however, was not the only cause of the desacralisation of the world. With reference to Max Weber,[5] de Benoist points to the process of the gradual rationalisation of human existence as another factor in the "disenchantment" (*Entzauberung*) of the world.[6] The key causes of gradual desacralisation are to be seen in the emergence and development of biblical monotheism, as well as rational thought.[7] De Benoist writes:

> Max Weber highlighted the role of 'ethical rationalisation' that spread once moral rules no longer originated from the cosmic order, but instead from 'commandments' proclaimed by God. The entirety of everyday life thus comes under the control of 'Law' [...]. Man no longer lives within the fold of myth or truth (*aletheia*) as unconcealment: those who are of the world must make do with reason.[8]

In other words, Yahweh demands obedience to the Law, whose source lies outside of the world. De Benoist points out that the origin of this rationalisation is the Covenant, the "rational contract" concluded between Yahweh and his chosen people.[9]

Rationalisation leads to perceiving the world of nature exclusively in categories of utility, and desacralisation takes place when a given thing or phenomenon begins to be seen exclusively in its utilitarian-rational dimension, i.e., seen exclusively as an object.[10] Christianity adopted this rationalisation, rooted in Jewish religiosity, and began to view God as a "first cause".[11] The world must have its cause — *nihil est*

---

5   See M. Weber, *Racjonalność, władza, odczarowanie* (Poznań: 2004).
6   de Benoist and Molnar, *Éclipse du sacré*, 156.
7   de Benoist, *Sacré païen*, 34–35.
8   Ibid., 35.
9   de Benoist, *Sacré païen*, 35–36: "The 'holiness' demanded by Yahweh ultimately boils down to obedience before the Law, which itself is an object of petty codification [...]. Religion thus changes into a kind of collection of legal-canonical commands."
10 Ibid., 35.
11 Ibid., 36.

sine ratione. "But to say that nothing happens without a cause is also to subjugate being to the rule of reason, to claim that 'being is an element of reason'."[12] De Benoist argues that Christianity identified being with God only to then see the latter as first cause. If God is the first cause, then being becomes synonymous with "reason". Thus, "from Aristotle, scholasticism adopted the idea that the first cause is the highest being, which was acknowledged to be God, while distinguishing between the sensual and the intelligible [...] is henceforth interpreted as a distinction between the real world and the divine intellect".[13] This, according to de Benoist,[14] is what Nikolai Berdyaev had in mind when he said that "St. Thomas desacralised the cosmos".[15]

The next stage was Cartesianism, which de Benoist defines as "the fullest expression of Western metaphysics".[16] If for Aquinas "reasoning was still bound to faith, which is the thread connecting human existence with the creator god, then in Descartes reason transcends itself and annexes faith as an ordinary mode of judgement".[17] In famously proclaiming "I think, therefore I am," Descartes made the ego into a condition of being, and the ego thereby became potentially autonomous. Henceforth, subjectivity became the source of modern Western thought. Descartes' writings, of course, still referred to God, but God himself is already a hypothesis which, for modern rationalism, is not necessary.

---

12 Ibid.

13 Ibid., 37.

14 What de Benoist does not mention are Dante's works, which are worth mentioning in this context for their contradiction to desacralisation. In his work *De monarchia*, the Italian poet postulated that the Empire is independent from the Church, and he formulated, for the very first time, the concept of a universal monarchy encompassing all of mankind irrespective of origin and religion. See M. Konik, *Filozofia polityczna Dantego w świetle traktatu 'De monarchia'*, Państwo i Społeczeństwo 1 (2008), 209–224.

15 de Benoist, *Sacré païen*, 37.

16 Ibid.

17 Ibid.

The Reformation only deepened these tendencies. The religious wars of the time compelled the institution of the State to find a different guarantee for social harmony than religion. This served as the pretext to make religion into a private affair, since Christianity, itself now divided, could no longer play the role of the social bond. Religion was pushed out of the public sphere, and it is here that de Benoist sees the origin of secularisation in Europe.[18] An analogous situation will later happen with liberalism, which demands neutrality of worldview for the State. Whereas in antiquity and the Middle Ages, "autonomy" was a political category, in the Reformation era it became a "category of spiritual and then moral life".[19] This time also saw the dawn of the bourgeois class and its values, whereby reason became the new basis of social life. God gradually became a convention instead of a real, living social conviction.

The Enlightenment took further steps in this direction: Christian theodicy "came down to earth". The aspiration for salvation turned into striving for happiness, the "state of nature" took the place of lost paradise, and entering into society took the place of original sin; likewise, God's place was taken by the Great Architect and the "laws of nature", and Adam Smith's "invisible hand" took the place of Providence. History retained its teleology through the idea of progress: everything moves towards ever greater rationality and towards the objectivity of the world, which entails the devaluation of cultural particularities in favor of an abstractly conceived humanity equipped with universal and inalienable rights — inalienable because they are due to the very fact of "being human", i.e., being logically more primordial than society.

Nineteenth-century historiosophy retained the monotheistic "structure" of directed, unilinear time watched over by a "divine intellect". Taking Hegelianism as an example, de Benoist exposes how reason replaces Providence and becomes the highest law: "Reason 'reveals

---

18   Ibid., 38.
19   Ibid.

itself' like God, just as God reveals himself as reason. In other words, reason 'is' the historical process."[20] It is in the Enlightenment era, de Benoist argues, that faith and reason are finally divided.[21] Separated from faith, reason naturally causes secularisation.

Interestingly enough, de Benoist maintains that the emergence of atheism in Europe was an effect of Christianity. The argumentation for this is that Western metaphysics excluded any authentic transcendence and thus unwittingly prepared the ground for atheism.[22] Secular rationalism turned against Christian rationalism.[23] Religion came to be defined as oppressive, as superstition, etc. The desacralisation of the world somehow "compromised" religious faith *in general*:

> Quietly wishing to link faith and reason, [Christianity] created the conditions in which the latter could turn against it. With [reason] being the creator of the essence of modern technology, science and technology analogously turned against it. Positioning God as an autonomous being in relation to the world, [Christianity] created the ontological rift between created and uncreated being; it put forth the conditions of reciprocity: in relation to a God who could get on without people (since people do not add any value to his perfection), people started to get on without him […]. Man, positioned as the subject of an objective world, could consequently begin to realise his dream of dominating being, which could not end otherwise than with positioning himself in the place of God.[24]

In summary, the distinction between created and uncreated being implied seeing the world as an "object" with which man enters into a purely "rational" interaction, an "objectifying" one (St. Thomas Aquinas). Modern science deepened the process of the world's desacralisation, and the world began to be seen in a qualitative manner as a collection of resources. After all, modern science is the "rationalistic

---

20 Ibid., 39.
21 de Benoist and Molnar, *Éclipse du sacré*, 174.
22 Ibid., 176.
23 Ibid., 173.
24 de Benoist, *Sacré païen*, 40.

activity *par excellence*"²⁵ (Descartes). It does strives towards precision rather than truth (*aletheia*). Desacralisation was carried out to the very end.

The Idea of Progress: The "Faith" of Modernity

Christianity, by creating the idea of a history that has a clear beginning and end, enabled the application of this principle to itself — it started and then it ended. The world moved on without it.²⁶ What remained was the Judeo-Christian manner of thinking, which manifests itself in secularised theological concepts that took on the form of secular ideas: "[..] if the Christian mission was partially betrayed, then it was also partially 'fulfilled'. The Western world is actually more 'Christian' than ever in the sense that it has internalised the values of biblical monotheism by separating them from the theological sphere and bringing them down into the sphere of the profane."²⁷

The flagship example of this is the idea of progress formulated in the era of the Enlightenment. The idea of progress significantly changed the way of thinking and *modus operandi* for subsequent generations of Europeans by changing the very meaning of the word "progress" from meaning development and perfection to meaning mere "growth". To this day, when the word "progress" is used, it ordinarily means a growth in value, such as growth in life expectancy or daily food consumption in terms of calculating the kcal per inhabitant.²⁸ It is also worth pointing out that the terms "progress" and "development" were originally treated solely as adjectives. In the Enlightenment, however, the notion of "progress" became an idea and was subsequently transformed into an ideology propagated by people who postulated the necessity of

---

25   de Benoist and Molnar, *Éclipse du sacré*, 164.
26   de Benoist, *Sacré païen*, 40.
27   de Benoist and Molnar, *Éclipse du sacré*, 195.
28   J. Żelazna, "Idea postępu, pojęcie rozwoju. Kilka uwag i pytań", *Humaniora. Czasopismo Internetowe* 3(19) (2017), 73.

radically accelerating changes for the onset of an anticipated era of "great people of the future".[29]

De Benoist regards the theory of progress as one of the theoretical presuppositions of modernity and sees it as the "religion of Western civilisation". It can be described as a kind of secular version of the messianic interpretation of history. De Benoist defines the term "progress" as "the culminating process in which each next stage is seen as more perfect, i.e., qualitatively better, than the previous one".[30] Understood in this way, "progress" contains a descriptive element (change is directed) as well as an axiological element (change is seen as improvement). In this regard, progress is the term for change that is directed (towards better), necessary (progress is unstoppable), and irreversible (returning to the past is impossible). In other words, the *novum* is seen as necessarily better in each and every case.

---

29 Nicolas de Condorcet, *Outlines of an Historical View of the Progress of the Human Mind* (Philadelphia: M. Carey, 1796): "There remains only a third picture to form, — that of our hopes, or the progress reserved for future generations, which the constancy of the laws of nature seems to secure to mankind. And here it will be necessary to shew by what steps this progress, which at present may appear chimerical, is gradually to be rendered possible, and even easy; how truth, in spite of the transient success of prejudices, and the support they receive from the corruption of governments or of the people, must in the end obtain a durable triumph; by what ties nature has indissolubly united the advancement of knowledge with the progress of liberty, virtue, and respect for the natural rights of man; how these blessings, the only real ones, though so frequently seen apart as to be thought incompatible, must necessarily amalgamate and become inseparable, the moment knowledge shall have arrived at a certain pitch in a great number of nations at once, the moment it shall have penetrated the whole mass of a great people, whose language shall have become universal, and whose commercial intercourse shall embrace the whole extent of the globe. This union having once taken place in the whole enlightened class of men, this class will be considered as the friends of human kind, exerting themselves in concert to advance the improvement and happiness of the species."

30 Alain de Benoist, "*Une brève histoire de l'idée de progrès*" in *Critiques — Théoriques*, 55.

De Benoist enumerates the following theses as being constitutive of the idea of progress: (1) the linear concept of time along with the conviction that history has meaning and is strongly oriented towards the future; (2) the conviction that humanity is fundamentally one and is supposed to develop as a whole in one and the same direction; (3) the conviction that the world can and must be transformed through affirming man as the sovereign over nature.[31] Progress, thus, has a vectoral, convergent, irreversible, and necessary character. De Benoist sees the origin of all three of these ideas in Christianity.[32] Starting in the 17th century, along with the development of science and technology, they underwent secularisation, laying the groundwork or the idea of progress in its modern form.

In contrast to the ancient Greeks, who saw history and time in a cyclical manner, Christianity interprets time and history as linear. The Bible dispensed with the ancient vision of history: "From the time of Adam and Eve, the history of salvation has been ongoing in accordance with a necessity from above, starting with the Old Covenant, then in Christianity, culminating in the Incarnation which cannot be repeated."[33] St. Augustine drew on this vision and was the first to lend this concept the form of a philosophical idea which postulates the existence of a humanity-wide history of salvation heading towards an end determined from above.

The secular idea of progress adopted Christianity's linear and vectoral concept of time, but with the difference that eternal life is replaced by the future and salvation is replaced by the pursuit of happiness.[34] What was eschatological in Christianity became historical within the framework of the idea of progress. Analogously to the case

---

31 Ibid.

32 Seeing the origins of the idea of progress in Christianity is by no means something controversial. See Z. Krasnodębski, *Upadek idei postępu* (Warsaw: 1991), 17–29.

33 Ibid., 56.

34 Ibid.

of divine will, man has no power over progress — he must submit to its "unexamined verdicts".

The roots of the secularised theory of progress can be seen in the 17th century, when some thinkers began to ponder whether faith in a "golden age" that allegedly existed in the beginning of human history had any sense whatsoever. As recently as the Renaissance period, authors like Niccolo Machiavelli and Giordano Bruno still leaned towards the ancient, cyclical concept of history.[35] The first to use the term "progress" in the temporal sense was Francis Bacon, who proclaimed the mission of man ruling over nature by knowing its laws. However, the progress he described pertained exclusively to knowledge of the natural world. Somewhat later, Blaise Pascal put forth that humans collectively effect progress in the sciences with the passing of time.[36] This thread was taken up and developed by Descartes and Galileo. These thinkers saw the world as an object, a mechanism that must be methodically worked out, dominated, and instrumentalised. Already in vain would we be searching here for any remnants of the ancient European understanding of the world in the categories of a cosmos, an order full of power and the divine. The cosmos-world is now bereft of meaning. The world becomes an object for the human subject (what Heidegger called the "metaphysics of subjectivity"). As Alain de Benoist puts it:

> For the Greeks, only eternity is real. Authentic being is unchanging: the cyclical movement that ensures the eternal return of the same in a series of progressing cycles is the most perfect expression of the divine. If there are flights and declines, progress and regress, then such happens within the cycle, which is always followed by the next one [...]. The cosmos of the ancients is then replaced by a new, geometric, homogenous and (most likely) infinite world, one ruled by the laws of cause and effect. The model of

---

35 P. Szymaniec, "*Condorcet i religia postępu*", *Wrocławskie Studia Erazmiańskie* (2007), 64.

36 Ibid.

this world is the machine, and more precisely a watch. Time itself becomes homogenous and quantifiable: 'merchant time' replaces 'peasant time'.[37]

It is also worth mentioning that the end of the 17th century saw the so-called "quarrel between the ancients and the moderns", which is of importance in the development of historiography. The "ancients" defended the primacy of classical, ancient models, while the "moderns" proclaimed the primacy of modern productions. One of the moderns, Charles Perrault, went so far as to claim that 17th-century artists and scholars had in every respect outstripped their ancient predecessors.[38]

De Benoist argues that the dynamic development of science and technology gradually lent the ground to optimism: science seemed to offer ever new possibilities. Enlightenment optimism and faith in the power of human reason shined with triumph, which weakened the influence of the primordial sin in Europeans' consciousness.[39] In the 18th century, in de Benoist's opinion, the classical economists like Adam Smith, Bernard Mandeville, and David Hume rehabilitated insatiable desire. They proclaimed that man will always want more and that the pursuit of maximalising business interest simply arises from human nature. This also concerns knowledge and science, whose constant progress is in demand: "The greater our knowledge, the better things will be."[40] Reason was put above tradition, which began to be seen as a dispensable ballast.

De Benoist that we can already find in St. Augustine the motif of framing humanity as a certain whole which has passed from the first ages of its "childhood" to the stage of its "adulthood".[41] This idea in-

---

37 de Benoist, "*Une brève histoire de l'idée de progrès*" in *Critiques — Théoriques*, 55–56.

38 Szymaniec, "*Condorcet i religia postępu*", 64.

39 de Benoist, "*Une brève histoire de l'idée de progrès*" in *Critiques — Théoriques*, 55–56.

40 Ibid.

41 M. Tomasiewicz, "*Przedaugustyńska filozofia dziejów — wybrane koncepcje*", *Krakowskie Studia z Historii Państwa i Prawa* 9(2) (2016), 183–184: "According

spired the modern category of "development", understood as ceaseless growth. In this French thinker's opinion, the 18th century was the beginning of the "idolatry of the *novum*", that is, the a priori appraisal of anything new as good for the very reason that it is new. It was in this century that the theory of progress was explicitly formulated by Jean Antoine Condorcet and Anne Robert Jacques Turgot, who claimed that humanity as a whole strives towards perfection. This view of humanity as a great whole exhibits, according to Benoist, the preservation of the Christian vision of humanity as aiming towards a determined goal established from above — the only difference being that reason comes to the fore instead of Providence. Reason is henceforth supposed to

---

to Augustine, the perspective is by all means optimistic. Humanity tends towards good and happiness. Of course, this advance does not proceed without difficulties, because the world has been condemned by original sin. The ultimate condition is that man cannot cope with the task of achieving salvation by his own efforts. Nevertheless, the aim of history remains within eschatological, and the greatest testimony to this is represented by historical events — the fate of the Jewish people, the fall of Persia and Greece, the later triumph of Rome and the emergence of the empire of the caesars, and thanks to this the brilliant blossoming of Christianity, the growth of communities of believers, their persecution and martyrdom, the monarchy of Constantine the Great, and then the triumph of Christianity as a state religion, the great councils, and the right against heterodox movements. In Augustine's eyes, all of these events fit into a logical chain of succession which manifests history's striving towards reaching the eschatological purpose that is the final victory of God." P. Wasyluk, "*Kategorie filozofii dziejów*", *Kultura i Edukacja* 4 (2007), 16: "Augustinian linearism broke with the ancient cyclicalism and expanded the perspectives of perceiving human history, which from this point on was understood as human history. Augustine's linearism can be finitist or teleological because human history is restricted by the apocalyptic perspective. Christ's second coming to earth meant the end of human history. Besides many such restrictions, this concept laid the ground for future concepts that expand the perspective of seeing the future. Infinitist linearism was most often associated with progressivist concepts. Voltaire, Turgot, Condorcet and Comte believed in the progress of mankind. Getting rid of the concept of Providence and original sin contributed to the subjectification of man. Human history was limited only by the possibilities of man himself, who became the sole creator of progress."

constitute the common denominator of every individual, regardless of geographical scope.[42] The new Enlightenment anthropology attributes to man a universal and abstract nature that is completely independent of any specific cultural context. Civilisational diversity is seen as a contingency, for the human is a *tabula rasa*, an essentially plastic, malleable being that can be shaped at will. The now dominant view is that humanity must be liberated from the supervisions, prejudices, and everything else that hinders "progress".[43] De Benoist concludes:

> The view becomes commonplace that politics must be rational. Politics must cease to be an art that obeys the principle of prudence, and become a science that obeys reason. Like the universe as a whole, society is seen as a machine in which the individual fulfils the function of one of the cogs. It must therefore be managed rationally, according to the rules as hard and precise as those of physics. The sovereign must be like a mechanic overseeing the evolution of 'social physics' with the aim of the 'greatest utility'. This concept lies at the foundations of the technocracy and administrative-managerial framing of politics of Saint-Simon and Comte.[44]

In turn, the 19th century becomes the peak of the popularity of the theory of progress. IT is in this time, the French thinker says, that the terms "progress" and "civilisation" became synonymous in the eyes of the people of the West. History was seen a sequence of stages, where each stage is a step forward on the road to progress — from the era of theology and magic to the era of reason and science (Hegel, Comte, Marx, etc.). Of course, Western civilisation was seen as the

---

42 de Benoist, "*Une brève histoire de l'idée de progrès*" in *Critiques — Théoriques*, 57–58.

43 Ibid., 58. It is in this view that de Benoist discerns the genesis of the Terror of the French Revolution.

44 Ibid., 59. It is also worth recalling that the origins of the concept of the "depoliticised" state can be found already in the 17th century, in Thomas Hobbes. See Carl Schmitt, *The Leviathan in the State Theory of Thomas Hobbes: Meaning and Failure of a Political Symbol*, trans. George Schwab and Erna Hilfstein (Chicago: University of Chicago Press, 2008).

peak of social evolution. Combined with the scientific positivism that dominated at the time, this view became, in de Benoist's opinion, the germ of racism. Traditional, "premodern" cultures were viewed from this universalist and hierarchicising perspective as lesser, worse, and backwards in relation to the West. From this very same view came the quasi-Christian conviction of the Western colonial powers that it is necessary to "civilise" ("baptise") backwards cultures (those which remain "ignorant of God"). Thus, in de Benoist's opinion, racism is directly bound to the postulated universalism of progress, which de facto exhibits a concealed or unconscious ethnocentrism.[45]

Nowadays, the idea of progress is no longer universally professed, especially in philosophy. The naive faith that the development of science and technology would automatically entail social emancipation has been seriously shaken. However, as Zdzisław Krasnodębski points out, even though no one any longer maintains or develops the idea of progress in philosophy, this idea is built into many contemporary, influential sociological and political theories.[46] In sociology, one significant example of this is the theory of modernisation,[47] which recognises development as evolutionary, consisting of stages, unilinear, and convergent, as though everyone is going down the same, only possible track of social development, in effect becoming more and more like each other. In the economic sphere, the idea of progress is the foundation of the ideology of development (Walt Rostow[48]), which is based on faith in the possibility of permanently increasing the production of goods, consumption, and the largest-scale globalisation of commerce through acquiring an ever-increasing quantity of markets.

---

45 de Benoist and Molnar, *Éclipse du sacré*, 164.
46 Z. Krasnodębski, "*Genealogia idei postępu*" [http://www.omp.org.pl/stareomp/index19e4.php?module=subjects&func=viewpage&pageid=732].
47 Krzysztofek and Szczepański, *Zrozumieć rozwój*, 29–54.
48 Walt Rostow, *The Stages of Economic Growth: A Non-Communist Manifesto* (Cambridge: 1991).

De Benoist's opposition to the idea of progress should come as no surprise. This idea was based on the Judeo-Christian linear framing of time whose adoption marks the symbolic break with the pagan *Weltandschauung*. It is noteworthy that de Benoist that was not the first to see the sources of the idea of progress in the Christian religion. Eric Voegelin's considerations (and his idea of "political gnosis"[49]) immediately come to mind: Voegel argued that the discernment of an inherent sense in history appeared only when the Christian concept of fulfilment was immanentised (the immanentisation of the eschaton). For Voegelin, one of the three types of immanentisation of the idea of salvation, besides "utopianism" and "mysticism", was "progressivism", which is characteristic of the idea of progress developed in the 18th century. The latter, according to Voegelin, concentrated on the desire to achieve fulfilment in the present world in the near but undefined future.[50] At the same time, Voegelin saw the idea of progress as decidedly unscientific.[51] Karl Löwith, in turn, wrote in his *World History and Salvation History*: "The Church Fathers developed out of Jewish prophecy and Christian eschatology a theology of history that is oriented towards supra-historical events like the creation of the world, the incarnation, the Final Judgement, and salvation. Modern man

---

49 Eric Voegelin, *The New Science of Politics: An Introduction* (Chicago: University of Chicago Press, 1987).

50 M.J. Czarnecki, "Człowiek wobec świata. Gnoza nowożytna Erica Voegelina", *Dialogi Polityczne* 8 (2007), 162.

51 Eric Voegelin, *From Enlightenment to Revolution* (Durham: Duke University Press, 1975), 84: "The problem of progress in its correct perspective: the idea of progress in general does not imply a scientific proposition which can be submitted to verification; it is an element in a doctrinal complex which purports to evoke the idea of an authoritative present. [...] A merely empirical present is a brute fact without superior authority in comparison with any past or future present. When the critical standards of civilizational values which stem from the *bios theoretikos* and the life of the spirit are abandoned, when the empirical process itself has to furnish the standards, then a special doctrine is needed to bestow grace on the present and to heighten an otherwise irrelevant situation of fact into a standard by which the past and the future can be measured."

thought up the philosophy of history by secularising the theological principles in the sense of a progressive march towards some kind of fulfilment."[52] Löwith claimed that it is this Judeo-Christian mentality that compelled European man to see an end and meaning in history. He also underscored the chasm between the ancient and biblical ways of thinking about history: for Christians and Jews, history is above all the history of salvation, and hence looking towards the future in an eschatological way means anticipating the promised prophecy. For the Greeks and Romans, the past was "present-*ed* as a constant beginning", whereas for Jews and Christians it is the promise of a future.[53]

This Christian-*cum*-modern concept of time constituted the basis for liberalism as well as Marxism (more broadly, the left). Just as history in Christianity begins with a primordial sin and exile from paradise, so does history in liberalism begin with a social contract and in Marxism with the end of primeval communism. In all of these cases, as Michael O'Meara argues, history is seen as progress from the slavery of the past to the realisation of freedom in the future.[54] Whether for salvation, economic development, or class struggle, this longing is the common denominator of a flight from, emancipation from, or end to history.[55]

Besides all of the above, the idea of a possible end of "history" implies the existence of a common history for all the peoples of the world, which de Benoist decisively rejects. Here we can see the influence of Oswald Spengler, who saw in the arena of history a plurality of peoples and civilisations, each with their own history and own path of development. According to Spengler, cultures go through several stages: from spring (a period of exuberant development) to summer and autumn (a period of completeness and maturity) to winter (a period of old age and decomposition). This is the law of history that Spengler assigns

---

52 K. Löwith, *Historia powszechna i dzieje zbawienia* (Kęty: 2002), 22.
53 Ibid., 10.
54 O'Meara, *New Culture, New Right*, 147.
55 Ibid., 148.

to all cultures, but he also sees and provides for differences in each individual case. It bears underscoring that there is no optimistic faith here, whether in the possibility of a permanent development/growth or ultimate fulfilment.[56] There is no faith in a historical "happy end". There is only *amor fati*. Man must come to terms with and face his own fate head-on. Where and when man is born has an absolutely fundamental influence on his destiny. "Everyone is born into a people, a religion, a class, an age, a culture"[57] — this is an incontrovertible fact. One cannot run away from one's destiny. But, for Spengler, this is not bound up with resignation or nihilism. On the one hand, we have cultural pessimism; on the other hand, we have the heroism of *amor fati*. It also bears recalling that the basic element of Spengler's historiosophical concept is the contrast between culture (*Kultur*) and civilisation (*Zivilisation*). Culture, in this German thinker's opinion, is characterised by immutability, organic nature, quality, and vitality, whereas civilisation is distinct for its artificiality, formality, and rigidity; at once being the refining and ossifying of "culture", "civilisation" is also its "agonising 'crystallisation' into a rationalistic, mechanical, rigid, 'petrified', and levelled reality".[58] In other words, once a culture has exhausted its "youthful" vital forces, it takes on the form of a "senile" civilisation and slowly heads towards crisis, decline, and collapse.

---

56 Oswald Spengler, "*Pesymizm?*" in idem, *Historia, Kultura, Polityka* (Warsaw: 1990), 95: "If the point is a 'goal of mankind', then I am a radical and decisive pessimist. I see no progress, no goal, no path for mankind besides that which exists in the heads of the Western philistines of progress. I see no spirit, not to mention unity of aspirations, feelings, and understanding in this mass of humans. I find a sensible orientation of life towards some goal and oneness of soul, will, and experience only in the histories of particular cultures. They are something organic and factual, and they contain something that is intended and achieved as well as a new task not in ethical phrases and generalisations, but in tangible historical goals."

57 Sunic, *Against Democracy and Equality*, 96.

58 Z. Mikołejko, *Mity tradycjonalizmu integralnego. Julius Evola i kultura religijno-polityczna prawicy* (Warsaw: 1998), 141.

Spengler was convinced that (his contemporary) Europe finds itself in such a crisis, in its decadent phase.

The conviction that Western civilisation is in a deep crisis was also shared by Martin Heidegger, another important figure who inspired de Benoist. The idea of progress is tightly bound up with faith in the emancipatory potential of scientific-technological development, of which Heidegger was extremely skeptical. Heidegger maintained that the technological mentality has become the fate of modern man. It has come to completely dominate man, reshaping man, and, along with man, has reshaped the world.[59] For Heidegger, technology is a way in which being reveals itself and a way of being human; in other words, it is a comprehensive kind of relation between man and his surrounding reality. It is both a relation to this reality and a way of interacting with it. The essence of technology is "enframing" (Heidegger's term *Gestell*) or "setting" (rendered in Polish *zestaw*) which is something deeper and more primordial than the division between theory and practice, something that precedes the latter. It can be defined as an ontological

---

59 Martin Heidegger, *The Question Concerning Technology and Other Essays*, trans. William Lovitt (New York: Harper Perennial, 2013), 14–15: "The revealing that rules in modern technology is a challenging [*Herausfordern*], which puts to nature the unreasonable demand that it supply energy that can be extracted and stored as such. But does this not hold true for the old windmill as well? No. Its sails do indeed turn in the wind; they are left entirely to the wind's blowing. But the windmill does not unlock energy from the air currents in order to store it. In contrast, a tract of land is challenged into the putting out of coal and ore. The earth now reveals itself as a coal mining district, the soil as a mineral deposit. The field that the peasant formerly cultivated and set in order [*bestellte*] appears differently than it did when to set in order still meant to take care of and to maintain. The work of the peasant does not challenge the soil of the field. In the sowing of the grain it places the seed in the keeping of the forces of growth and watches over its increase. But meanwhile even the cultivation of the field has come under the grip of another kind of setting-in-order, which sets upon [*stellt*] nature It sets upon it in the sense of challenging it. Agriculture is now the mechanized food industry. Air is now set upon to yield nitrogen, the earth to yield ore, ore to yield uranium, for example; uranium is set upon to yield atomic energy, which can be released either for destruction or for peaceful use."

process. It means "the collecting, accumulating, and uniformising of the diverse means of technological extracting out of nature of the world".⁶⁰ Heidegger thought that it is through technology that the world is reduced to resources. Through technology, nature manifests itself as a "supplier" of goods and resources, as an energy warehouse. Man's relation to the world thus becomes strictly instrumental and calculative. Man is the manager, and nature is the resource for management. As Jan Galarowicz puts it:

> Technology frames and arranges nature as a totality. This is simply our comprehensive surveying of nature and a way of dealing with it. The essence of technology lies in a determined relationship between man and the world. The world appears therein as material for ordering from the standpoint of man, yet man thereby treats himself as a functionary of this order. Contemporary (modern) technology [...] is the special form of any and all technology. What constitutes this specificity? It is bound up with modern metaphysics and the positioning whose essence is expressed by the thesis that man is the *subiectum*, the subject, across from which is the world, treated like an image, a representation, an object. Man appears to himself to be the lord and master of being, and reality and the world remain at his disposal. Man is characterised by the will of dominating: everything is mine, by me and for me. Nature is treated as material that must be dominated and used. This disposition towards reality, which transforms nature into disposable material, is what Heidegger calls the 'enframing' [*zestaw*]. It is this 'enframing' that constitutes the essence of technology.⁶¹

According to Heidegger, technology is characterised by intensification (technology demands increasingly more technology), globality (technology covers the whole Earth), and enormous destructive potential.⁶² The manifestations of technology include not only modern science, but

---

60 J. Urban, "*Co Martin Heidegger rozumie pod pojęciem 'technika'? Na ile jest ona poddana roszczeniu zasady, z
e
wszystko ma swoją przyczynę?*", Studia Redemptorystowskie 2 (2004), 166.
61 Galarowicz, *Martin Heidegger — genialny myśliciel czy szaman?*, 206.
62 Ibid., 207.

also the totalitarian state. In Heidegger's opinion, technology harbours all kinds of negative effects. It exploits nature, tears man away from the earth and tradition, and dominates relations between humans. The technological way of thinking influences not only man's relation to nature itself, but everything around man, including other people. The technological way of thinking has dominated the entirety of human life. In this regard, we treat other people in a technological manner as "human resources". Moreover, amidst the dominance of technology, man has lost his ability to experience reality as such, in and of itself, in the ways that it wants to reveal itself to us in its fullness.[63]

To sum up, instead of liberation, technology has brought enslavement. The rule of the "enframing" means that man is disposed, exploited, and used by a power that he does not rule over. In this light, modern faith in progress seems to be but one big oddity, a joke of dark humour. Technological-scientific progress not only enslaves but destroys man's sensitivity to the beauty of the world. It kills his "poetic" relation to the world, which it reduces to a resource base.[64] This should come as no surprise, for modern science is based precisely on modern metaphysics, and the latter on Christianity. In other words, technology

---

63   Ibid., 208.

64   Ibid., 204. A very similar perspective is visible in the thought of the Frankfurt School, particularly Max Horkheimer and Theodor Adorno, who saw in the "Enlightenment" as they understood it (i.e., positivism, logic, deductive sciences, empirical sciences, capitalism, the rule of money, mass culture, liberalism, fascism) everything that is negative. Besides their critique of mass society and their typically Marxist critique of capitalism and reification, they also discerned a threat in science itself (as understood in the extreme positivist sense). Going further than Marx, they accused the Enlightenment of "severing man's ties with nature and taking nature to be a pure object for exploitation, whereby man himself, as part of the natural order, is ultimately treated as an object for exploitation. The ideological counterpart of this process is science, which is not interested in the qualities of things, but only in what the world has to offer in quantitative form and whatever might be useful in technological operations." — L. Kołakowski, *Główne nurty marksizmu*, vol. 3 (Warsaw: 2009), 376.

is the continuation and complementation of the mentality expressed in Genesis 1:28: "Subdue the earth."⁶⁵

For the ancient Greeks, discerning any inherent sense of progress in history would be absurd, for time flows cyclically. In such an arrangement, there can be no historical "progress" understood as passing from one (less advanced) phase to another (more advanced). Of course, time flows on and changes ensue, but there is no "progress". There is no history rolling towards a designated end set from above. History does not strive towards final fulfilment or completion. There is only the Eternal Return.⁶⁶

De Benoist would say that the "aftermath" of Christianity is the conviction that humanity must necessarily be heading somewhere, establishing some kind of ultimate, temporal goal. The Bible teaches that the world has a beginning and an end. Pagan thought, for its part, has never been fixated on "history-time".⁶⁷ Instead, paganism concentrates more on the world-space, on what passes and yet is eternally ongoing. For *Homo paganus*, the past is not a burden from which one

---

65 Scholarly debate on Christianity's alleged influence on the contemporary ecological crisis was sparked in 1967, when the American mediaevalist Lynn Townsend White Jr. published "The Historical Roots of Our Ecological Crisis" in *Science*. He argued that the present crisis has been caused by the combination and reciprocal influence of science and technology, which is characteristic of the West and is based on a specific attitude towards nature of Judeo-Christian origin. This article caused a wide-reaching polemic and remains a source of controversy to this day. See R. Łętocha, "Chrześcijaństwo i współczesny kryzys ekologiczny", *Nowy Obywatel* 32(83) (2020), 112–127.

66 de Benoist, *On Being a Pagan*, 11–12: "We must reach an understanding of just what this word 'past' means. We refuse to give any credence whatsoever to the Judeo-Christian problematic that posits the past as a definitively passed *point* on a *line* that would necessarily conduct humanity from the Garden of Eden to Messianic times. We do not believe this has any historical meaning. For us the past is a *dimension*, a *perspective* that is totally relevant to the present. [...] We believe in the Eternal Return. [...] In fact, it is not a question of *going back* to the past, but of *connecting with it* [...] in a *spherical* conception of history."

67 Ibid., 79; Löwith, *Historia powszechna i dzieje zbawienia*, 8.

wants to free oneself (in order to reach a "Promise Land"). The past is heritage, legacy, memory, that which gives man an identity and roots him in the earth. It is a value that must be nurtured, not a burden to be cast off. De Benoist concludes:

> Pagan man feels the *place* of his birth through its relation to his ancestral lineage. He has a 'mother-country.' In biblical monotheism, to the contrary, there is no native land; there is only a final land, the land of destination that does not derive from any founding myth but clearly from a finality [...]. The people of Israel are not children of a land; they are the sons of Yahweh.[68]

The Ethnocidal Ideology of Human Rights

Alain de Benoist writes: "The religion of human rights, based on monohumanism, seems to be bound up with [...] egalitarianism on the one hand, and monotheism on the other. Biblical thought is monohumanistic and monogenistic 'for the same reason that it is monotheistic'. This is the obsession with the Same [...]: all people are the same before Yahweh."[69] Thus, de Benoist calls into doubt the obviousness, inalienability, and universality of human rights. He treats human rights as an ideology (or civic religion[70]) that is "ethnocidal" (sic!) In nature. This ideology, in his view, "inherited" the typical features of Christianity: universalism, monohumanism, egalitarianism, individualism, etc. As Christianity has increasingly disappeared from the Western public sphere, its place has been taken by human rights. In de Benoist's opinion, the ideology, or religion, of human rights is based on four tenets:

1. Belief in the oneness of humankind and the mortal gravity of this fact;

---

68 de Benoist, *On Being a Pagan*, 82.
69 de Benoist and Guillaume Faye, "*La religion des droits de l'homme*", 6.
70 De Benoist uses the terms "ideology of human rights" and "religion of human rights" interchangeably.

2. Belief in the existence of the "human person" regardless of the specific traits of each particular individual;
3. Belief in one "human nature" that provides the ground for "natural law";
4. Belief in the primacy of the individual over organic and historical communities like cultures, peoples, and nations.[71]

In contemporary Western political discourse, human rights function as something indisputable and self-evident. De Benoists points to how the very fact of doubting human rights incites the same reactions that one once received for denying the existence of God.[72] This is the case not because human rights are seen as a common ideology, but because they seem to be self-evident, and they are treated as self-evident because they have become the undoubtable, quasi-religious dogma of Western politics.

However, de Benoist draws attention to the fact that human rights — contrary to what is taken to be common knowledge — are not at all universal or timeless, as they arose in a very specific time and place as part of a specific cultural circle. De Benoist argues that even though human rights are ahistorical, they nonetheless have their own history:

> The ideology of human rights is a product of the thought of the Enlightenment and [...] the very idea of human rights belongs to the specific context of Western modernity. The question then arises of knowing if the narrowly circumscribed origin of this ideology does not implicitly contradict its pretensions to universality. Since every declaration of rights is historically dated, does not a tension, or a contradiction result from it, between the historical contingency that presided at its elaboration and the demand of universality which it intends to affirm? It is clear that the theory of rights, with respect to all human cultures, represents the exception rather than the rule — and that it even constitutes exception within European

---

71 de Benoist and Faye, "*La religion des droits de l'homme*", 5.
72 de Benoist, *Beyond Human Rights*, 9.

culture, since it appeared only at a definite moment and relatively late in the history of this culture. If the rights have been 'there' always, present in the very nature itself of man, one may be surprised that only a small portion of humanity has perceived it, and that it has taken it so long to be perceived.[73]

Moreover, de Benoist underscores that human rights cannot be treated as an expression of the European spirit per se, but at most as a certain "clip" cut out of the latter. Before the doctrine of human rights appeared, there already existed morality, ethics, law, rights, etc. In ancient Greece, de Benoist recalls, justice was understood as proper proportion, i.e., as the proper relation in the distribution of goods and duties.[74] In ancient Rome, "[t]he *ius* of Classical Roman law aimed equally at determining the 'good distribution' that should exist between men, the just share that should be attributed to everyone: *suum cuique tribuere.*"[75]

Attention should be drawn to the fact that in the ancient cultures of Greece and Rome, justice was based on a proportionally structured network of ties — social relations oriented towards the common good. Justice was treated as the right proportions that are the condition of harmonious coexistence within a given community. In other words, it was not the individual that was the source of rights and law, but the community. In antiquity, there was no concept of the individual as a bearer of universal and inalienable rights by virtue of the very fact of existing. According to the idea of human rights, justice is based on the rights of the individual, that is, an abstract individual seen as independent of the context of his specific culture and tradition. In this framework, the abstractly conceived individual is the source of law and rights. From this perspective, the basis of harmonious coexistence is the law of free commerce and the invisible hand of the market, whereby man is seen as not as a being within a specific national community, but

---

73 de Benoist, *Beyond Human Rights*, 61.
74 de Benoist, "*L'idéologie ethnocidaire de l'Occident*", 29.
75 de Benoist, *Beyond Human Rights*, 26.

as a participant in a free game of interests that is tempered only by the "juridisation of social ties".[76]

In de Benoist's opinion, behind this model of justice lurks the dream of a humanity united by the very same norms and under the rule of the same law[77] (implying that all people have the same nature).[78] For de Benoist, this is an obvious offshoot of the Christian mentality of salvation (the salvation of all mankind). In other words, behind this model lurks the rejection of the Other that is typical of the monotheistic mentality and doctrine. De Benoist summarises: "The imposition of human rights certainly bears the hallmarks of acculturation, and implementing them in life creates the risk of a collapse of the very community identities that have their own part in the creation of individual identities."[79]

The universalist claims of the "ideology" of human rights, in de Benoist's opinion, exhibit a concealed Western ethnocentrism and represent a relict of the "colonial mentality". This mentality is exhibited in how human rights are seen as principles which are universal to all humans, and therefore in the desire to impose them upon the whole world. Such a perspective, whether consciously or not, divides people into "civilised" and "barbarians" (those to whom the tradition of liberal individualism is foreign). Moreover, as de Benoist argues, this discourse goes hand in hand with the expansion of the Western market. For these reasons, this French thinker writes off human rights as an "ideology of the Western bourgeoisie".[80]

In de Benoist's judgment, the ideology of human rights is unwilling to acknowledge cultural diversity for two fundamental reasons. First, this is an effect of its inherent individualism and the abstract

---

76 de Benoist, *Au-delà des droits de l'homme: pour défendre les libertés* (Paris: 2016), 43.

77 Ibid., 46.

78 It is this tendency that de Benoist calls the "ideology of the Same".

79 de Benoist, "*L'idéologie ethnocidaire de l'Occident*", 32.

80 de Benoist, *Au-delà des droits de l'homme*, 20–21.

character of its subject; second, this is because it is tightly bound up with Western culture. Human rights, therefore, are a product of the European Enlightenment, and the very idea of human rights is a part of the specific horizon of Western modernity.[81] In this respect, human rights are seen as a "Western construction with limited applicability", one that is incompatible with cultures to whom the tradition of liberal individualism is alien.

Moreover, the ideology of human rights entirely ignores the fact that what is specifically human, what defines man as human, can arise out of history and culture.[82] Man cannot be treated like any other animal, i.e., man is not definable exclusively as belonging to a species. De Benoist emphasises that man, unlike other animals, is not determined by belonging to a species:

> What is specifically human [...] arises out of culture and history. Man is not merely an animal; he does not define himself exclusively in terms of belonging to a species [...]. Man is a cultural being. In other words, there is no common paradigm for all of mankind. To put it historically, cultures always crystallise in the plural.[83]

Thus, in de Benoist's opinion, the absolutisation of the abstract individual leads to tearing asunder the social ties that are constituted by a concrete cultural community with its own history and tradition. It is for this reason that human rights are described as "ethnocidal": they are supposed to "override" what is given by concrete, extant national communities and hold all cultures according to a "one and only right model", and thereby destroy real diversity.

It is beyond any doubt that human rights became the basis of the Western political, social, and legal order after the Second World War. They became the most important moral doctrine regulating practical

---

81 de Benoist, "*L'idéologie ethnocidaire de l'Occident*", 29.
82 de Benoist and Faye, "*La religion des droits de l'homme*", 6.
83 Ibid.

affairs, and they are treated by many as something holy.[84] Nor is it controversial to say that human rights seem to be an incontrovertible element of democracy today — more often than not, the two are uttered together in one breath.[85] What determined this state of affairs? It bears recalling that the implementation of human rights on such a broad scale became a kind of response to the criminal politics of the Third Reich (and later also as a counter to the USSR). Human rights were supposed to be a certain, constant reference point for all states and societies with the aim of protecting man from the abuse of government power.

Although human rights do not have any established philosophical ground dominated by universal agreement, one can nevertheless point to their historical roots. The fact that the contemporary idea of human rights has its genesis in the Western individualist-liberal philosophy of the Enlightenment is a widespread perspective today.[86] Like de Benoist, some even acknowledge that this ideology's egalitarianism already existed in embryonic form in Christian ethics,[87] hence natural law is sometimes seen as having anticipated human rights. However, the secularisation that became widespread across Europe brought the divine instance of authority into doubt. Hence the constantly present problem of the universalist claims of the idea of human rights — since

---

84 See Michael Freeman, *Human Rights: An Interdisciplinary Approach* (Cambridge: Polity, 2002); P. Bała and A. Wielomski, *Prawa człowieka i ich krytyka: przyczynek do studiów o ideologii ponowożytnych* (Warsaw: 2016), 16.

85 Bała and Wielomski, *Prawa człowieka*, 23. See the European Parliament's webpage, "Democracy and human rights" [https://www.europarl.europa.eu/about-parliament/en/democracy-and-human-rights].

86 Freeman, *Human Rights*; M. Rakusa-Suszczewski, "*Prawa człowieka — między krytyką i apologią europejskiego modelu politycznego*", *Studia Europejskie* 1 (2016), 12; K. Przybyszewski, *Prawa człowieka w kontekstach kulturowych* (Poznań: 2010); K. Stępniak, "*Koncepcja jurydyzacji czwartej generacji praw człowieka w międzynarodowym systemie ochrony*", *Przegląd Sejmowy* 2(151) (2019), 108.

87 Rakusa-Suszczewski, "*Prawa człowieka*", 12.

they have no philosophical substantiation, their pretences to universality are unfounded.

In this regard, the idea of human rights is not accepted by everyone without reservation. One can find voices critical of human rights in the Western cultural circle as well. Adam Wielomski and Paweł Bała distinguish two basic categories of critique of human rights: accidental and substantial. Accidental critiques pertain to situations in which the idea of human rights itself is accepted, but particular manifestations of human rights (or subgroups of manifestations) are critiqued as being perversions of the original idea. Substantial critiques concern the very idea of human rights. Examples of the latter include critiques from the standpoint of (a) traditional Catholic thought, (b) conservative thought, and (c) totalitarian ideology. The conservative critique of human rights is concentrated on opposing the universalism of human rights on the grounds of the concept's excessive abstraction (Edmund Burke), from the standpoint of local cultures and their traditions (Joseph de Maistre), as well as from seeing in human rights an American ideological weapon that is inconsistent with European tradition (Thomas Molnar).[88] Thus, human rights "are the culmination of the philosophical tradition of the Enlightenment and nothing more".[89] De Benoist's views can be situated in this current.

Critics argue that the universality postulated by human rights is an illusion produced by the dominance of Western countries after the Second World War. In other words, the universalism of human rights is a cover for the cultural imperialism of the West.[90] Advocates of the idea of universal human rights might respond that it is absurd to accuse an idea of imperialism when this idea is rooted in opposition to Nazism.[91] The essence of this dispute lies largely in the difference in

---

88 Bała and Wielomski, *Prawa człowieka*, 173.
89 Ibid., 212.
90 Freeman, *Human Rights*.
91 Ibid.

the philosophical anthropologies which the advocates and critics of human rights maintain.

The idea of human rights is based on the implicitly adopted hypothesis that all people are naturally and inherently equal and the same (what Benoist calls "monohumanism"). In the optic of human rights, every Pole, Frenchman, Chinese, Nigerian, and Vietnamese is entitled to exactly the same human rights, for all of them are identical as humans. This hypothesis can be relatively easily called into doubt, basically in two ways. First, one can question the biological oneness of humankind. The Jews and Greeks did so in antiquity, and after the Christian era (in which the thesis of the oneness of all humans appeared in Europe for the first time) this view lived on in racist doctrines (e.g., Arthur de Gobineau, Alfred Rosenberg, Houston Steward Chamberlain). As a result of the Second World War, racial theories became morally bankrupt and are no longer accepted as worldviews or political options. However, this by no means proves that the conviction that biological traits make people unequal (which is suggested by studies of IQ[92]) is fallacious. The second counterargument against monohumanism is the empirical fact of the existence of different cultures — there is no "human culture", only many different cultures (which consist of religion, morality, ideas of the truth, the good, beauty, justice, etc.), and each of them has its own concept of man.

Part of the contemporary Western left sees a masked form of racism in highlighting cultural differences.[93] This is up for discussion. One could equally well wonder whether viewing all of the peoples and cultures of the world through the prism of Western European standards (with the simultaneous aspiration to impose these standards) is itself not racist. Indeed, this charge is formulated by Alain de Benoist.[94] It is worth drawing attention to the fact that the strongest

---

92 Bała and Wielomski, *Prawa człowieka*, 144.

93 P. A. Taguieff, "*Le néo-racisme differentialiste*", *Langage et société* 34 (1985).

94 Alain de Benoist, "*Contre tous les racismes*", *Éléments pour la civilisation européenne* 8–9 (1974–1975), 13–23.

resistance to human rights exists in the countries of the Third World, where the conviction is to be found that human rights are a form of Western ideological imperialism.[95] Furthermore, attention should be paid to the often categorical proclamations of human rights advocates themselves.[96]

The problematic nature of this issue can be seen whenever we are dealing with a cultural custom that is condemned by human rights ideology, but enjoys recognition among a country's native population. One good example of this is ritual female circumcision in the states of Black Africa. This is a cultural custom that constitutes a form of initiation. After undergoing this ritual, a girl becomes a woman capable of marrying and having children. Not sending one's daughter to this custom condemns her to social exclusion. It is very likely for this reason that mothers and other adult women in the tribe, motivated by care, aspire to uphold this tradition.[97] Presuming that this practice is condemnable from the point of view of human rights, de Benoist poses the question: in whose name could one prohibit such a custom which itself is not imposed from the outside? Since "my" freedom should not

---

95   Bała and Wielomski, *Prawa człowieka*, 145.

96   Freeman, *Human Rights*, 127: "The principle of respect for persons does not entail that we ought to respect all cultures, and therefore cultures that endorse human-rights violations cannot demand our respect simply because they are cultures. [...] Human-rights supporters should, therefore, realize that they are committed to not respecting some cultures, or at least some features of some cultures." G. Lohmann, "Różne kultury—dlaczego więc uniwersalne prawa człowieka?", *Principia* 57–58 (2014), 121, 139: "Human Rights do not protect culture as such, but rather every individual person as a value in and of themselves, completely irrespective of the culture in which they live. [...] The universal regime of human rights is not reconcilable with all cultures; rather, it demands that cultures change until they are compatible with human rights. [...] A pluralism of cultures is acceptable only when the minimal demands of the regime of human rights are applied, which means that the equal legal value of every individual person is recognised, since this is demanded by the notion that human dignity is one human right."

97   de Benoist, *Au-delà des droits de l'homme*, 95.

violate others' freedom, on what basis could one forbid other people from observing such customs?[98]

The preaching of the universality of human rights ideology is based on the tacitly adopted presumption that the majority of countries in the world (if not all) are pursuing a universal track of development from "mythical" community to "modern" community, analogous to that of Western countries. From this presumption arises the belief that human rights ideology is a universal solution. In de Benoist's opinion, this functions as a self-fulfilling prophecy: in the name of such postulated universalism, human rights are simply imposed. In other words, they are a "Trojan horse of the West",[99] the latter's ideological weapon.

De Benoist also draws attention to the fact that every law requires a certain political force to execute it. The role of the global police could only be fulfilled by armed forces that cannot be opposed. Given that armies always belong to concrete states, the result would be the de facto acceptance of the hegemony of the great powers of the world. In de Benoist's opinion, it would be naive to presume that a great power would not use its position to pursue its own particular interests, especially as it is able to do so under the cover of rights and morality. In effect, only the weaker states would be punished, while the great powers — whom it would be impossible to hold accountable — would have nothing to worry about at all. As de Benoist argues, any "justice" that is not the same for all does not deserve the name.[100] Even good intentions can yield bad consequences, as can be seen in the interventions in Kosovo, Afghanistan, Iraq, and Libya. De Benoist maintains that democracy and "freedom" cannot be compelled from the outside. They can only be the result of endogenic evolution, never coercion. In his opinion, the spread of human rights ideology does not yield a more just or peaceful world. The only thing it does cause is increasing

---

98 Ibid.
99 Ibid., 96.
100 Ibid., 127.

economic inequality whose beneficiaries are transnational corporations and financial markets.[101] Let us quote de Benoist:

> To accept cultural diversity demands a full recognition of the Other. But how to recognise the Other if his values and practices are opposed to those that one wishes to inculcate? [...] But what compatibility is there between human rights and the plurality of cultural systems and religious beliefs? If the respect for individual rights passes through a non-respect for cultures and peoples, should one conclude from this that all men are equal, but that the cultures that these equals have created are not equal?[102]

We can arrive at this conclusion by taking into consideration the very fact that human rights are not adopted by every state on their own, but are established within the politico-economic centre (the West) and are then imposed on all the rest. Wielomski and Bała therefore put forth the conclusion that this is a blatant violation of the principle of state sovereignty, or, speaking more plainly, the implementation of "might is right" in the international arena.[103]

When it comes to the West's relations with the Third World, de Benoist distinguishes four possible models of relations:

(a) The West's superiority over the Third World: this is the classical right-wing framing based on the uncritical cult of everything Western;

(a) The Third World's superiority over the West: this is the left-wing framing based on guilt felt before the Third World;

(b) The West and the Third World as equals, but cultural differences and peculiarities are devalued: this is the liberal, universalist framing of human rights;

---

101 Ibid., 128.
102 de Benoist, *Beyond Human Rights*, 68.
103 Bała and Wielomski, *Prawa człowieka*, 212.

(c) The West and the Third World are equal alongside affirming and respecting cultural differences: this is the framing of the New Right, which rejects universalism.[104]

In Georg Lohmann's opinion, human rights are "comprehensive and, above all, abstract rights" as well as a "project in defence of the individual person".[105] In other words, the idea of human rights recognises the primacy of the (abstract) individual over the community. Human rights ideology asserts the existence of a uniform, universal human nature, knowable through reason, that is independent of era and place. This entails a threefold separation: (a) between man and other living beings, (b) between man and society, and (c) between man and the entirety of the cosmos. This division, de Benoist remarks, is not a part of most non-Western cultures, yet these cultures recognise the existence of a human nature.[106] In the majority of cultures (including premodern Europe), man was never conceived as a monad. The notions of justice, harmony, and order were not derived from the abstract rights of the individual, but emerged from tradition, culture, or a given model of social relations. In other words, in holistic cultures, speaking of any freedom of the individual in and of itself is completely pointless and senseless.[107]

The idea of human rights was intended to protect the individual from abuses of power. However, in de Benoist's opinion, human rights themselves have become a potential source of oppression. Whenever a culture believes that it manifests a universal decree, it begins to see others as worse, as foolish, and as irrational,[108] which gives it the moral right to intervene in a foreign culture.

---

104 Robert de Herte (Alain de Benoist), *"Pour un autre tiers-mondisme"*, *Éléments pour la civilisation européenne* 48–49 (1983–1984).
105 Lohmann, "Różne kultury", 122.
106 de Benoist, *Au-delà des droits de l'homme*, 92.
107 Ibid.
108 Ibid., 106.

One of the central threads of de Benoist's thought is the right to difference (*droit à la différence*), the opposite of which is the ideology of the same (*l'idéologie du même*) that arises out of monotheistic conceptual cliches (the desire for the uniformity of everything in accordance with one right model). The French thinker maintains the standpoint that there exists something more important than the abstract rights of the individual: the ethnocultural integrality of the community. De Benoist sees culture as a good in and of itself, and it is culture that shapes man as a human being.

It is also worth underscoring that contesting the idea of human rights does not mean praising despots or questioning whether people possess any rights. What de Benoist contests is the thesis that human rights are the best means of ensuring the rights of humans. He sees freedom as a cardinal value, but freedom should not, in his opinion, be based on universalism and subjectivism. The question of freedom is not to be resolved by means of abstract rights or universal morality, but is to be a political question and therefore resolved politically.[109]

When it comes to a more concrete form of guaranteeing rights, an alternative to human rights, de Benoist points to the example of the Universal Declaration of the Rights of Peoples adopted in Algeria on 4 July 1976, in which the category of "people" is in the first place.[110] In this context, it is worth reading Section IV, Article 15: "Every people has the right not to have an alien culture imposed upon it."[111] In the opinion of our French thinker, the imposition of human rights is a blatant violation of this right.[112]

To sum up, human rights are for Alain de Benoist not the universal, inalienable rights of every individual, but rather an ideological instrument that serves to uphold the cultural hegemony of liberalism.

---

109 Ibid., 21.

110 Ibid., 99.

111 "Universal Declaration of the Rights of Peoples" [https://permanentpeoplestribunal.org/algiers-charter/?lang=en].

112 de Benoist, "*L'idéologie ethnocidaire de l'Occident*", 32.

Liberalism: The Negation of Democracy

In and of itself, liberalism as a doctrine is entirely opposed to collective identities. It is based on an individualist anthropology resultant of the secularisation of the Christian concept of man, who is understood above all as an abstract moral subject (whereby the value of the individual soul results from its having being created by the one God). As already mentioned, Alain de Benoist maintains that Christianity bears responsibility for European societies' shift from being traditional and holistic to modern and individualistic.[113]

The individualism present within Christianity *in potentia* expressed itself explicitly in the time of the Reformation, in the form of the personalisation of religion. It was the Reformation that broke the mediaeval order in which the individual was seen through the prism of the greater whole. As Rafał Łętocha writes: "The Reformation's individualism, which over time underwent secularisation, supported the process of the emancipation of the individual ongoing since, and thanks to, the Renaissance."[114] In de Benoist's words, Christianity by way of secularisation still "infected" social life with its individualist-universalist component.[115] Thus, the individual started to constitute the basic component of society instead of the family, guild, or estate. Organic society of the holistic type disappeared. The old conception of man as a part of the greater whole was replaced by a vision of a collection of individuals linked together by a rational contract.

An important stage in this process was the nominalism of William Ockham, who postulated that only individual entities exist. The next important stage was Cartesianism, which grounded individualism in philosophy, later to become the basis of the idea of human rights and

---

[113] de Benoist, "*Critique de l'idéologie libérale*" in idem, *Critiques — Théoriques*, 13–14.

[114] R. Łętocha, "*Polityczne dziedzictwo Reformacji*" in K. Pilarczyk and W. Gajewski (eds.), *Dziedzictwo kulturowe Reformacji w perspektywie polskiej i europejskiej: w 500-lecie wystąpienia Marcina Lutra* (Kraków: 2017), 202.

[115] de Benoist, "*Critique de l'idéologie libérale*" in idem, *Critiques — Théoriques*, 14.

Enlightenment thought. Starting in the 18th century, the emancipation of the individual from traditional ties began to be seen as progress and the human striving towards the stage of "adulthood". "With individualism at its basis, modernity should be understood above all as the process of the disintegration of lineage-based and local groups, as well as broader communities, for the sake of 'liberating the individual', i.e., destroying any organic relations of solidarity."[116]

In the contemporary sense of the word, individualism is a philosophy that takes the individual to be the only real entity and only evaluative criterion.[117] This individual is always seen as abstracted from its particular socio-cultural context. The opposite of this would be the holistic perspective, which views society in relation to its hereditary values passed down from generation to generation — which, from the standpoint of individualism, is void of any significance. In de Benoist's opinion, the individualist perspective does not recognise any reality or autonomous status for peoples, nations, or cultures, which are instead seen as an ordinary sum of (competing) individuals.

Liberalism, which is based on individualism, regards the individual itself as being the source of its own rights, regardless of cultural belonging. In this framework, the individual is logically more primordial than the community. Society has no value in and of itself; instead, society is reduced exclusively to individuals' pursuit of their own interests. In this respect, liberalism takes freedom to mean independence.[118] This contrasts the ancient notion of freedom as the possibility of participating in public life (as per Benjamin Constant). In the liberal understanding, freedom is reduced to the individual being able to do what it wants as long as it does not violate the freedom of another individual (as per John Stuart Mill[119]). Especially important in liberalism

---

116 Ibid., 15.

117 Ibid.

118 Ibid., 16.

119 M. Małek, "*Liberalizm etyczny J.S. Milla: współczesne nawiązania i kontynuacje (analiza poglądów Johna Graya i Petera Singera*", PhD dissertation (Katowice:

is the idea that the individual's interest should never be pursued in the name of the interest of the community, that is, the so-called "common good". The aim of freedom is not the common good, but the pursuit of happiness and the maximisation of the individual's interests.

In de Benoist's opinion, this conception of freedom is destructive of national communities, as it erodes social ties. "Modern liberalism [...] destroyed the organic relations of closeness that were first and foremost relations of mutual aid, and in so doing it caused the disappearance of old forms of social welfare."[120] Society no longer has any common goal — the only thing that binds together the people inhabiting it is the market. Individuals are thus reduced to being consumers and lose their social, cultural, and other traits. Upholding the market as the main reference point and regulatory of social life, next comes the complete transvaluation of all values. In Europe, commercial values have "since time immemorial" been seen as values of the lowest rank. "On the moral level [liberalism] idealises the spirit of rational calculation and egotistical behaviour, which traditional societies always condemned."[121] Liberalism thus reduces individuals (and the whole of society) to their market values — liberalism acknowledges no other value. De Benoist writes: "Liberal authors believe that society can be based solely on individualism and commercial relations. This is a delusion. Individualism has never been the sole basis for social behaviours and never will be. There is much that suggests that individualism can function only insofar as society remains holistic to some extent."[122]

De Benoist takes the standard-bearing example of a liberal author to be Friedrich von Hayek, who, without a doubt, is an authority of liberal thought. Already telling is that de Benoist deems him to be the

---

University of Silesia, 2007), 57.
120 de Benoist, "*Critique de l'idéologie libérale*" in idem, *Critiques — Théoriques*, 26.
121 Ibid., 22.
122 Ibid., 27.

"theoretician of the law of the jungle".[123] For this French thinker, Hayek represents liberalism taken all the way to its extreme consequence of being a *vide* doctrinal rejection of the idea of social justice. The market, de Benoist recapitulates, occupies the key place in liberal thought, or rather the place of the Absolute. In effect, out of an abstract model of commercial relations between individuals (who are supposed to be guided by the invisible hand in accordance with allegedly objective laws, rights, and independence from any human control), a normative model is created which is unquestionable and is transplanted into all other spheres (the social, political, etc.). Instead of setting up the market in accordance with social needs, society is set up according to the needs of the market. In effect, the market absorbs the social dimension in its entirety. Yet, it is not treated as a model of human activity, but rather only as human activity as such, in and of itself.[124] In this perspective, ideas of social justice, national sovereignty, and socio-cultural integrity seem to be completely pointless, if not altogether absurd.

For these reasons, de Benoist does not consider liberalism to be an adequate foundation for democracy. To the contrary, liberalism is antinomian to democracy, as a contradiction between them exists on the level of the concepts themselves (as per Carl Schmitt).[125]

The liberal perspective sees society simply as a collection of individuals, each of which pursues his own interests. Democracy, however, in de Benoist's eyes, is supposed to be based on an organised, collective deed, by virtue of which society attaches importance to collective undertakings, and therefore, thanks to common work and the fusion of individual will, democracy takes on an "organic" character. Whereas democracy is based on the sovereignty of the people (as per

---

123 Alain de Benoist, "*Hayek: la loi de la jungle*", *Éléments pour la civilisation européenne* 68 (1990), 5.

124 Ibid., 7.

125 See Carl Schmitt, *The Crisis of Parliamentary Democracy*, trans. Ellen Kennedy (Cambridge: MIT Press, 2000).

Jean-Jacques Rousseau), liberalism is based on the rights of the individual. For de Benoist, this is an obvious contradiction, as the principle of common will conflicts with the principle of the individual's primacy over the community.

Authentic democracy, then, in de Benoist's opinion, cannot be based exclusively on a formal contract. Authentic democracy is possible only when "the people are so homogeneous that there is essentially unanimity [...]. The state therefore rests not on a contract but essentially on homogeneity [...]. The democratic identity of the governed and governing arises from that."[126] An homogenous, organic community (a people, *peuple*, *Volk*) is the *sine qua non* condition of authentic democracy.

However, if we look at democracy from the liberal perspective, then the situation changes diametrically. In the absence of a bond with a concrete cultural community, its tradition and history, democracy needs to be based on something else. In the case of the liberal version of democracy, this function is fulfilled by the rule of law. In this arrangement, democracy attains a strictly juridical-formal meaning.[127] The emphasis falls on procedure, not on content (this is the "proceduralism" of liberalism).[128] The rule of the people is replaced by the rule of law, which is indifferent towards questions of an explicitly axiological shade, such as national identity, ethnic homogeneity, or any definite concept of the good. Any strictly political project therefore becomes aimless, as democracy, instead of being an instrument of the national community in the pursuit of its destiny (as per Arthur Moeller van den Bruck),[129] is reduced to being an "incubator of enterprise".

---

126 Ibid., 13–14.

127 de Benoist, "*Hayek: la loi de la jungle*", 10.

128 K. Jasiński, "*Liberalizm a dobro wspólne*", Studia Koszalińsko-Kołobrzeskie 23 (2016), 305–319.

129 See Bielawski, "*Arthura Moellera van den Brucka konserwatywno-rewolucyjna krytyka liberalizmu*".

It is beyond any doubt that the assertion of an equivalence of identity between liberalism and democracy (in common thinking as well as in political practice) is a fact in today's Western world. However, this does not mean that the relation between democracy and liberalism is natural, necessary, or even obvious.[130] It bears highlighting that the roots of democracy reach back to antiquity, whereas liberalism is a creature of the Enlightenment. Popular assemblies were widespread in Europe since the most ancient times, monarchies (including elected ones) did not necessarily have a despotic character, and kings often co-governed with parliaments. The oldest parliament in the West of Europe arose in 930 (the Icelandic *Althing*). The legitimisation of authority, as well as the political rights of individuals, from below was never something alien to the European mentality.[131]

De Benoist takes Athenian democracy to be the touchstone of democracy. In his opinion, when it comes to evaluating the "democratic nature" of a democratic system, it is necessary to apply this reference point, not contemporary liberal democracies. The crowning argument is that democracy as a system was already constituted in antiquity. In other words, Athenian democracy is original democracy. De Benoist highlights:

> To some extent, *demos* and *ethnos* coincide: democracy is conceived here in relation not to the individual, but to the *polis*, which is to say the city as an *organised community*. [...] To be a citizen meant, in the fullest sense of the word, to belong to a homeland — that is, to a homeland and a past. One is born an Athenian — one does not become it (rare exceptions notwithstanding). [...] Political equality, established by law, derived from a common

---

130 T. Sawczuk, "*Czy demokracja może być liberalna?*", Rocznik Historii Socjologii 8 (2018), 131–138; P. Beniuszys, "*Ocena demokratycznego ładu w myśli liberalizmu*", Studia Gdańskie. Wizje Rzeczywistości 9 (2012), 201–215; Z. Stawrowski, "*Liberalizm a demokracja*", Ośrodek Myśli Politycznej [https://omp.org.pl/artykul.php?artykul=26].

131 Bielawski, "*Demokracja organiczna Alaina de Benoist jako alternatywa dla globalistycznej demokracji liberalnej*", 484.

origin [...]. Democracy was rooted in a notion of *autochthonous* citizenship [...].[132]

Indeed, Athenian democracy functioned as a community governed directly, not by a caste of delegates.[133] Citizenship was not an abstract, legal-administrative category, but something very concrete: belonging to the *polis*, which was an ethnic and cultural community in which citizens were bound together by ties of values, religion, language, custom, and tradition. Citizenship arose from origin, not law. The notion of freedom was understood not in the liberal way (as "emancipation", "freedom from"), but as the capacity and privilege to participate in the life of the community. Equality was also understood differently: it was not "natural" (as in the idea of human rights), but rather a means for serving the optimal functioning of the democratic system. It was derived from belonging to the Athenian people, not from essential equality between (all) people. In other words, the equal right to participate in the popular assembly was not taken from "inalienable individual rights", but from common origin. In addition, it was not nominal equality before the law that mattered; rather, it was relative equality of wealth that was of significance. Economic stratification was not as large for the realities of the day. Moreover, wealth entailed greater civic duties. On the most profound level, the difference between Athenian democracy and liberal democracy lies in the philosophical anthropology upon which the whole vision of a democratic system is based. As Ryszard Kulesza summates:

> Ancient democracy was communitarian and "holistic", whereas contemporary democracy is above all individualistic. Ancient democracy defined citizenship through origin and gave citizens the possibility to participate in the life of the city. Contemporary democracy organises atomised individuals into citizens, viewing them above all through the prism of abstract egalitarianism. Ancient democracy was based on the idea of the organic

---

132   de Benoist, *Problem of Democracy*, 23–24.
133   R. Kulesza, *Ateny Peryklesa* (Warsaw: 1991), 11.

community; contemporary democracy, as an heir to Christianity and the philosophy of the Enlightenment, [is based on] the individual.[134]

At this stage, it should be clear why de Benoist is an advocate of the "original" model of democracy and is critical of the liberal version. As Tamir Bar-On rightly notes, de Benoist rejects a social order that is based on Judeo-Christian decrees (universalism, egalitarianism, individualism, etc.). The ideal society, according to the *Nouvelle Droite*, is instead based on the Indo-European heritage, i.e., it is "pagan", "organic", and hierarchical, rooted and homogenous, non-liberal, decentralised, and therein the political sphere has primacy over the economic sphere, as the market is subordinated to the needs of society.[135] Athenian democracy was, according to de Benoist, built precisely on this foundation, and this is why it should be recognised as democracy *tout court*. Today's version of democracy (where it is de facto representatives who govern, not the people) would certainly have been seen by the ancient Athenians as a parody of democracy.[136]

De Benoist's considerations fit well within the still ongoing dispute[137] between communitarians and liberals, which is one of the most essential polemics in contemporary political philosophy and concerns issues like the conceptualisation of freedom, individualism, and the

---

134 Ibid., 28.
135 Bar-On, *Rethinking the French New Right*, 54–55.
136 R. Kulesza, "*Demokracje antyczne i współczesne*" in P. Fiktus, H. Malewski, and M. Marszał (eds.), *"Rodzinna Europa": europejska myśl polityczno-prawna u progu XXI wieku* (Wrocław: 2015), 26.
137 Interestingly enough, this dispute is not confined to academic discussions, as it has spilled over into the sphere of practical political issues concerning liberal (Western) and illiberal (Jarosław Kaczyński's Poland, Viktor Orbán's Hungary) models of democracy within the European Union. See É. Zemmour, "Europa Wschodnia przypomina nam czym powinna być Europa", Wszystko co najważniejsze [https://wszystkoconajwazniejsze.pl/eric-zemmour-europa-wschodnia-przypomina-nam-czym-powinna-byc-europa/].

common good.[138] The occasion that gave rise to this debate was John Rawls's work *A Theory of Justice*, published in 1971. The beginning of communitarianism is recognised to be Michael Sandel's response to Rawls's thesis as contained in his work *Liberalism and the Limits of Justice* (1982). The most important representatives of this current include Alasdair MacIntyre, Charles Taylor, Michael Walzer, Robert N. Bellah, and, of course, Sandel.

Recalling this dispute is important insofar as de Benoist himself (like MacIntyre[139]) thinks that today's political discussion is to a large extent confined to a closed circle, as its actual participants are not even left-wing or right-wing as much as they are left-wing liberals, centrist liberals, or right-wing liberals. De Benoist, however, is above all anti-liberal, as Krzysztof Tyszka-Drozdowski rightly points out.[140] What de Benoist and the communitarians have in common is anti-modernism, anti-individualism, anti-contractualism, emphasising the common good, and postulating a society that is based on shared values. As de

---

138 See A. Miętek, "*Spór liberałów z komunitarystami*", Dialogi Polityczne 7 (2007), 101–111; J. Miklaszewska, "*Liberałowie i komunitaryści o wolności i sprawiedliwości*", Prakseologia 158(2) (2016), 15–33; K. Sosenko, "*Komuntarianizm i liberalizm. Uwagi w związku z prawami człowieka*", Prakseologia 158(2) (2016), 53–74.

139 Alasdair MacIntyre rejects liberalism on three fundamental grounds: (1) the rules of parliamentary democracy and the principle of respecting private property in the liberal spirit are uncritically accepted by workers' unions, which is de facto a political forfeit in their struggle for social justice; (2) liberalism is a political ideology of the parliamentary, media, and financial elites, and these elites play a key role in shaping possible political options for voters, which demands increasing political passivity on the part of voters and sees the use of democratic rhetoric for non-democratic ends; (3) the moral individualism proclaimed by liberal ideologists has a destructive influence on the social ties that are the condition for real participation in a political community oriented around a definite understanding of what is good. In summary, MacIntyre accuses liberalism of de facto upholding a politics that takes away people's subjectivity and autonomy. See A. Chmielewski, "*Filozofia moralności*" in A. MacIntyre, *Dziedzictwo cnoty* (Warsaw: 1996), xvi–xvii.

140 Tyszka-Drozdwoski, "*Alain de Benoist. Ponad lewicą i prawicą*", 46.

Benoist himself emphasises, besides the differentiations inside this current itself, practically all communitarians are characterised by their problematisation of the concept of the citizen being reduced to the role of a consumer and occasional voter, by a common critique of centralism and statist bureaucracy, as well as, perhaps first and foremost, by their belief that the only alternative to a society founded on shared values and a concept of the common good would be either authoritarianism or disintegration.[141]

It bears remembering that de Benoist's anti-liberalism has roots in the Conservative Revolution. This current of thought is one of his most important sources of inspiration.[142] As has already been underscored in the present work, the *Nouvelle Droite* can be seen as a kind of continuation of the German Conservative Revolution, but also as a development of it, and the latter current saw liberalism as the main political enemy.[143] On the matter of their common approach to democracy and liberalism, it bears especially recalling Arthur Moeller van den Bruck[144] and Carl Schmitt,[145] both of whom were exceptionally explicit in emphasising their negative view of liberalism. The Conservative Revolution itself is the subject of a whole book by de Benoist: *Quatre figures de la révolution conservatrice allemande: Werner Sombart, Arthur Moeller van den Bruck, Ernst Niekisch, Oswald Spengler.*[146]

---

141 Alain de Benoist, "*Communautriens vs. libéraux*" in *Critiques — Théoriques*, 446–447.

142 Bar-On, *Where Have All the Fascists Gone?*, 29–30.

143 Bielawski, "*Arthura Moellera van den Brucka konserwatywno-rewolucyjna krytyka liberalizmu*", 186.

144 Alain de Benoist, "Arthur Moeller van den Bruck" [https://s3-eu-west-1.amazonaws.com/alaindebenoist/pdf/arthur_moeller_van_den_bruck.pdf].

145 Alain de Benoist, *Carl Schmitt Today: Terrorism, 'Just' War, and the State of Emergency*, trans. Alexander Jacob (London: Arktos, 2013).

146 Alain de Benoist, *Quatre figures de la révolution conservatrice allemande: Werner Sombart, Arthur Moeller van den Bruck, Ernst Niekisch, Oswald Spengler* (Paris: 2014).

To the above should be supplemented the clear influence of Jean-Jacques Rousseau, whom de Benoist interprets from a somewhat more "right-wing" perspective. Essential here is the link between the idea of direct democracy, anti-liberalism, anti-progressivism, admiration for antiquity, and seeing the geneses of individual rights in social relations rather than in abstract theories. For de Benoist, what is essential in Rousseau is the argument that a people cannot renounce its own sovereignty, which emphatically means that if power is handed over to representatives, then a people ceases to be sovereign: "It is clear [...] that democracy can fully exist only in direct form: the citizen who delegates his right to recognise or reject a given law to a representative, even one he has elected, deprives himself of his own autonomy and uses his freedom only to renounce it."[147]

At the turn of the 1980s-90s, Francis Fukuyama proclaimed his vision of the "end of history",[148] in which he foretold the final triumph of Western liberalism as a universal ideology. Liberal democracy was seen as a "new universal church" in which only the "market liturgy" had effected large schisms.[149] However, the beginning of the 21st century has shown that this American political scientists' predictions have not come true. A serious crisis of liberal democracy is being discussed not only within the academic community, but also in the mainstream press, such as in the *New York Times, The Times, The Financial Times, The Washington Post,* and *The Economist* in English, *Le Figaro* in French, *Frankfurter Allgemeine Zeitung* in German, and *Dziennik Gazeta Prawna* and *Do Rzeczy* in Polish.[150] As Krzysztofek and Szczepański write:

---

147 Alain de Benoist, "*Relire Rousseau*" in *Critiques — Théoriques*, 323.
148 Francis Fukuyama, *The End of History and the Last Man* (New York: Free Press, 1992).
149 Krzysztofek and Szczepański, *Zrozumieć rozwój*, 259.
150 J. Y. Chung, "Globalization and the Crisis of Liberal Democracy: The Political Dynamics of Neoliberalism and Populism", *The Journal of Inequality and Democracy* 2(1) (2019); S. Kubas, "*Globalny nieład demokratyczny — współczesne*

Liberal democracy functioned thanks to a canon: religious and ethical systems whose implantation was the engagement of institutions ensuring responsible socialisation and control through social roles, such as the family, churches, school, the army, and political parties. This was accompanied by the conviction that European values are better. Today this has been laid on the altar of egalitarianism and tolerance. The democracy of tolerance has been suspended in a vacuum. It cannot manage to function effectively in this way.[151]

Or as Yascha Mounk writes:

[...] because people's views exhibit an illiberal tendency and the preferences of the elite remain undemocratic, a conflict emerges between liberalism and democracy. Liberal democracy, a unique mix of individual rights and rule of the people, which has long since characterised the majority of governments in North America and Western Europe, is starting to fall apart. Instead of it, we are observing the development of illiberal democracy, or democracy without rights, and undemocratic liberalism, or rights without democracy.[152]

The above-quoted diagnoses to a certain extent seem to harmonise with de Benoist's analyses. Following Arthur Moeller van den Bruck, this French thinker argues that the essence of democracy is the participation of a people in its fate ("*Demokratie ist Anteilnahme eines Volkes an seinem Schicksal*"). In other words, democracy is founded not on a form of state system or its procedures, but on the participation and

---

perspektywy", *Studia Krytyczne* 5 (2017), 14–47; L. Dorn, "Na Zachodzie alarm. Kończy się świat jaki znamy", *Magazyn TVN24* [https://tvn24.pl/magazyn-tvn24/na-zachodzie-alarm-kon- czy-sie-swiat-jaki-znamy,151,2652]; A. Szahaj, "Nie-demokratyczny kapitalizm", *Dziennik Gazeta Prawna* [https://edgp.ga- zetaprawna.pl/e-wydanie/57254,24-kwietnia-2020/70499,Dziennik-Gazeta-Prawna/718830,Niedemokratyczny-kapitalizm.html]; Alain de Benoist, "*Jak liberalizm uprowadził demokrację*", *Do Rzeczy* [https://dorzeczy.pl/swiat/106566/jak-liberalizm-uprowa-dzil-demokracje.html]

151 Krzysztofek and Szczepański, *Zrozumieć rozwój*, 258.
152 Yascha Mount, "Stracone złudzenia", *Kultura liberalna* [https://kulturaliberalna.pl/2019/09/17/yascha-mounk-lud-kontra-demokracja-ksiazka-wprowadzenie/].

influence of the *demos* on the life of the State.¹⁵³ It is people, not procedures, that are supposed to decide what democracy is. De Benoist argues that liberal democracies have been based on the principle of freedom and the "people's democracies" were based on equality. The organic democracy that he proposes would be based on the principle of fraternity.¹⁵⁴ For the sake of clarifying and ordering his views on democracy, de Benoist presents "ten theses on democracy", which we can summarise thusly:

1. The model of democracy and the fundamental reference point for understanding this term is the system that emerged in antiquity. Our understanding of democracy should be referenced above all to the way in which it was understood by those who first created it.

2. Liberalism and democracy are not synonyms. Democracy is based on the sovereignty of the people, whereas liberalism is based on the rights of the individual. Liberal democracy (representative) implies delegating sovereignty to someone else, the effect of which is the people's abdication of their sovereignty.

3. Democracy should not be confused with the rule of number or the tyranny of the majority. Its basic principle is the affirmation of the people as the holder of political prerogatives. Equality before the law does not imply natural equality — it is only a certain convention that gives individuals the right to participate in governance.

4. Political competence (the capacity to govern) is unrelated to technical competence (specialised knowledge from a given field); it is related to the capacity to make decisions. The principle of technocracy conflicts with the principle of the sovereignty of the people.

---

153 Alain de Benoist, "*Vers une démocratie organique*", *Éléments pour la civilisation européenne* 52 (1985), 34.
154 de Benoist, *Problem of Democracy*, 99.

5. The citizens of a democratic system have equal political rights by virtue of their belonging to one political community (citizenship), not by virtue of alleged, inalienable "human" rights. The foundation of democracy is not abstract "society", but the community of citizens who are heirs to a common history and a shared will to shape the future.

6. The basis of democracy is participation — not the right to vote, general elections, or representation. Democracy is the participation of a people in its fate (as per Moeller van den Bruck). It is not institutions that create democracy, but the participation of the people in institutions that makes democracy. The maximum of democracy is neither maximal freedom nor maximal equality, but maximal participation.

7. The principle of the majority is binding in practice because the unanimity (general will) implied in theory cannot possibly be made into reality. The principle of the majority can be seen as a dogma or technique. The latter yields a relative space for minorities. However, the plurality of opinions should not be confused with a pluralism of values, which is incompatible with the notion of a "people". Pluralism should be secondary to the common good.

8. Contemporary liberal democracy is a degeneration of the idea of democracy: parties act undemocratically, the tyranny of money depraves and corrupts, elected representatives have no motivation to fulfil promises, etc. The media messaging that constitutes the groundwork of elections is standardised and partisan. Political life thus becomes a constant choosing of a lesser evil, hence general elections come to be treated with increasing indifference. The result is political apathy, which itself is a negation of participation and therefore of democracy.

9. Democracy is irreducible to general elections. Democratic procedures need to be reevaluated and revised so that they correspond

to the original spirit of democracy, i.e., so that they strengthen the direct relationship between the people and the government (e.g., through referenda, local and workplace assemblies). The idea of brotherhood should be put above ideas of freedom and equality.

10. Democracy mens rule of the people, that is, the authority and power of the organic community historically shaped within a given political structure (e..g., city, people, empire). If there is no "people", and instead only a collection of atomised individuals, then there is no democracy. Any political system that dilutes and disintegrates organic community is undemocratic.[155]

America: Anti-Europe

From the *Nouvelle Droite*'s perspective, the United States of America is an "anti-Europe". It is such because, from the very beginning, i.e., ever since the "pilgrim fathers", America took shape *in opposition* to Europe.[156] At the ideational sources of America lies not the creation of a new, better Europe, but rather the creation of a New Jerusalem free from Europe's history of errors and distortions. Alain de Benoist writes:

> The Americans did not merely want to break away from Europe. They wanted to establish a society capable of recreating all of mankind. They wanted to create a new Promised Land that would simultaneously become a universal republic. This biblical thread consists the *leitmotiv* of all of American history since the time of the Founding Fathers.[157]

In connection with the fact that the American people took shape out of individuals from different ethnic soils, creating a citizenship

---

155 Ibid, 100–103.

156 O'Meara, *New Culture, New Right*, 176; Alain de Benoist, "*L'Amérique*" in *Critiques — Théoriques*, 141.

157 de Benoist, "*L'Amérique*" in *Critiques — Théoriques*, 142.

independent of ethnos meant that even removing cultural particularisms in the private sphere became a necessity. This fit very well with the individualist philosophy of the Founding Fathers. In the end, de Benoist argues, it was in America that a society made up of individuals, rather than social groups, was constituted for the first time.[158]

From the latter condition also arises Americans' distance from history. After all, reaching into history always leads them back to the European roots from which they wanted to cut themselves off. Thus, at the very origins of America stood the desire to create a new society from scratch, one that could then turn to lead the rebirth of all of humanity and liberate mankind from sin.[159] The first Puritan immigrants saw themselves as chosen by God to be the inhabitants of the new Promised Land. De Benoist remarks: "It was this Puritan theology of 'Providence' that inspired the doctrine of 'Manifest Destiny': if God has chosen Americans, then they thereby have the right to convert other peoples to their model."[160]

Although the Christian religion has played and still plays an essential role in American public life,[161] it has little in common with the European experience of Christianity. In contrast to the state of European Catholicism or Lutheranism, Calvinist Puritanism was supposed to purge Christianity of the pagan elements that had settled in its rich, transcendent and sacred robes and reduced Christian religiosity to moral imperatives. In other words, American Christianity sought to rid itself of the specifically European layer of aesthetics and symbolism, and thereby cut itself off from the European spirit.[162] American Christianity draws abundantly from the Old Testament, especially given the predominant conviction that Americans have been chosen by

---

158 Ibid.
159 Ibid.
160 Ibid., 143.
161 Tomislav Sunic, *Homo Americanus: Child of the Postmodern Age* (London: Arktos, 2018), 109–144.
162 Ibid., 114.

Providence to be the model for other nations. The colonial community in Massachusetts was supposed to be a result of a new Covenant between God and his chosen people on the new Promised Land, like the old one with the biblical people of Israel. Their religiosity thus turned "outwards", i.e., it concentrated on labor in this world more than on the inner life, as God's grace is evident in the material successes one achieves.[163] Comparing Christian religiosity in Europe and the United States, Michael O'Meara argues that while the first fits into the first function of Dumézil's trifunctional ideology (with its strong state and Church), the latter fits into the third function (with its concentration on the material sphere of commerce).[164] Tomislav Sunic, for his part, defines the two pillars of Americanism as "the Bible and business".[165] In other words, Americans turned the traditional, European hierarchy of values upside down, one example of which would be the higher social position of the "semi-illiterate basketball player" over the classical philologist.[166]

De Benoist points out that the American political system is based on the philosophy of the Enlightenment, but filtered through Puritanism. The United States is a state based on the contractual theory of governance, which puts the emphasis on individual freedom and free commerce. For the Founding Fathers of America, the *raison d'être* of government was first and foremost to guarantee inalienable rights to individuals who are created equal. Thus, the state is not an emanation of the people or nation supposed to serve the realisation of the people's

---

163 O'Meara, *New Culture, New Right*, 177–178.

164 Ibid., 179.

165 Sunic, *Homo Americanus*, 117.

166 O'Meara, *New Culture, New Right*, 183: "The Puritan/liberal notion that an individual's merit is synonymous with his material success is alien to the European spirit: the aristocrat, whose standards still inspire, values that which does not have a price. The priest, the magistrate, the scholar, the artist, the man of letters — all of whom figured in the upper ranks of European society (at least until a generation ago) — are formed by spirit, not industry, commerce, or intellectual specialization."

destiny, but is *cosmopolis*, a state in which every individual is a potential citizen. The American political system is based on rationalistic premises, which means that the individual is the main reference point, not the nation, tradition, or common history.[167] The New World was supposed to be built "from zero" and based on the commandments of the Bible. This forms a consensus which is never to be doubted by any political faction. Moreover, this creates what Alexis de Tocqueville described as political and cultural monotony throughout the United States of America.[168] At the same time, Americans are supposed to see this consensus as the ideal worth imitating for the whole world.

From the *Nouvelle Droite*'s perspective, the United States is the crystallisation of liberal modernity. Nowhere else have the principles of the Enlightenment — rationalism, egalitarianism, individualism, universalism, economism, the theory of progress — been implemented so consequently. Based on these liberal-individualist and rationalist foundations, the American conception of politics proclaims the supremacy of the private over the public and civil society over political life, while politics itself, or "political nature" as such (including the institution of the state), is treated with suspicion and is replaced by morality and the economy. Americans want to free themselves from history — the "end of history" anticipated and announced by Francis Fukuyama is a testimony to this. In contrast to the traditional European understanding of the State as an emanation of the will of the people and a tool for realising the people's destiny, American thought conceives of the state nomocratically, which means that the political is replaced by the legal.[169] American jurisprudence treats law as if it were the expression of reason itself, completely impartial and independent of any cultural background.[170]

---

167 Ibid., 184–185.
168 de Benoist, "*L'Amérique*" in *Critiques — Théoriques*, 142.
169 O'Meara, *New Culture, New Right*, 186.
170 Ibid., 187: "[The American] nomocratic state accordingly reduces the political to the judicial. But once constitutional principles are substituted for a political

In de Benoist's opinion, this Puritanical-Enlightenment ideological mixture is also the cause of the rather peculiar approach of American foreign policy, which can be summarised as "what is good for America is good for the rest of the world". This is simultaneously the reason for Americans' ignorance of the rest of the world: "For Americans, the external world simply does not exist or does not exist until it is is Americanised."[171] Americans are so deeply convinced of the exceptionalness of their country that they see no need to be interested in the outside world.

The above-mentioned "nomocratic flight from the political" has monumental consequences in the American approach to war: war is seen not simply as an extension of politics, or even a temporary suspension of the rule of law, but as something extraordinarily unnatural.[172] Americans ordinarily cannot accept that conflict is an inherent part of life and that, in an extreme situation, it is violence, not reason, that settles a dispute. In connection with accepting this fact, European tradition provided for certain limitations to waging wars, the aim of wars being to pacify an opponent, not to utterly destroy him.[173] In contrast, Americans fight in the name of "fighting evil itself", and hence their opponent is not understood to be a rival on the other side of the barricades, but as embodied Evil which must be liquidated.[174] [175] This

---

concept of its people's will and individual rights take precedent over communal norms, the state's main function becomes the arbitration of domestic conflicts on the basis of 'the supreme law of the land' — not the defense of a specific national ontology grounded in tradition and culture."

171   de Benoist, *"L'Amérique"* in *Critiques — Théoriques*, 144.
172   O'Meara, *New Culture, New Right*, 188.
173   Ibid., 189.
174   Ibid.
175   De Benoist cites as examples the Soviet Union being termed the 'Evil Empire' and the US policy of genocide against the Indians, the effect of which was the death of around 10 million indigenous Americans. See de Benoist, *"L'Amérique"* in *Critiques — Théoriques*, 151.

is seen as a reflection of their "Hebraic-Puritan" conviction as to their chosenness and mission.[176]

Yet, de Benoist concludes: "The truth is that the United States, contrary to what they preach, is not a universal model. It is a particular model, 'their' model, one which they push to impose upon the whole world, and this is not the same thing [as a universal model]."[177]

In the *Nouvelle Droite*'s eyes, America is an extreme version of modern Western civilisation — insofar as the modern West is seen, as the *Nouvelle Droite* does, as a crystallisation of liberal modernity based on the premises of the Enlightenment. At the same time, the *Nouvelle Droite* underscores the clear distinction between the West and Europe, where the term "West" is to be understood as Europe being in an asymmetrical, non-sovereign relationship with the United States, and "Europe" in the proper sense of the word is what they postulate to be the authentic Europe — Europe based on its own identity and axiology, its own cultural formations, and free from American (which means liberal) hegemony.

The strong anti-Americanism present in de Benoist's thought as well as the *Nouvelle Droite* in general is multidimensional. Besides the anti-Christianity that is typical of the *Nouvelle Droite*'s thought, we can enumerate two of this anti-Americanism's fundamental sources: (1) counter-Enlightenment (counter-revolutionary) thought and (2) French culture.

It bears pointing out that anti-Americanism is essentially nothing new in European conservative and right-wing thought. It has deep historical roots.[178] America, supposed to be a crystallisation of the ideas of the Enlightenment, was already made into the subject of critique in Europe by the thinkers of Romanticism who wanted to reverse the effects of the rational "disenchantment" of the world. This was most

---

176 O'Meara, *New Culture, New Right*, 188–189.

177 de Benoist, "*L'Amérique*" in *Critiques — Théoriques*, 152.

178 L. Nowak, "*Kontrooświeceniowe korzenie antyamerykanizmu*", *Studia Politologiczne* 14 (2009).

visible of all in German culture, where critiquing Enlightenment ideas led to questioning Germany's belonging to the West.[179] Thus arose the concept of *Sonderweg*, or the idea of Germany's special path of development divergent from the Western track followed by the English or the French.

Johann Gottfried Herder, in turn, was the author of the distinction between *Kultur* and *Zivilisation* later adopted by Oswald Spengler. "Culture" is like the blood of an organism: it is the stream of moral energy that upholds the vitality of social ties. The German Romantics saw culture as the spiritual energy that defines a people and manifests itself in the people's beliefs and customs. "Civilisation", in turn, describes the external layer composed of customs, law, and specialised technical knowledge. Culture is typical of "young", dynamic peoples who, although they are not (yet) refined, are full of youthful energy. "Civilised" peoples, on the other hand, are characterised by a subtle, refined culture, but also by a certain tiredness, weariness, boredom, and spiritual "oldness". The German Romantics described themselves as a *Kulturnation* in contrast to the "old" Western nations.

In light of this vision, America is seen as ambivalent. On the one hand, it is a young nation, energetic and free from the burden of tradition. On the other hand, it exhibits many of the typical symptoms of bourgeois *Zivilisation*, such as utilitarianism, superficiality, "practicalism", materialism, etc. Americans are also seen as not being an authentic national community, as only a collection of people without a fatherland who do not share any common origin, language, memory, culture, history, etc. The only thing that connects them is the utilitarian, rational contract based on the pursuit of interests. In other words, Americans are fused together not by "blood", but by calculation — they are not a people or nation *sensu stricto*, but rather a collectivity of interests.

---

[179] Ibid., 141. Ernst Niekisch, *"Prawo Poczdamu"* in W. Kunicki (ed.), *Rewolucja konserwatywna w Niemczech 1918–1933* (Poznań: 1999), 198; Bielawski, *"Arthura Moellera van den Brucka konserwatywno-rewolucyjna krytyka liberalizmu"*, 194

The current of so-called cultural pessimism that emerged in Germany in the 19th-20th centuries restarted and sharpened the old negative image of America. Special attention here should be paid to the representatives of the Weimar Cultural Revolution, such as Oswald Spengler, Ernst Jünger, and Arthur Moeller van den Bruck. Besides them, it is worth recalling Friedrich Nietzsche and Martin Heidegger. All of these thinkers saw in Americanism a threat to (higher) European and especially German culture.[180] Each of these thinkers, as already mentioned, became a source of inspiration for Alain de Benoist.

Besides German thought, we can also mention traditionalist, counter-revolutionary thinkers from the Romance world, such as Joseph de Maistre and Julius Evola. The former doubted the possibility of creating a nation, or any greater institution, "out of ink" — such is the work of many generations, for which there is no "shortcut" by one-off, rational legislation.[181] Evola described Americans as characterised by a spiritual vacuum, thoughtless conformism, vulgarity, materialism, and as reducing human existence to economic interests.[182]

In addition to the principal causes rooted in philosophical thought, it is necessary to mention the cultural context, namely, the dislike for the United States that is typical of and to this day remains strong in French society.[183] Philippe Roger holds that the origins of anti-Americanism in France can be seen in the 19th century, in the "aesthetic and intellectual" outlook of the intelligentsia, which saw Americans as mediocre, backwards, and petty-bourgeois. It was at this time that

---

180 Nowak, "*Kontrooświeceniowe korzenie antyamerykanizmu*", passim.
181 Joseph de Maistre, "*Nicość republiki francuskiej*" in J. Trybusiewicz (ed.), *De Maistre*, 135–136.
182 Julius Evola, "American Civilization" [https://www.juliusevola.com/julius_evola/writings/reader.html?text=american_civilization.txt].
183 M. Lakomy, "*Czynnik kulturowy w relacjach francusko-amerykańskich*", *Horyzonty Polityki* 1(1) (2010), 39–48; Philippe Roger, "*Généalogie de l'antiaméricanisme français: Entretien avec Philippe Roger*", *Esprit* 287(8/9) (2002), 176–194.

the ethnocultural stereotype of "Yankees" took shape in France, a stereotype that was supposed to describe allegedly English character traits, such as miserliness, greed, business flair, and dishonesty. This stereotype, which generalised and exaggerated "Anglo-Saxon" traits, was quite lively in popular writing and French literature of the time. Of course, the many-centuries-long English-French rivalry was a factor here.

Mirosław Lakomy sees the beginning of anti-Americanism in the first large-scale encounter between the two nations in 1917–1918, when two million American soldiers sailed to France. The initially warm French attitude towards the Americans changed after more or less one year, when the deep cultural differences between the two nations made themselves known. Also of significance were the disputes that arose during the war as well as the discussions intending to establish the new, post-WWI order. A similar situation took place around the end of the Second World War, when General Charles de Gaulle disagreed with President Roosevelt on the shape of postwar France. Traces were also left by decades of dependence on material aid from the United States, which must have been embarrassing for the French, who were used to being a great power. According to public opinion polls, in 1957 only 27% of Frenchmen had a positive opinion of the US.[184] Dislike for Americans on the part of French society also found reflection in political anti-Americanism, which was exhibited unanimously (albeit for different reasons) by virtually every French political faction, left, right, and center.

Anti-American sentiments in France do not seem to have lessened around the turn of the 20th-21st centuries, as studies conducted by the French-American Foundation in 2000 seem to confirm. According to Stanley Hoffman, the reasons for anti-Americanism in contemporary France include Frenchmen's critical approach to the American model of a multicultural society, American mass culture, American social

---

184 Lakomy, "*Czynnik kulturowy w relacjach francusko-amerykańskich*", 42.

ethics based on free commerce, individualism, the central role of money, American capitalism's lack of any adequate social policy, and America's "imperial" foreign policy.[185] [186]

Besides the fact that both countries regard themselves as the leading representatives of universalist values (democracy, freedom, human rights, etc.), and besides both countries' conviction as to their exceptionalness and to the need to messianistically spread their civilisational achievements everywhere, the actual role of the promoter of these values looks altogether different in these countries' practices. Whereas France focuses on diplomatic actions, the United States often resorts to coercive solutions. Besides the nominally similar values that these states promote, the French attach incomparably greater importance to the concept of equality, whereas Americans insist above all on freedom.

The above-mentioned conflict between "two universalisms" finds expression not only in foreign policy, but also in the economic sphere. While the American economic system is based on affirming the logic of the market, the central role of money, and restricting the role of the state to being a "night watchman" (which also causes significant social inequalities), the French economic model asserts the central role of the state in ensuring citizens' equality and social protection in the name of solidarity and equalising chances. It is also worth adding that French society views "chasing after money" as a rather distasteful and unpleasant affair, instead placing greater importance on other spheres of life, such as art.

Krzysztof and Szczepański write:

> One simple consequence of the civilisational triumph of America is, according to the common belief, Americanisation. The cultural influence of the US is enormous, and dozens of arguments can be waged around this

---

185 Ibid., 43.

186 It is striking that practically all of the these criticisms of the US are repeated in de Benoist's writings.

thesis. [...] Americans really want to spread their culture on the world scale, a culture which turns its recipients into its consumers, because they want to spread the culture of the market and the open society across the world, without which there is no '*pax americana*' — and hence no control. Americans' dream is for this type of consumption of culture to take over all people [...] and give them a popular life philosophy. In the strategic sense, this is more significant than any military or economic arms.[187]

This is precisely what Alain de Benoist is against. He opposes the unipolar "Jacobinisation" of international relations, especially considering how the convergent trajectory of globalisation leads to Europe's dependence on America and its use on a fundamentally "anti-European" axiology. De Benoist rejects Euro-Atlanticism, of course. Instead, he proposes that Europe draw closer to Russia[188] and establish an alliance with the Third World against American hegemony.[189]

Modernity: Secularised Christianity

Alain de Benoist writes:

> The world has never been as Judeo-Christian as it is today. The moral God is dead, but the values he has bequeathed are more present than ever... God is dead, but the modern world continues to claim him as its authority, precisely because it cannot and does not *want* to rid itself of his carcass.[190]

At the same time, as de Benoist notes, the Christian religion is experiencing a deep crisis in Western Europe. It has been reduced to merely one possible opinion among others and is no longer the fundamental reference point as an institution regulating social life. But this

---

187 Krzysztofek and Szczepański, *Zrozumieć rozwój*, 259–260.
188 Alain de Benoist, "*Russie, Europe, même combat!*", *Éléments pour la civilisation européenne* (2009). Before the collapse of the USSR, GRECEists put forth a policy of maintaining equal distance from both liberal America and communist Russia.
189 See de Benoist, *Europe, Tiers monde — même combat*.
190 de Benoist, *On Being a Pagan*, 196.

does not at all mean that Christianity has disappeared. It still exerts a colossal influence, only in a secular form. All of the component elements of modernity enumerated in this chapter (human rights, the idea of progress, liberalism, etc.) have their roots in Christianity. The sources of modernity lie in secularised Christian metaphysics. In other words, what the Christian religion has lost on the level of dogmas, it has gained on the ideological level. Individualism, egalitarianism, progressivism, and universalism — all of these elements are inherited by modernity from Christianity. Secularisation is not only the loss of the Church's influence or religious indifference, but the transplanting of Judeo-Christian content and structures into the socio-cultural sphere.[191] Even if the majority of people in Europe no longer believe in the Christian God or no longer regularly go to church, there still persists the homogenising-uniformising, monotheistic-universalist, totalitario-genic way of thinking that destroyed the feeling of tolerance once characteristic of Europeans.[192] Alain de Benoist does not argue that totalitarianism arose directly out of Christianity, but the latter religion prepared the soil for it with religious intolerance that was unprecedented in the history of Europe. Paganism, to the contrary, recognised a world of diverse confessions among different peoples. It was with Christianity that there appeared the notions of absolute good and evil, one and only one god, and all the dogmas, heresies, inquisitions, and religious wars. Christianity's aspiration was to convert the whole of humanity to its model.[193]

The situation is analogous with modernity, which strives for global uniformity. Consequently, it is predisposed antagonistically towards all collective identities which hinder its desire for a homogenous humanity ("neither Jew nor Greek").[194] The crisis of identity that has plagued

---

191 de Benoist and Molnar, *Éclipse du sacré*, 195.
192 Sunic, "*Wywiad z Tomislavem Suniciem*", 39.
193 Sylvain, "Interview with Alain de Benoist", 76–77.
194 de Benoist, "*Nowoczesność jako wróg tożsamości*", 9.

Europe for 1,500 years has not been solved, since the Judeo-Christian conceptual cliches have remained intact despite secularisation. Modern man, like Christian man, is characterised by a predisposition to rejecting the Other, whom he is incapable of confronting positively. In connection with this, he strives to "convert" him. All differences are to be levelled (the "ideology of the same"), and all individuals torn from their traditional communities. The world composed of different cultures is supposed to be transformed into a uniform global market.

The driving force of modernity and its crystallisation was global capitalism. It functions as a cultural bulldozer — it must flatten down everyone into uniform consumers. Individuals are uprooted from their native cultures for the sake of becoming *Homo oeconomicus*, the new type of man that modernity brings into history. This type of man is uprooted, a calculating merchant, and his sole *raison d'être* is to accumulate capital. For him, the totality of social relations boils down to market relations.

The worldview of the *Nouvelle Droite* recognises the value of diversity (the existence and keeping of cultural differences), which it sees as constituting the richness of the world ("political polytheism").[195] For this same reason, the *Nouvelle Droite* opposes any ideas that want to destroy this diversity ("political monotheism"): "Modernity will not be transcended by returning to the past, but by means of certain premodern values in a decisively postmodern dimension. It is only at the price of such a radical restructuring that anomie and contemporary nihilism will be exorcised."[196]

This "restructuring" is what lies at the heart of the founding of the *Nouvelle Droite* as a movement which puts forth an idea: the idea of endeavouring to establish a positive connection with a premodern (pre-monotheistic, Indo-European, polytheistic) axiology which can serve as the basis for a renaissance of European civilisation.

---

195 Ibid., 11.

196 de Benoist and Champetier, "Manifesto", in Sunic, *Against Democracy and Equality*, 212.

CHAPTER VI

THE *NOUVELLE DROITE* AND ISLAM

THE *Nouvelle Droite*'s relation to Islam is a multi-leveled and complex topic in the very least because it is not possible to speak of Islam in complete separation from the issue of the phenomenon of mass immigration of Muslim populations to Europe around the turn of the 20th-21st centuries. By the dint of affairs, a politically leaning intellectual movement will not look at Islam in a purely academic and abstract way. It bears starting from the fact that Islam is seen in diverse ways within the *Nouvelle Droite sensu largo*. GRECE with Alain de Benoist at the head does not devote excessive attention to Islam, which it treats as a rather secondary question. It is an entirely different case in the later thought of Guillaume Faye (as well as Pierre Vial), who regards this religion as a fundamental problem.

The works of the *Nouvelle Droite sensu stricto* do not come around to dwelling on the topic of Islam as such. This religion is not to be found in the centre of GRECE's interests. Faye only laconically referred to this question in 1985 when he said: "We will not judge the value of Islam 'itself'."[1] In connection with the fact that Islam is, like Christianity, a monotheistic, universalistic religion which is "close to the Judeo-Christian project of unifying the Earth", the *Nouvelle Droite* treats Islam with certain reservations. However, taking into account the fact that the "Arab-Islamic awakening" represented a chance for

---

1 Guillaume Faye, "*Pour une alliance euro-arabe*", *Éléments pour la civilisation européenne* 53 (1985), 15.

a "serious perturbation" of the Atlanticist-Communist bipolarity and posed a hindrance to the monolithicisation of the whole world along the Western model, then it is an objectively positive factor.[2] Alain de Benoist framed this matter in a similar way when he said that the awakening of Islam is more of a hope than a threat.[3] Let us recall that the *Nouvelle Droite* has a negative stance towards Western modernity, and the Arab world, united under the standard of Islam, could act as a dam upon the Western monolithicising model, which wants to turn the whole world into one big market with a motley collection of consumers instead of a diversity of peoples and cultures. In de Benoist's eyes, only Islam can unite the Arab world and protect the region's culture from forced Westernisation, the prime mover of whose modern-universalising tendency is the United States. In line with the doctrine of right-wing Third-Worldism, de Benoist as well as Faye postulated a Euro-Arab alliance: "We reject, in the name of the rights of peoples to remain who they are, nostalgia for the Battle of Poitiers as well as advocates of the Tower of Babel."[4] Pierre Vial, for his part, draws attention to how the Islamic revolution in Iran, of which he speaks with a certain respect, was against the Westernisation pursued by the Shah.[5]

De Benoist treats the thesis of the "clash of civilisations" advanced by Samuel Huntington with far-reaching reservations. He regards it as a reformulation of the old motif of conflict between North and South, as well as the conflict between modernity and traditional social forms.[6] Significantly more essential than strictly religious issues is

---

2   Ibid.
3   Robert de Herte (Alain de Benoist), "*Le réveil de l'Islam*", *Éléments pour la civilisation européenne* 53 (1985), 2.
4   Ibid.
5   P. Vial, "*L'intégrisme musulman: une vraie révolution culturelle*", *Éléments pour la civilisation européenne* 48–49 (1983–1984), 77.
6   Alain de Benoist, "*Un débat sur le 'choc des civilisations'* " in *C'est-à-dire*, vol. 2, 83.

the demographic-economic question, that is, the issue of mass migration of the Afro-Maghreb population to Europe, especially to France. On this issue, the *Nouvelle Droite* holds an unambiguously negative stance. De Benoist called immigration the "reserve army of capital", which to a great extent speaks for itself. Immigration is supposed to cause, among other things, wage dumping, the first victim of which is the local workforce. Another problem is the fact that immigration is too fast and is not controlled in any way. The French state did not create a corresponding integration model. The "Jacobin" model, which sees masses of immigrants as only a collection of individuals who are supposed to assimilate into European society and renounce their native cultures, has failed the test. The young generation of immigrants is, on the one hand, cut off from the local culture; on the other hand, they do not put down roots in European society for economic reasons (significantly worse status) as well as ethnic reasons (cultural distance). The effect is "ethnic apartheid".[7] For these reasons, immigration gives rise to a large amount of social frustration, whose symptoms are, among other things, unrest and crime committed by the young descendants of immigrants who do not see any prospects for themselves. In de Benoist's opinion, what is important is that such unrest does not have a religious background. For such young people, Islam is only a kind of substitute identity. The fact of the matter is that Islam is not the cause for unrest and riots.

In the loud debate over the Muslim women's right to wear Islamic headscarves in public places, de Benoist advocates the permissibility of such practices.[8] The French thinker is opposed to the aggressive secularisation that arises out of Jacobin republican formalism, which demands that Muslim students cut themselves off from their culture and identity. He believes that secularism should recognise all beliefs instead of rejecting them *en bloc*. Secularism is supposed to be based

---

7   Alain de Benoist, "*Les émeutes des banlieues*" in *C'est-à-dire*, vol. 2, 66.
8   Alain de Benoist, "*Foulard islamique et laïcité*" in *C'est-à-dire*, vol. 2, 49.

on neutrality, not hostility. De Benoist assesses the law banning Islamic headscarves as being extraordinarily intolerant and excessively invasive of conscience. In his opinion, it would lead to "school apartheid".[9] According to de Benoist, this whole dispute is a substitute war arising out of virtually the entire political class's reluctance to raise and consider the fundamental problem that is immigration. Like the majority of Frenchmen, de Benoist is aware that immigrants of Afro-Maghreb origin will not leave France en masse and that assimilation policy has been a fiasco. He believes that such immigrants have the right for the symbols of their cultural identity to be visible in the public sphere. In turn, when it comes to caricature cartoons of Muhammad, he stands for the right to publish such, although he does not believe such to be prudent or necessary.[10]

However, not all members of the *Nouvelle Droite* share de Benoist's opinion. In his later years, after leaving GRECE in 1986, Guillaume Faye made a 180-degree turn in his views, as is expressed in his works *La colonisation de l'Europe* [*The Colonisation of Europe*] (2000) and *Comprendre l'islam* [*Understanding Islam*] (2015). The New Right's orthodoxy says that liberalism and the US are the main enemy of Europe. For Faye, in turn, Islam has taken the place of liberalism. He proclaims such from the standpoint that Islam is a religion that is by its very nature aggressive, rigid, totalitarian, and has an explicitly conquistadorian zeal. He rejects all of this religion's claims to being peaceful, which he regards as ordinary propaganda intended to lull the vigilance of its opponents. He sees a clash between the West and the Islamic world as inevitable, which fully fits in with Samuel Huntington's schema of the "clash of civilisations". Faye does not even try to look at the Muslim religion objectively. He is consciously partisan.[11] He puts forth four fundamental theses on Islam:

---

9   Ibid., 50.
10 Alain de Benoist, "*Les caricatures de Mahomet*" in *C'est-à-dire*, vol. 2, 70.
11 Guillaume Faye, *Understanding Islam*, trans. Roger Adwan (London: Arktos, 2016), ix: "This criticism of Islam does not stem from a Judeo-Christian

1. Islam is colonising Europe;
2. Islam is by its very nature totalitarian;
3. There is no difference between Islam and "Islamism" (radical political Islam);
4. Islam is incompatible with European culture.

Faye writes:

> Despite its divergences, internal struggles and schisms, Islam has, ever since the 7th century, embodied one whole and represented a global threat, regardless of the conflict between the Sunnis and Shiites. Its utopian goal is to conquer all continents. Unlike Christianity, whose universalistic essence rests (or rested, rather) upon the world's *spiritual* conversion, Islam's ambition is none other than the religious, ideological and political *conquest* of our planet, in an effort to form a single unified ensemble abiding by the same Law, a universal caliphate [...].[12]

Hence, Faye believes that we are presently dealing with an "anthropological disfiguring", a deep change in the ethnic substrate of France.[13] This is how he assesses the relatively large amount of immigrants, mainly of Afro-Maghreb origin, and their constant influx. He estimates the number of immigrants to be at 5–8 million, not counting illegal immigrants and citizens of France who are not of European origin but who have been "designated" French on the basis of *ius soli*.[14] By the end of the 20th century, according to the figure indicated by the President of the National Institute for Demographic Studies (INED),

---

perspective nor that of any other religion, nor is it due to an atheistic mental position or one's ideological belonging. My reflection is a personal one, the only difference being that I am inspired by the principles of Aristotelian thought, namely experience, common sense and balance."

12 Ibid., 245.
13 Guillaume Faye, *The Colonisation of Europe*, trans. Roger Adwan (London: Arktos, 2016), 1.
14 Ibid., 3.

Jean-Claude Barreau, around 100,000 immigrants were arriving in France each year. In 1997, the INED estimated that around 12 million citizens of non-French origin live in France, which is around 20% of the country's population.[15] The number of naturalisations is increasing (45,000 in 1987, 73,000 in 1993), to which should be added the descendants of immigrants who are legally French by being born on the country's territory.[16] In addition, Faye claims that around 30% of children born in France are born in Afro-Maghreb families of first- or second-generation immigrants, and 11% of marriages are ethnically mixed, the woman being of European origin.[17] For the author of *The Colonisation of Europe*, the assessment is clear: "Europe is undergoing a demographic and ethno-cultural tragedy, one that is concealed by the fragile screen of economic illusions."[18] The problem, however, is not the quantity of immigrants, but the fact that they retain their culture, customs, language, religion, and historical memory.[19] In connection with this, Faye interprets mass immigration as a kind of colonisation. The difference between the old form of colonisation carried out by Europeans is that the latter was colonisation "from above" and brought civilisation, whereas Islamic colonisation is "from below" and, instead of civilisation, brings primitivisation.[20] According to Faye, complicit in this procedure are the "traitorous" French elites who "collaborate" with the enemy and uphold a pro-immigrant position which is rooted in moral blackmail and "ethnomasochism",[21] or hate for one's own culture

---

15 Ibid. According to the 2018 report of the *Institut national de la statistique et des études économiques*, the total population of France was approximately 67 million.

16 Ibid., 4.

17 Ibid., 5.

18 Ibid., 5.

19 Ibid., 11

20 Ibid., 12.

21 The conservative philosopher Roger Scruton used the term "oikophobia" in a similar context. See K. Brzechczyn, "*Patriotyzm — nacjonalizm — ojkofobia w*

and heritage.²² French Muslims supposedly call such unproblematic colonisation a "miracle from Allah".²³

Generally speaking, Islam divides the world into two zones: *dar al-islam* (the zone of peace in which Islam is dominant) and *dar al-harb* (the zone of war).²⁴ In Faye's perspective, these terms are not as much spatial as they are temporal, which means that they refer to a given region's stage of Islamisation. Faye lists three stages in the colonisation of Europe:

1. *Dar al-suhl* (the stage of truce) is the phase of relative peace in which actions are undertaken to gradually settle a Muslim population in the area.

2. *Dar al-harb* (the stage of war) is the phase in which decisive steps are taken: in the name of fighting alleged discrimination and Islamophobia, there follows an escalation of demands, rights, and privileges, accompanied by anti-discriminational, moral blackmail as well as active aggression and attacks intended to intimidate.

3. *Dar al-islam* (the stage of Islam): any opposition is pacified; the "*pax islamica*" ensues.²⁵

Faye concludes: "Since Islam literally means 'submission' and advocates the *jihad*, the holy war, will it not bring an end to all conflicts once it has achieved final victory and imposed global submission, thus leading to peace? Therefore ... Islam means peace!"²⁶

It is significant that Faye regards Islam as a religion that is "totalitarian" in character. He judges it to be such because Islam fuses faith

---

myśli Rogera Scrutona", *Przegląd Filozoficzny — Nowa Seria* 1(113) (2020), 51–62.
22 Faye, *Understanding Islam*, 100.
23 Ibid., 52.
24 M. Ruthann, *Islam: A Very Short Introduction* (New York: 1997), 119–120.
25 Faye, *Understanding Islam*, 52.
26 Ibid., 18.

and law, religion and politics — all spheres are connected into a single, rigid system. The individual does not count and is of no significance. The only thing that matters is the *umma*. Faye compares this to the Marxist "proletariat", highlighting the similarity between Islam and Communism as well as Nazism.[27] All three of these systems have an aggressive, totalitarian, collectivistic character that does not take the individual human into account. They are also characterised by a moral relativism (in the case of Islam, morality is only in force within the *umma*). Non-Muslims are treated worse, i.e., morality applies to them only to a limited extent. In the final analysis, "idolaters" must choose between adopting Islam or death. Faye summates: "The very essence of Islam lies in its aggressive and boundless expansion, along with an ethic of violence, intolerance, and exclusion involving a belief in the inferiority of both women and disbelievers, the practice of legal murder, and more. All this is stated in the Qur'an [...]."[28]

To support his theses, Faye refers to the example of the Prophet Muhammad, the moral model for all Muslims. He describes him as a preacher of commands, the voice of a god, a political conspirator, a brutal warrior, and an autocratic leader with almost unlimited power. Muhammad, according to Faye, personifies "a cynical and uncompromising morality in the expansion of Islam".[29] Autocracy, anti-Semitism, and moral relativism — Islam shares all of these traits with Nazism.[30] One religion, one law, one leader — this is the schema of Islam. Thus, Faye sees in the example of Muhammad the source of Islam's politico-religious totalitarianism.[31] According to him, this schema has been in force throughout the whole history of Islam, and remains in place to this day.

---

27 Ibid., 31.
28 Faye, *Colonisation of Europe*, 113.
29 Faye, *Understanding Islam*, 8.
30 Ibid., 21.
31 Ibid., 8.

To summarise, Faye sees the Muslim religion as a totalitarian system *par excellence*. The following traits are decisive in this direction: (a) a doctrine that uniformises everything, (b) a fusion of faith and law, (c) the criminalisation or discrimination of infidels, (d) an intention to dominate all of mankind through jihad, (e) a social life that is entirely innervated by the official religion, (f) a prohibition on all publications and studies which contradict the Quranic truth, (g) a will to make social life homogenous by authoritarian means, (h) a monopoly of power and authority — the Caliph, (i) idealising and sacralising Quranic dogmatism, (j) the use of holy scripture as an absolute reference point, (k) aggressive rhetoric calling for the extermination of internal as well as external opposition.[32]

If we understand the term "Islam" to mean a religion, and "Islamism" an integral political system, then in Faye's opinion, we are speaking of one and the same. Any differences boil down to a matter of tactics. From the Islamic perspective, generally speaking, the concept of a religion-less state is incomprehensible.[33] With reference to the Aristotelian theory of essence, Faye underscores that upon the moment a religion or secular doctrine becomes explicitly formulated, there is the high chance that its premises can be implemented in full. Faye concludes that since totalitarian tendencies are present in the very premises of Islam, there is nor reason to doubt that Islam as such, in and of itself, is totalitarian.[34] Moderate representatives are not representative of the doctrine, for they present only the "watered-down" version. In the case of an epidemic, Faye remarks, there are people who

---

32 Ibid., 25–27.

33 Nicholas Birch, "'Islamism is an interpretation of Islam in step with the modern world': An Interview with Professor Ismail Kara", *New Age Islam* (18 July 2010) [https://www.newageislam.com/interview/islamism-interpretation-islam-step-with/d/3327]; Republished in Polish as: Ismail Kara, "*Islamizm kontra islam*", interview by Nicholas Birch, *Znak* (2011) [https://www.miesiecznik.znak.com.pl/6692011-nicholas-birch-islamizm-kontra-islam/].

34 Faye, *Understanding Islam*, 47.

are less or more affected by the virus (and they can exhibit different symptoms), but this says nothing about the virus itself.[35] For Faye, moderate Islam is nothing other than a smoke screen — and it is very difficult to the moderate in the case of such a strict, rigid system. Faye concludes that a moderate Muslim is either a hypocrite or someone living a delusion. Only the naive can believe in a "secular", rational, moderate Islam. In Faye's opinion, believing that Islam could take a path similar to that of Christianity, stepping back from totalitarian zeal and intolerance, is a fundamental mistake:

> Through its open dogmatism, its lack of Faustian spirit, its fundamental negation of humanism (which is to be understood as the autonomy of human will) in favour of absolute submission to God, its extreme rigidity regarding both obligations and social prohibitions, its theocratic merging of civil society, political state, and religion, its absolute monotheism, as well as its profound reluctance to- wards allowing free artistic and scientific creation, Islam is irreconcilable with traditional European mental traits, which are all fundamentally polytheistic.[36]

Faye calls into doubt any chances of an eventual "Europeanisation" of Islam. In his conviction, Islam is too implacable and uncompromising to adjust to European standards and fit into a secularised public space. This is not a matter of the "polytheistic aspect" of European culture alone. The mistake, Faye argues, lies in perceiving any symmetry between Islam and Christianity: unlike insidious Islam,[37] Christianity continued the European traditions of honour and integrity that were present since ancient times. Also essential are the differences

---

35 Ibid.
36 Faye, *Colonisation of Europe*, 107–108.
37 Guillaume Faye, "The Third World War is About to Begin: An Interview with Guillaume Faye" in Michael O'Meara, *Guillaume Faye and the Battle of Europe* (London: Arktos, 2019), 66: "It is often forgotten that Islam is deceptive on principle. The Koran says that it is perfectly permissible to lie in certain circumstances, whenever, for example, one is in a weakened state or whenever it would serve Islam's interests to do so."

pertaining to their religious leaders. Jesus never cared for his own personal wealth, never called for killing others, and, most importantly, did not insert himself into politics. His kingdom was "not of this world". Muhammad, in Faye's assessment, was a political conspirator and brutal conqueror. These fundamental differences translate into the political sphere. In the Christian world, there took shape a division between secular authority (the emperor) and spiritual authority (the papacy). In the Muslim world, the Caliph was an undivided, secular and spiritual authority. For this reason, Faye maintains, with reference to Alain Besançon, that Islam is irreconcilable with Western democracy and the secular state.[38] Faye summates that Islam denies the "European traditions inherited from ancient Greece and Rome" and simultaneously contradicts "Slavic and Scandinavian Germanic customs, as well as those of the Enlightenment, which all originate in the principial assumption of the superiority of both public debate and majority opinions over any doctrine whatsoever".[39]

In addition, Islam is seen as negating the value of the individual and national identity, as the only really essential category is the *umma*. Categories like family and nation do not matter. European thought is based on the philosophy of the subject, whence originates the value attached to such categories as the individual, the people, the *polis*, etc.[40] This "subjective", pre-Christian mentality was preserved in Europe by Christianity, within which there took shape the idea of a personal relationship with God, which Islam lacks. According to Faye, the central concept in Islam, absolute "submission", leads to abolishing the freedom of the individual as well as collective creativity.[41] Thus, Faye sees Islam as "a source of mental impoverishment and a decivilising

---

38 Faye, *Understanding Islam*, 19.
39 Ibid., 35.
40 Ibid., 31.
41 Ibid., 22.

factor".[42] As follows, the Muslim religion leads to low artistic and scientific creativity.

Faye sees three basic possible scenarios for the development of Islam in Europe. The first scenario is the slow death of France, the gradual implosion of state structures, progressive uncontrolled immigration, deepening economic crisis, rising unemployment, increasingly widespread street riots, and the gradual installation of Sharia. Finally, by around 2040, more than 50% of the population will be of non-European origin. The second scenario is the territorial partition of France: in addition to the above factors, an ethnic civil war of middle intensity will break out, armed jihad will spread, and entire French territories will secede from the state, ending around 2030–2040 with an EU/US/UN intervention that would divide France along ethnic lines. The third potential scenario is a "Second French Revolution" or "Reconquista": around 2030, a revolution will break out as the French, side-by-side with part of uniformed forces, will rise up against the passive state and form a revolutionary party that would eventually seize absolute power and introduce (with democratic legitimacy) an authoritarian government, immediately deport all illegal immigrants, and instate a final end to mass immigration.[43]

There can be no doubt that Faye sees Islam as a fatal threat to Europe and European identity. In his opinion, there is no chance that Islam would adjust to European norms on any macro-scale. The chances that Muslims will Islamicise Europe are greater than those of Islam being Europeanised. According to Faye, Islam is de facto the banner under which the peoples of the "Global South" are colonising Europe while the latter finds itself in a state of identity and moral crisis. In the opinion of this French thinker, Europe stands before an alternative: either be conquered by Islam and lose its identity, or rise up to fight Islam.

---

42   Ibid., 23.
43   Ibid., 264.

In this context, the differences between Alain de Benoist and Guillaume Faye can, only somewhat simplifying, be boiled down to the divergence between ethnopluralism (ethno-differentialism) and ethno-nationalism (ethnocentrism).[44] The former's stance is based on the postulate that every people has the right to maintain and cultivate its culture and particularity (regardless of geographic location). The latter proclaims the need to defend not only culture, but the ethno-racial homogeneity of a given territory.[45] According to Faye, "ethnopluralism" (a concept which arises from the polytheistic spirit) was originally meant to be a slogan for defending ethnocultural heterogeneity in the world, i.e., upholding that all peoples (and nations) are different and that these differences must be respected, provided that all of them should live in their own lands. However, the original meaning of this term (which was also, by default, equivalent to opposing the phenomenon of mass immigration) has been distorted, one example of which was the defence of wearing Islamic headscarves in public schools.[46] Faye maintains that the notions of "ethnopluralism" and the "right to difference" were forged by the *Nouvelle Droite* mainly for the sake of justifying the right of European peoples to preserve their identity and cultural particularity and avoiding accusations of racism.[47] However, this is unconvincing to some researchers (e.g., Taguieff) who regard ethnopluralism as a masked version of racism. Such a "tactic", according to Faye, did not yield any of the desired results, and focusing on the rights of all peoples is now, in the current situation (the colonisation of Europe by Islam), Faye concludes, a misconception. Moreover, here we can notice a certain lack of consequentialness. In contrast to the *Nouvelle Droite*'s declared anti-egalitarianism, it is

---

44 Michael O'Meara describes this difference as "communitarianism vs. ethnonationalism".
45 O'Meara, *Faye and the Battle of Europe*, 27.
46 Guillaume Faye, *Archeofuturism: European Visions of the Post-Catastrophic Age*, trans. Sergio Knipe (London: Arktos, 2010), 39.
47 O'Meara, *Faye and the Battle of Europe*, 32.

alleged to have adopted a narration of the fundamental equality of all peoples, which is typical of the Marxist and Christian left.[48] In Faye's opinion, GRECEists began to treat all peoples and nations as museum exhibits, not as living organisms, thereby forgetting that "in the selective process of History and Life, all must make do on their own. There are no gracious protections [...] The turbulent process of selection carried out by History leaves no place for 'protection' — only for competing subjectivities".[49] The survival of every people is decided by its own willpower, not to mention the fact that the world bends down to lend an ear to everyone — except Europeans. The situation, however, is such that Europe presently finds itself under the pressure of belligerent Islam — in this arrangement, Europe cannot worry about the fate of the Other, but only take care of its own survival. However, De Benoist argues:

> If Europeans are less dynamic in demographic terms, then this is not the fault of those who are. If they have lost their identity, then, once again, this is not the fault of those who haven't. In relation to peoples with a strong identity, those who are lacking such could very well stop to think about the cause of the loss of their own. To this end, they could very well think about the planetary spread of the values of the market or the nature of Western nihilism.[50]

---

48 Guillaume Faye, "From Dusk to Dawn: Guillaume Faye speaks in Moscow" in O'Meara, *Faye and the Battle of Europe*, 58: "We need to break with all forms of 'ethnopluralism', which is simply another kind of egalitarianism, and reclaim the right to 'ethnocentrism', the right to live in our own lands without the Other. [...] Besides, only Westerners believe race-mixing is a virtue or envisage the future as a melting pot. [...] Francis Fukuyama's 'end of history' will never happen. Instead, we're going to experience an acceleration of history with the 'clash of civilizations.'"

49 Guillaume Faye, "*Soupçons sur la cause des peuples*", *Terre et Peuple* 18 (2003), 27.

50 Alain de Benoist, "*Le 'communautarisme' n'est plus rien d'autre que la caricature de l'esprit communautarien*", *Terre et Peuple* 18 (2003), 26.

This bone of contention between both thinkers is equally a reflection of whom they take to be the main political enemy of Europe (as per Carl Schmitt's friend-enemy distinction). In de Benoist's case, the enemy is the US. In Faye's case, the enemy is Islam. This does not mean that the latter is enthusiastic about America. He is still critical of what he calls the "New American Imperialism". On this mater, he is very much in agreement with de Benoist. He is aware of the US's negative influence on Europe in the cultural as well as political sphere (promoting the ideology of human rights, multiculturalism, pressuring the EU to accept Turkey into its orbits, to intervene in the Balkan civil wars on the Muslim side, etc.). At the same time, Faye does not stand on the side of those whom he calls "Obsessive, Hysterical Anti-Americanists", i.e., those whose anti-American obsession leads them to lose sight of the greater threat that is the Islamic invasion of Europe. Such obsessive anti-Americanists even go as far as solidarity with Islam, which they sometimes perceive as a potential ally in the fight against Americanism. This, in Faye's opinion, is a cardinal mistake, for they do not take into consideration that over the past 1,400 years, Islam has consistently striven to conquer and destroy Europe.[51] Although Faye acknowledges that American plutocratic liberalism has caused the mass immigration of Third World peoples to Europe, he maintains that it is a mistake to concentrate on the US in a situation when the real threat is "right under one's nose". Moreover, designating America as the main enemy somehow puts the European in a role similar to that of the "poor African", i.e., as a victim of colonisation, adopting the victim mentality and targeting another white man as the enemy.[52] To sum up, Faye sees the US as more of an adversary of Europe rather than the enemy, insofar as an adversary is one who strives to dominate, whereas an enemy is one who strives to kill.[53] Islam is the enemy of Europe.

---

51 O'Meara, *Faye and the Battle of Europe*, 50.
52 Ibid.
53 Faye, "From Dusk to Dawn" in O'Meara, *Faye and the Battle of Europe*, 60: "America, specifically its ruling class, is Europe's and Russia's 'principal

On the philosophical level, the difference between both of these thinkers can be described in the following way: while Guillaume Faye presents a Nietzschean bearing, Alain de Benoist adopts a more Heideggerian perspective. Moreover, Faye focuses on anti-egalitarianism, while de Benoist concentrates on anti-liberalism. Finally, Faye is, to a certain extent, an apologist of the West, while de Benoist is a critic of the West.

---

adversary' at the level of geopolitics, economics, and culture. Europe's 'principal enemy' is the peoples of the South, increasingly assembled under the banner of Islam, whose invasion of the Continent is already well underway, facilitated by a political class and an intelligentsia who have opened the gates and who seek a miscegenated, non-European Europe (to Washington's delight). Like Atlanticists, the hysterical anti-Americans overestimate the United States, without understanding that it is only as strong as we are weak. The Americans' catastrophic and counterproductive occupation of Iraq, to which they have brought nothing but chaos, makes this all indisputably evident. In the twenty-first century, the U.S. will cease to be the premier world power."

CHAPTER VII

THE *NOUVELLE DROITE* AND RELATED CURRENTS

The *Nouvelle Droite* and French Integral Nationalism

THE NOUVELLE DROITE was not the first revision of traditional conservatism in France to combine elements of conservatism and revolution. Without a doubt, the first was the integral nationalism represented by *Action Française* (AF). Interestingly enough, it is in *Action Française* that René Rémond sees the precursor of the *Nouvelle Droite*.[1]

The most important representatives of this current were Charles Maurras (1868–1952) and Léon Daudet (1867–1942). *Action Française* was its own kind of attempt at bringing traditionalism, ultra-royalism, and French legitimism from the 19th century into the 20th century. It bears emphasising, however, that this traditionalism was only nominal. The political thought of *Action Française* is far more revisionist in nature in terms of hitherto conservative thought, for it was based on modernist ideas drawn from Jacobin nationalism and positivism.[2]

What connects both currents is certainly the "conservative-revolutionary" character of the attempt to reformulate conservatism after

---

1 René Rémond, *Les Droites en France* (Mayenne: 1999), 284.
2 Adam Wielomski, *Nacjonalizm francuski 1886–1940. Geneza, przemiany, i istota filozofii politycznej* (Warsaw: 2007), 532.

the "death of God".³ Both currents are right-wing, but in a decisively unorthodox way. Both abundantly draw from left-wing thought as well, thereby adjusting the intellectual conservative core to the conditions of modernity.

Neither of these currents appeals to a religious, divine origin of power, nor do they construct a metaphysical system to their needs. In both cases, their political philosophy is based on scientific grounds: the conservative worldview is described in scientistic-positivist categories. It is worth qualifying that Charles Maurras himself was one of the first ideologists of the right to bring scientific methods "into the workshop" and renounce religious argumentation.⁴

Besides these currents' relative "modernness", both decisively critique modernity itself. In general, they reject the legacy of the Enlightenment and the Revolution in the form of liberalism, individualism, capitalism, the idea of progress, as well as the bourgeois ethos. Progress is seen as factor in the disintegration of social ties. It is interesting to note that both Maurras and de Benoist advance the thesis of a de facto alliance between the left and big business, and thereupon indicate that the real opposition to the liberal-capitalist system must be anti-bourgeois.⁵ The ethos of liberal and progressive bourgeoisness is rejected in favour of emphasising the gravity of rootedness in tradition.

If we look into the systematic concepts of both currents, however, we can discern a certain divergence. For *Action Française*, the ideal is the *ancien régime*, which is interpreted as the combination of absolutism on top and decentralisation at the bottom.⁶ Nominally, the model they proposed was monarchy, but de facto dictatorship with a king occupying the highest state office. Monarchy was a symbol and

---

3   As Adam Wielomski puts it, conservatism has gone through the Mohlerian "axial age" (referring to Karl Jasper's concept). See Adam Wielomski, *Konserwatyzm* (Warsaw: 2007), 45.
4   Wielomski, *Nacjonalizm francuski 1886–1940*, 496.
5   Ibid., 530.
6   Ibid., 437.

alternative to democracy. Moreover, Maurras advocated a decisionist concept of authority in which the only real political category is force, not the rule of law or the sovereignty of the people. Political decision stands above any legal norm.[7] The future France will have a decentralised federation of mini-republics fused together by an absolutist government.[8] The *Nouvelle Droite*, on the other hand, postulates a model that is nominally imperial but actually (directly-)democratic and federalist, where the state organism would take on the form of autonomous regions. There is no talk of an absolutist or even authoritarian government, for the "empire" is only a symbol intended to be the antithesis to the "Jacobin" centralism characteristic of the (monolithic) nation-state. The only acceptable concept of the origin of power is the sovereignty of the people. In addition, the concept of seizing power by revolutionary force is absent in the *Nouvelle Droite*. The *Nouvelle Droite*'s *modus operandi* is to attain cultural hegemony by means of intellectual work and publishing activity.

These two currents also define their political enemy differently. In the case of *Action Française*, the enemy is the "plutocracy" or "four confederated states" of Jews, Masons, Protestants, and *meteques* (naturalised foreigners).[9] The *Nouvelle Droite*, for its part, does not define its enemy in terms of specific social groups, but as the liberal-capitalist system. In other words, the *Nouvelle Droite* does not seek scapegoats, but points to problems of the system. This is a rather essential difference.

Also of interest is comparing *Action Française* and the *Nouvelle Droite*'s relation to Catholicism and Christianity in general. To put things as simply as possible, *Action Française* recognises Catholicism, but not Christianity.[10] Maurras saw Catholicism as the certain founda-

---

7 Wielomski, *Konserwatyzm*, 295.
8 Wielomski, *Nacjonalizm francuski 1886–1940*, 436.
9 Wielomski, *Konserwatyzm*, 294.
10 Wielomski, *Nacjonalizm francuski 1886–1940*, 482.

tion of social harmony and the Church as the reservoir of tradition, hierarchy, and authority. Catholicism defies individual pride, excessive individualism, and revolutionary inclinations.[11] What matters is the Catholic *system*, not the Christian *faith*. Jesus Christ is thus seen as a democrat, individualist, and subversive.[12] The Gospel is not seen as a source of truth or values. In other words, the Christian vision of the world was alien to Maurras, who saw the world as a place of evil dominated by the Darwinian struggle over existence.[13] In summary, *Action Française* was pro-Catholic and clerical, but distanced from Christianity.

The case of the *Nouvelle Droite* is completely different. Neither Catholicism nor Christianity are seen as a dam holding out against the legacy of the Revolution; rather, Christianity itself was the ember of revolution! The *Nouvelle Droite* sees the Enlightenment as the secularisation of Christian doctrine which, in the end, has led to the crisis of the European culture. At the same time, it bears pointing out that de Benoist does not condemn Christianity in any fanatical way, since, as he himself claims, he sees certain positive elements in the social teaching of the Church (although he does not specify which ones). He distinguishes between the Church of St. Francis and the Church of Thomas of Torquemada, and suggests that he prefers the former.[14]

If one wanted to find the difference between these conservative-revolutionary currents on the level of ideational foundations, one could advance the thesis that *Action Française* is to a greater extent strictly French, whereas the *Nouvelle Droite* is more pan-European. *Action Française*'s accomplishments pertained first and foremost to the situation in France at the time. The *Nouvelle Droite*, however, is a broader current oriented more towards the totality of European

---

11   Ibid., 483.
12   Ibid., 487.
13   Ibid., 492.
14   Sylvain, "Interview with Alain de Benoist", 74.

history, tradition, and culture. In addition, it is worth pointing out what Jakub Stobiecki has noted: to a large extent, the *Nouvelle Droite* appropriated German political thought (the Weimar Conservative Revolution, Althusius, etc.),[15] which is, in the very least, evident in their symbolic appeal to empire instead of monarchy.

The *Nouvelle Droite* and Integral Traditionalism

Integral Traditionalism is an esoteric current whose origins can be dated back to the 1920s. The founder of the current is regarded to be the French thinker René Guénon (1886–1951), the author of, among other works, *Introduction to the Study of the Hindu Doctrines* (1921), *The Crisis of the Modern World* (1927), *Man and His Becoming According to the Vedānta* (1925), and *The Reign of Quantity and the Signs of the Times* (1945), in which he formulated the basic canons of Traditionalist thought. Mircea Eliade described Guénon as the most distinguished contemporary representative of esotericism. The second important figure of Traditionalism is the Italian thinker Julius Evola, the author of, among other works, *Revolt Against the Modern World* (1934), *Orientations* (1950), *Men Among the Ruins* (1953), and *Ride the Tiger* (1961), which shifted the emphasis on applying the principles of Traditionalism to the realities of political life.[16] In Polish, Evola's publications include *Orientacje* (*Orientations*),[17] *Etyka aryjska* (*Aryan Ethics*),[18] and a collection of articles entitled *Na antypodach modernizmu. Pisma wybrane* (*At the Antipodes of Modernism: Selected Writings*),[19] as well as a number of translations featured in

---

15 J. Stobiecki, "*Alain de Benoist I Francuska Nowa Prawica*", 34.

16 M. Tondera, "*Inna, dziwna prawica*" [https://klubjagiellonski.pl/2018/02/07/inna-dziwna-prawica/]; B. Kozieł, "*Sacrum et profanum — Integralny Tradycjonalizm a idee Nowej Prawicy*" [https://tradycjonalizm.net/juliusevola/artykuly/sacrum-et-profanum-integralny-tradycjonalizm-a-idee-nowej-prawicy].

17 J. Evola, *Orientacje* (Chorzów: 1991).

18 J. Evola, *Etyka aryjska* (Chorzów: 1993).

19 J. Evola, *Na antypodach modernizmu. Pisma wybrane* (Biała Podlaska: 2014).

the journal *Reakcjonista* (*The Reactionary*). In addition to these two figures, Frithjof Schuon, Titus Burckhardt, Ananda Coomaraswamy, and Miguel Serrano can be counted among the representatives of Traditionalism.

Zbigniew Mikołejko describes the basic themes of Guénonian Traditionalism as:

— the belief in the existence of a Primordial Tradition that preceded the empirically existing religions and civilisations and is the source of the particular manifestations of "secondary traditions" in extant reality;

— the study of initiatic reality, rituals, and symbols, i.e, everything that concerns the sphere of the *sacrum* conceived as a singular whole;

— analysing the contemporary world as the final phase of history (the "Dark Age") from the perspective of esoteric sciences;

— the thesis that the West needs to return to the metaphysical "Principles" of the East in order to regain Tradition (which it has lost);

— negating the privileged position of the human individual, who represents only a transitory and accidental manifestation of real being.[20]

Evola, who was evidently dependent on Guénon's thought, differed from his master in several respects. First, Guénon, based on the model of the East, emphasised the primacy of contemplation and the figure of the *brahmin*, whereas Evola, based on the model of West, emphasised the superiority of the man of action, the *kshatriya*. For Guénon, the East was the only depository of Tradition, whereas Evola believed that the West possesses its own, specific Tradition. Finally, for Guénon the only structure that could enable the rebirth of European Tradition was the Catholic Church, whereas Evola judge this institution to be a symbol of the Semitic degeneration of the primordial matrix that led

---

20 Z. Mikołejko, *Mity tradycjonalizmu integralnego. Julius Evola i kultura religijno-polityczna prawicy* (Warsaw, 1998), 131–132.

to the destruction of the mediaeval imperial and Ghibelline Tradition, the last expression of the Tradition of the West.[21]

Mikołejko distinguishes the following elements as typical of Evolian Traditionalism:

— the Guénonian definition of Tradition as a supra-historical, universal principle;

— opposition between the traditional world ("normal in the higher sense") and the modern world (which is regressive compared to the traditional world);

— the qualification that traditional civilisation is organic, differentiated, and hierarchical, whereby all types of human activity are oriented "from top down" (traditional civilisation is based on transcendent order).[22]

It is worth recalling that the *Nouvelle Droite* has on more than one occasion raised the topic of Evolian Traditionalism in its publishing activities.[23] The following comparison will focus on the Evolian variation of Traditionalism, as de Benoist himself cites Evola whenever he refers to Traditionalist thought.

The first difference between these two currents that catches the eye is that Traditionalism is an esoteric doctrine that, as its name suggests, draws on "sacred", traditional wisdom from ancient myths and legends which it does not treat to analysis by modern scientific methodology, but rather approaches in an uncritical manner, taking them to be the fundamental reference point and measure of all things. The existence of the Primordial Tradition is assumed a priori and is treated as the starting point for all further considerations. The *Nouvelle Droite*, for its part, is stripped of any mystical, esoteric, transcendental elements. It does not create a metaphysical system. Instead, it puts an immense

---

21 Ibid., 133.
22 Ibid., 139.
23 Besides articles in *Éléments* and *Nouvelle École*, a work on Evola was published by Copernic, a publishing house affiliated with the *Nouvelle Droite*: *Julius Evola. Le visionnaire foudroyé* (1977).

emphasis on the scientific foundation of the theses it voices. Much attention is devoted to studies from disciplines like sociobiology, ethnology, sociology, religious studies, anthropology, linguistics, history, etc. On the question of the existence of the Primordial Tradition, de Benoist has spoken out with far-reaching reservation. Put simply, he regards such to be a product of the imagination.[24] The *Nouvelle Droite* sees tradition above all in the plural and concentrates its attention and references on Indo-European tradition.

Evola refers to a mythical understanding of history that sees history as a process of involution from "higher" initial stages to decline, from the Golden Age to the Silver, Bronze, and Iron Ages, a motif taken from Hesiod. Also overlaid on this division is the Hindu doctrine of four eras, the *Satya-yuga*, *Treta-yuga*, *Dvapara-yuga*, and *Kali-yuga*, not to mention references to Iranian and Chaldean mythology.[25] According to his own statements, de Benoist sees time as a spherical, not linear, i.e., neither in the evolutionary (the idea of progress) or devolutionary (Traditional), fashion. This does not mean, however, that the *Nouvelle Droite* creates a new categorisation of eras or temporal phases (like Evola), or that it rejects the Gregorian calendar. This is rather a reference to the symbolic, intellectual, ideational level intended to refer to ancient mentalities.[26] Besides this, the *Nouvelle Droite* regards

---

24 de Benoist, *Les Idées à l'endroit*, 115.

25 F. Frerraresi, "Julius Evola: Tradition, Reaction, and the Radical Right", *European Journal of Sociology* 28(1) (1987), 112–113; Mikołejko, *Mity tradycjonalizmu integralnego*, 154.

26 Mikołejko expresses the opinion that the *Nouvelle Droite* does not actually operate with a cyclical concept of history, as it seems to make "too many concessions to historical determinism" under the influence of Nietzsche and Heidegger. Thomas Sheehan, in turn, discerns certain similarities between these two thinkers' concepts of time: Evola's is cyclical (the periodical return of the *arche*) and de Benoist's is spherical (past and future constitute dimensions of the present). See Mikołejko, *Mity tradycjonalizmu integralnego*, 194; Thomas Sheehan, "Myth and Violence: The Fascism of Julius Evola and Alain de Benoist", *Social Research* 48(1) (1981), 64–65.

Evola's knowledge in the history of religions to be obsolete — for them, George's Dumézil is a greater authority in this field.[27] It bears highlighting that the *Nouvelle Droite* — unlike Traditionalism — does not refer to any lofty or mystical historiosophical conceptions.

Central to the Evolian worldview is a strong elitism and the idea of social hierarchy — ideas which are antithetical to modern society, based as it is on liberalism, egalitarianism, rationalism, individualism, etc. The egalitarian ideal is seen as a degeneration, for society, according to Tradition, should be based on castes. Hence also the devastating Evolian critique of democracy and the "politicisation" of the "masses". The modern idea of society is contrasted to the idea of the State. Mikołejko writes:

> Society is the fruit of a naturalistic involution, the opposite of the essence of the true State. The social sphere is thus defined by the values of pacifism, pure economics, and material well-being, while the political sphere (the sphere of the State) is described in terms of 'hierarchical, heroic, ideal, and anti-hedonistic values' [...] which separate it from the order of naturalistic and vegetative existence.[28]

This antinomy is presented figuratively by attributing society and the people to the feminine element, whereas the State represents the masculine element.[29] Compared to Evola, de Benoist presents a more ambivalent approach to elitism. In the *Nouvelle Droite*, the idea of eliteness and hierarchy functions above all on the symbolic-aesthetic level — (post-)Enlightenment, egalitarian, liberal-capitalist society is framed within Dumézil's trifunctional model, which functions in principle as the archetype of the structure of authentic Indo-European society. Thus, the Brahmins are on top, followed by the Kshatriyas, and the Vaishyas are at the bottom. The modern "bourgeois" world has departed from the "authentically Indo-European", as the whole of society

---

27 Mikołejko, *Mity tradycjonalizmu integralnego*, 194.
28 Ibid., 163–164.
29 Ibid., 179.

has been "levelled" and the economic function (the third) has been absolutised (put in the place of the old elite) and made the model one. From this arises the New Right's critique of the liberal, pro-market right, as the latter defends the bourgeois (anti-aristocratic) status quo. What is essential in the *Nouvelle Droite*'s case is that this does not entail a critique of democracy. Why? First, because democracy is a system that was created within the framework of the Indo-European tradition. Second, (authentic) democracy is in its very essence anti-liberal (Carl Schmitt). Third, in connection with the fact that the current status quo is bourgeois, the New Right critique is closer to the socialist than to the liberal,[30] since the former want to change the status quo. Fourthly, as the *Nouvelle Droite* evolved, its elitist (anti-egalitarian) elements grew quieter over time in favour of anti-liberal emphases. This is connected with the decisive bet hedged on direct democracy from the bottom up, since democracy is above all the participation of the people in their fate (Arthur Moeller van den Bruck).[31] This position is entirely opposite to the idea found in Evola of building the State "from above" by an elite, an idea which is contemptuous of the people.[32]

---

30 Here we can see an obvious echo of Moeller van den Bruck, who postulated an alliance between conservatives and revolutionaries (against liberals) with the aim of creating an "organic socialism". See Bielawski, "*Arthura Moellera van den Brucka konserwatywno-rewolucyjna krytyka liberalizmu*", 193.

31 In recent years, de Benoist has gone so far as to support a "populism of the people" (not to be confused with party populism) against the exploitative liberal-capitalist "elite". One great example of this is his support for the Yellow Vest protests in France. See "*Alain de Benoist, à propos des Gilets Jaunes*" [https://www.youtube.com/watch?v=hSbPdzKTw44].

32 De Benoist has directly referred to his differences with Evola on this matter: "Certainly, [Evola], with his absolute rejection of modernity [...] might seem to be such [a revolutionary]. However, we cannot forget the great disgust he felt for 'the masses' (which he did not distinguish from the people) getting involved in history. He never hid that he considered monarchy to be the best system. Of course, he hated the bourgeoisie, but he preferred the bourgeoisie to any populism or socialism [...]! In this regard, he seemed to be more of a reactionary [...]. We can argue that Evola was above all an elitist and, like all elitists, he had

The differences between these thinkers becomes even clearer if we compare their attitude towards totalitarianism and racism (often connected with fascism). Evola was an advocate of a "military" state based on the ethic of the warrior and legitimised from above, which obviously led to the conviction of the need for authoritarian, if not absolute, power.[33] At the same time, Evola believed that the State must be based on a spiritual foundation, not a purely political one. He believed that the organic state should not be confused with the totalitarian state, since the latter is a modern idea while the former is a traditional idea. Totalitarianism, although it arose out of a positive reaction to social atomisation and individualism, is based on inorganic principles differing from the "organic and qualitative" principles of tradition, and it strives for a "raw and mechanical" unity.[34] Nevertheless, Evola approved of the fascist governments and hoped that they would at one point implement the idea of government based on the "higher order". In other words, he was an apologist of totalitarianism. He dreamed of a fascism that would be more radical and more absolute. In his opinion, Italian fascism lacked an ideology containing such a complete vision of the world that could become the antithesis to the rationalist-liberal reality.

For Evola, the element that could transform ordinary fascism into such a "super-fascism" was racism (or "racialism").[35] This Italian thinker did not conceive of race in the biological, "scientific" way in currency in the Third Reich. Rather, he understood racism in a psycho-cultural way: for him, races were categories of the spirit. Having a negative attitude towards nationalism (as an ideology that is

---

> big problems with seeing that there are moments in history when the people manifests greater value than the 'elites' who are supposed to be leading them." Alain de Benoist, "*Entretien sur Julius Evola*" in *C'est-à-dire*, vol. 2, 271.

33 Mikołejko, *Mity tradycjonalizmu integralnego*, 177.
34 Ibid., 180.
35 Adam Wielomski, *Faszyzmy łacińskie. Sen o rewolucji innej niż w Rosji i w Niemczech* (Warsaw: 2011), 125.

too plebeian), Evola wanted fascism to be based on a less egalitarian, more lucidly hierarchical idea. As Adam Wielomski argues, racism for Evola was the myth of superiority of some people over others: not the superiority of one people (as in nation) over another, but of a certain part of the people, i.e., the aristocracy, over the rest, i.e., "the people".[36] The case with the *Nouvelle Droite* is completely different: this current is unambiguously against totalitarianism in any form, whether secular, religious, or political. It sees the monotheistic idea *par excellence* at work in totalitarianism. It also distances itself from racism, which it assesses to be an erroneous doctrine rooted in evolutionism and scientific positivism, both of which it also sees as negative.[37]

Besides the above-mentioned differences, we can discern some points of contact between these currents. The first that catches the eye is the explicitly critical approach to the Christian religious tradition, paired with seeking normative sources in the most ancient past of European culture. It is worth pointing out that Evola distanced himself from strictly naturalistic neo-paganism, and de Benoist directly adopted this view from Evola.

Moreover, constitutive of both currents is their critical approach to the Enlightenment, modernity, and the crystallisation of the latter in individualism, egalitarianism, liberalism, universalism, etc. Of course, this is bound up with a negative evaluation of Americanism, capitalism, economism, the "ideology of labor", and the bourgeois ethos, which are critiqued from "right-wing aristocratic" positions.

Evola and de Benoist also share a similar vision of Europe. Both thinkers are skeptical of the centralised, "Jacobin", unitarian nation-state. In this context, the model of the *Imperium*, which is characterized by decentralisation, internal diversity, and a conditionally large extent of local autonomy, rises to the level of a symbol. Both would be most pleased to see a Europe shaped along the lines of an "organic

---

36 Ibid., 127.

37 de Benoist and Champetier, "Manifesto for a European Renaissance", in Sunic, *Against Democracy and Equality*, 230.

federalism", in which "every people can preserve its particularity and its own sovereignty thanks to taking part in the sovereignty of the Empire".[38]

Alain de Benoist assesses Evolian Traditionalism as cognitively fruitful and inspiring, but he does not subscribe to its system.[39] This is a good summation of the *Nouvelle Droite*'s relation to Traditionalism. On the deepest philosophical level, the difference between these currents can be defined in terms of their relation to Platonism: Traditionalism is a current of thought that is strongly Platonist in character, whereas the *Nouvelle Droite*'s thought is far from Platonism.[40]

The *Nouvelle Droite* and Dependism

The usefulness of comparing the *Nouvelle Droite* to "dependency theory" (Spanish: "*teoría de la dependencia*") is justified by the extent to which it allows for bringing into relief the ambiguity of the alleged "right-wingness" of the *Nouvelle Droite*.

The beginning of dependism is recognized to have been 1966, when Andre Gunner Frank published the article "The Development of Underdevelopment", which laid the foundations for interpreting the phenomenon of "dependent development". The subsequent year saw the publication of *Capitalism and Underdevelopment in Latin America: Historical Studies of Chile and Brazil*, which developed the train of thought contained in the article. This work describes the structure of the contemporary world economic system as consisting of a global metropolis (the "Center") and its class that rules over its satellites (the "Periphery"). The development of dependism involved numerous intellectuals from different regions, including Latin Americans (e.g., Fernando Cardoso, Celso Furtado, Enzo Falletto, Osvaldo Sunkel, Orlando Caputo), Africans (Samir Amin, Walter

---

38 Mikołejko, *Mity tradycjonalizmu integralnego*, 176.
39 de Benoist, "*Entretien sur Julius Evola*" in *C'est-à-dire*, vol. 2, 270.
40 Sunic, "*Wywiad z Tomislavem Suniciem*", 38.

Rodney), Asians (Ranjit Sam, Sanjaya Lall), Americans (Immanuel Wallerstein), Englishmen (Gavin Williams, Edwin Brett), Frenchmen (Alain Touraine), and Poles (Ignacy Sachs, Jan Kieniewicz, Witold Kula, Marcin Kula, Henryk Szlajfer, Michał Chmara).

We should begin with recalling that the "left-wing" theory of dependency appeared as a counter to the "liberal" theory of modernisation, which is practically based entirely on the idea of progress.[41] One of the distinctive traits of dependism is the rejection of the progressivist-unilinear perspective.[42] Already here we can see an ideational colligation with the *Nouvelle Droite*, which *ex definitione* rejects the "political monotheism" (the "ideology of sameness") that is manifest in, among other things, attempts at creating a world system in accordance with a monolithic (the "only right") model that excludes the possibility of any other alternatives.

Another distinctive trait of dependency theory is the postulate of overcoming Eurocentrism (although it would be more accurate to describe such as "Western-centrism"). This perspective is adopted counter to the theory of modernisation's presumption that the Western model of development (from traditional, pre-industrial society to industrial to the postmodern, information society[43]) is essentially the only possible one (as simply established by its adoption virtually

---

41   Krzysztofek and Szczepański, *Zrozumieć rozwój*, 34: "Theorists of modernisation regard development as an evolutionary, stage-based, unilinear [...] as well as convergent [...] process of social changes. It is evolutionary because it brings in stages — distributed over time — changes from the stage of backwardness to the industrial stage or even to the stage of information. It is unilinear and convergent because it proceeds most often in a similar way in all societies and leads to similar — even if not identical — effects."

42   Ibid., 108: "Theorists of dependism understand development as evolutionary, non-stage-based, multilateral, and divergent. It is evolutionary because it is based on secular trends and is extended over time; it is multilateral because it proceeds differently in particular cases; it is divergent because it leads to differing results in central, peripheral, and semi-peripheral countries."

43   Ibid., 36.

everywhere). In the opinion of dependists, the modernising approach has the aim not of helping peripheral countries develop, but of making them dependent, both economically and ideologically-culturally. As Krzysztofek and Szczepański write:

> This means recognising such economic, political, and cultural structures and institutions as complementary, although the relations binding them are asymmetrical and, in ethical categories, unjust. The material success of the capitalist centre is conditioned by the reproduction of dependency (the development of underdevelopment or the underdevelopment of development), which does not mean the unconditional impoverishment of the periphery, but does mean the disproportionate division of profits flowing from this asymmetrical complementarity.[44]

De Benoist sees the state of affairs in a similar way. Offering non-Western countries a no-alternative path of development, one that is *de facto* Westernisation, is an echo of the old chauvinism of the colonial mentality. The French thinker recalls how in colonial times, European missionaries in the New World operated with very similar motives.[45] Of course, there is no longer talk of "converting and civilising savages", but of "assisting development". Naturally, dependent development is effected not only on the economic level of the market, but also on the socio-cultural level.[46] The end effect is the degradation and disintegra-

---

44 Ibid., 108.
45 de Benoist, de Benoist, *Europe, Tiers monde — même combat*, 104.
46 Krzysztofek and Szczepański, *Zrozumieć rozwój*, 117: "[…] and its most essential manifestation in this case is 'symbolic rape'. It consists in repeated attempts to transfer to the Third World ideological and doctrinal systems, broadly understood values and norms, as well as institutions which were born in European cultural circles and are alien to the Third World. Symbolic rape can lead to a partial and at times complete loss of cultural identity. It inevitably degrades a native culture and deprives it of social sense, condemning African, Asian, and Latin American societies to accept a foreign culture that is often incomprehensible and illegible to them. Then collapses […] the legible system of culture which, as Edward Shils wrote, plays the role of the central nervous system of society and constitutes the first and foremost condition of its existence." This

tion of the indigenous identity, traditional social structures, native culture, way of life, and developmental paths that differ from the Western one. In summary, de Benoist agrees with the dependants that adopting the Western model of development is not the proper way to solve the problem of the Third World's "underdevelopment".

The theoreticians of dependism have a negative relation to liberalism,[47] one example of which would be their suspicious approach to the theory of comparative advantage (David Ricardo), according to which everyone benefits from international exchange. They understand the world economy (relatively) as a zero sum game, which means the unequal division of profits ("unequal exchange"[48]) more than the unconditional impoverishment of the periphery. This is naturally bound up with inflating the active role of the state in the economy — which runs counter to the liberal concept of the "minimal state".[49] Key here is the emphasis that the entire system of liberal capitalism exists thanks to the maintenance of asymmetrical relations between states. In the dependists' opinion, one must also emphasise that the internationalisation of economic activity is profitable first and

---

symbolic rape can have the effect of cultural servility (slowly accepting the transmitted values), rebellion, or even revolution (e.g., the Islamic Revolution in Iran).

47 According to Samir Amin, the liberal worldview can be summarised in the following points: (1) social efficiency is wrongly identified with economic efficiency; (2) the spread of the global market and the spread of democracy are treated as complementary; (3) the US is treated as the most developed country and the model to be imitated, because it is in the US (to a greater extent than anywhere else) that politics has been reduced to being a tool for the economy (and hence politics is subordinated to capital); (4) there is no alternative to the model of equating the market and democracy and reducing politics to an auxiliary role for the economy. See Samir Amin, *The Liberal Virus: Permanent War and the Americanization of the World* (New York: Monthly Review Press, 2004). This perspective is strikingly similar to de Benoist's.

48 Krzysztofek and Szczepański, *Zrozumieć rozwój*, 34.

49 R. E. Kelly, "No 'return to the state': dependency and developmentalism against neo-liberalism", *Development in Practice* 18(3) (2008), 319.

foremost to big capital, which constantly tries to obtain ever greater profits through wage dumping, such as that made possible by importing economic immigrants.[50]

The negative assessment of liberalism is thus another common trait of the *Nouvelle Droite* and dependism, although the emphases are somewhat shifted. De Benoist much more strongly underscores the cultural and social consequences of capitalism. For him, liberal capitalism is not only an economic system, but an anthropological one which creates the model of a man (*Homo oeconomicus*) whose "rationality" has strictly economic connotations, i.e., is oriented towards the maximisation of personal profit. Yet, it bears highlighting that the French thinker critiques liberalism not only in ideological terms, but also according to strictly economic criteria.[51]

Besides the above similarities, the differences between both currents are obvious. First, the *Nouvelle Droite* attached great weight to religious questions and to the socio-political consequences of one religious confession on the macro-scale. Dependism, however, does not treat this question in any way whatsoever. Second, dependency theory busies itself with exclusively economic questions, while the *Nouvelle Droite* is a multi-dimensional, interdisciplinary ideational current. Third, dependism, as a current connected with the left, draws on Enlightenment axiology (oriented towards emancipation), whereas the *Nouvelle Droite* completely rejects such in favour of the postulate of "rootedness". Such an idea is explicitly counter-Enlightenment, and in this respect is "right-wing". However, the most fundamental and most expressive difference lies in what constitutes the foundational reference point when it comes to understanding the economy. In the case

---

50 J. Tomasiewicz, "*Wojna światów. Wokół teorii zależności*", *Nowy Obywatel* [https://nowyobywatel.pl/2019/12/22/wojna-swiatow-wokol-teorii-zaleznosci-2005/]

51 See Alain de Benoist, *Au bord du gouffre. La faillite annoncée du système de l'argent* (Paris: 2011).

of dependism, this foundation is Marxism.[52] However, even though Karl Marx is also an inspiration for de Benoist, he draws on a much farther-reaching institutional approach, namely, that of Karl Polanyi.[53]

Both currents see similar ways out of the trap of dependent development. Dependists recommend that Third World countries liberate themselves from the role of passive receivers of the values, ideas, and cultural goods imposed by the "colonisers", and instead reconstruct their own past, their own "self-creation", reproducing the special model of identity that is typical of their own peoples, and carrying out restructuring that leads to restricting their bonds with the highly developed capitalist countries.[54] De Benoist proposed endogenous development within the framework of semi-autarkic economic spaces.[55]

The *Nouvelle Droite* and Third Positionism

Let us recall that the essence of Third Positionism, or *terceryzm* in Polish, means seeking a "third way", that is, an alternative to both capitalism and Marxism. The Third Positionist credo can be encapsulated in the slogan "National Freedom is Social Justice."[56] This current draws from miscellaneous and at times even contradictory sources. It has a clearly right-wing character on matters of worldview, yet it adopts a number of left-wing postulates on the political and socio-economic levels, such as on matters of social justice (equality of opportunity), the affirmation of the people (the lower social strata are seen as the "salt

---

52 Kelly, "No 'return to the state'", 321.Tomasiewicz, "*Wojna światów. Wokół teorii zależności*".
53 On the question of comparing Karl Marx and Karl Polanyi's concepts, see B. Selwyn and S. Miyamura, "Class Struggle or Embedded Markets? Marx, Polanyi and the Meanings and Possibilities of Social Transformation", *New Political Economy* 19(5) (2014), 639–661.
54 Krzysztofek and Szczepański, *Zrozumieć rozwój*, 119–120.
55 de Benoist, "*Pour le Tiers monde, quelles solutions?*", 39.
56 K. Karczewski, *Miecz i Krzyż. Doktryna polityczna Trzeciej Pozycji i jej geneza na tle zjawiska terceryzmu* (Warsaw: 2019), 246.

of the earth" opposed to the oppressive bourgeoisie), and direct democracy ("grassroots"). The left as such is, however, outright rejected. In Jacek Bartyzel's categorisation, Third Positionism is situated on the "extreme left" of the right.[57]

Third Positionism and the *Nouvelle Droite* come very close to each other in terms of doctrine. The difference is in the details. In comparing the *Nouvelle Droite* to Third Positionism, it first and foremost bears noticing the secondariness of the latter to the former. The *Nouvelle Droite* is one of the main sources of ideational inspiration for Third Positionism. An even more significant difference is that the *Nouvelle Droite* is an intellectual current, not a strictly political one. The *Nouvelle Droite*'s attention is predominantly focused on metapolitical questions, often even academic ones, whereas the Third Position is above all engaged in strictly political, social, and economic issues. In other words, Third Positionists attempt to implement in practice what the *Nouvelle Droite* has created on the theoretical level. Krzysztof Karczewski presents the following as the most important inspirations that the Third Position takes from the *Nouvelle Droite*:

A. Support for the national-liberation movements of Latin America;

B. Anti-racism, understood as rejecting the hierarchisation of human races and ethnic groups and, at the same time, rejecting the mixing of ethnic groups in cultures in the likes of the Western model of multicultural society;

C. The primacy of the "rights of peoples", which means proclaiming, among other things, the right to preserve one's own identity;

D. Affirming the cultural and ethnic differentiation of the whole world, accepting the right of every culture or ethnic group to preserve its own traditions and identity (ethnopluralism);

E. Opposing uniformisation and centralisation;

---

[57] Bartyzel, "*Próba teoretyzacji pojęcia 'prawica'*", 62–63.

F. Propagating decentralisation and direct democracy based on traditional communities (organic democracy);

G. A vision of a united Europe in the form of an empire, a "Europe of a Hundred Flags", which is to maintain geopolitical and civilisational unity alongside preserving the particularities of its cultural, linguistic, and ethnic components.[58]

Besides the above-listed, we should also mention anti-Americanism and anti-imperialism, which are basically treated synonymously, as well as the heroic ethos as opposed to the bourgeois ethos (materialism and the cult of money).[59]

The most important difference on the level of doctrines is the lack of any explicit nationalism in the *Nouvelle Droite* (which emphasises localism, regionalism, etc.).[60] In the case of Third Positionism, nationalism is a key element.

When it comes to religion, we can enumerate three worldview options within the scope of Third Positionism: (a) Christian, (b) rationalist-materialist, and (c) neo-pagan and esoteric.[61] However, it needs to be pointed out that basically all of these worldview variations are linked by a common search for a new spirituality, which leads to rejecting openly affirmed materialism as well as organised religion.[62] Third Positionist organisations generally present themselves either as officially, even integrally Christian (nationalism is thus fully

---

58 Karczewski, *Miecz i Krzyż*, 115. It should be pointed out that in the case of the *Nouvelle Droite* the basic components of the imperial Europe they postulate are regions, ethnic groups, and 'small nations' like the Basques, Welsh, Bretons, Corsicans, etc., as opposed to the centralist and "Jacobinist" nation-states.

59 Karczewski, *Miecz i Krzyż*, 248.

60 De Benoist has issued rather expressive criticisms of nationalism. See Alain de Benoist, "*Nationalisme: phénoménologie et critique*" in *Critiques — Théoriques*, 85–88.

61 Karczewski, *Miecz i Krzyż*, 125.

62 Ibid.

subordinated to the principles of the Christian religion), or as secular, drawing a boundary between religion and politics (religion as a private matter) — the latter also pertains to neo-pagan groups (which do not wish to create unnecessary divisions). In other words, religion is not one of Third Positionist groups' main points of interest. This differs from the case of the *Nouvelle Droite*, for whom the religious sphere has since the very beginning been among their main interests. In addition, this current has always openly declared a "pagan" worldview.

To summarise, the *Nouvelle Droite* is an intellectual and metapolitical current focused on creating theoretical foundations with the aim of overcoming the paradigm of modernity, whereas Third Positionism is a political current and an attempt at creating a practical alternative to liberal capitalism and Marxist socialism.

The *Nouvelle Droite* and the Fourth Political Theory

The Fourth Political Theory is a concept created by Alexander Dugin, a Russian thinker, historian, and geopolitician. Maintaining the position that the hitherto political doctrines have become somewhat anachronistic since the onset of postmodernity, which declared the end of history and the end of ideologies, Dugin recognises three main (modernist) political ideologies:

1. Liberalism (right and left)
2. Communism (socialism, Social Democracy, Marxism)
3. Fascism (Italian Fascism, German National Socialism, Spanish National Syndicalism, Peron's Justicialism, the Salazar regime, etc.).[63]

---

63 K. Karczewski, *Tradycja, imperium, geopolityka. Eurazjatyzm w ujęciu Aleksandra Dugina jako alternatywa wobec liberalizmu oraz demokracji liberalnej* (Toruń: 2017), 412.

From today's perspective, the 20th century can be seen as an arena of clashes between these three ideologies. The Second World War ended with the victory of liberalism and communism over fascism. The Cold War ended with communism's defeat by liberalism, which in the final accounting gave liberalism global triumph. Although we officially live in the reality of postmodernism, i.e., in the era of the "end of any ideologies," this is, according to Dugin, a "ruse" on the part of liberalism. The slogan of the "end of ideologies" does not mean the end of any ideologies whatsoever, only the end of non-liberal ideologies. In other words, this means the end of the ideological battle inasmuch as one ideology (liberalism) now rules indivisibly, even if discreetly. Dugin calls this situation the "absent center", that is, the illusion of a lack of any doctrines in the political domain.[64] The epicentre of liberal ideology, and hence the global hegemon is, of course, the United States.

Dugin assesses the current constellation of conditions, to put it mildly, as unfortunate and undesired. The two above-mentioned competitors of liberalism have been defeated; therefore, in Dugin's opinion, it is necessary to create a fourth ideology, or a fourth political "theory", that would constitute an adequate response to liberalism in the 21st century.

At first glance, the New Right and Fourth Political Theory exhibit far-reaching similarity. First and foremost, both currents take liberalism to be the political enemy par excellence — political compromise is entirely ruled out. Next, both currents try to go beyond the conceptual limitations of modernity and endeavour to build a completely new form of political spectrum (among other things, leaving behind the typical opposition of left vs. right). Both Alain de Benoist and Alexander Dugin see the "Mecca of liberalism" in the United States, and for this reason they recognise this state to be the main enemy in the geopolitical sense. Moreover, both de Benoist and Dugin draw

---

64 Ibid., 415.

handfuls from different ideational currents and branches of science to make their own authorial "ideational blocs" into a coherent whole.

The similarity between the New Right and the Fourth Political Theory is decided above all by what they are both against, i.e., modernity, liberalism, the international politics of the US, etc. However, if we look closer into the positive programmes of each current, it turns out that there are more differences than there might seem at first glance.

It bears starting from the fact that both currents originate out of completely different civilisational circles. The New Right is a product of "Western" (as per Samuel Huntington) or "Latin" (as per Feliks Koneczny) civilisation, whereas the Fourth Political Theory arises out of Byzantine (Huntington) or "Turanian" (Koneczny) civilisation. It should immediately be added that the Fourth Political Theory is the direct successor of Dugin's Neo-Eurasianism, and therefore should not be examined in separation from it. One could even put forth the thesis that the Fourth Political Theory is nothing more than freshly "repainted"[65] Neo-Eurasianism trying to uphold the appearance of a universal theory. The question arises: what is this meant to serve? Certainly, this can be assessed in different ways, but according to Leszek Sykulski, Alexander Dugin's ideology is an element of information war ("reflexive management") which, in turn, is an element of the Russian Federation's policy orientation towards rebuilding the Russian Empire.[66] In the end, this is very logical if we take into consideration the fact that Russian imperialism is an inseparable, even constitutive element of Dugin's Neo-Eurasianism. Alain de Benoist, on the other hand, as already discussed, explicitly distinguishes between empire and imperialism, appeasing the former positively and the

---

65 Ibid., 426: "Summing up Dugin's concept of the Fourth Political Theory, it is obviously evident that the Eurasianist is once again recreating a certain new formula expressing the very same content as before."

66 See L. Sykulski, "*Koncepcja radykalnego podmiotu i 'Czwarta Teoria Polityczna' Aleksandra Dugina w kontekście bezpieczeństwa Polski i Unii Europejskiej*", Przegląd Geopolityczny 8 (2014), 229–242.

latter negatively. This is a very essential difference. The New Right's ideal is a European "empire" that is internally decentralised, directed towards building a certain international harmony, and is based on balance against disorder. The ideal of Neo-Eurasianism is a state that is ostensibly decentralised, but is in fact strongly authoritarian and unambiguously oriented towards expansion.[67] This should come as no surprise if we take into consideration the fact that on the symbolic level, Neo-Eurasianism refers not only to the Byzantine heritage, but also the Mongol heritage which, let us recall, is seen by Dugin as unambiguously positive. According to this Russian thinker, the entity called "Eurasia" is supposed to be a European-Mongol synthesis (additionally complemented by the political myth of the Third Rome[68]). The political "radical centrism" and "imperative of expansion" in currency in Russian culture are seen as being from precisely this Mongol legacy.[69] The New Right, however, appeals to the strictly European heritage, particularly the Europe of antiquity. The essence of the New Right is the aspiration to go to the essence of Europe, free from

---

67 A. Dugin, "*Czekam na Iwana Groźnego*", interview by G. Górny, *Fronda* 11/12 (1998), 133: "We Russians and Germany think in terms of expansion and we will never think differently. We are simply not interested in the preservation of one's own state or nation. We are interested in absorbing, by way of the pressure we exert, the maximal amount of categories that complete us."

68 Boris Uspenskij and Victor Zhivov, *Tsar and God and Other Essays in Russian Cultural Semiotics*, trans. Marcus C. Levitt, David Budgen, and Liv Bliss (Boston: Academic Studies Press, 2012), 7: "The Florentine Union and fall of Byzantium, as a result of which Russia found itself the single Orthodox kingdom [...] introduced a new element into Russian religious and political thinking. [...] The conception of Moscow as Third Rome defined the Russian grand prince as successor to the Byzantine emperor and at the same time put him in a position that had no direct precedent in the Byzantine model. The conception of Moscow as Third Rome was eschatological, and in this context the Russian monarch as head of the last Orthodox kingdom was endowed with a messianic role."

69 J. Breczko, "*Eurazjatyzm — rosyjska idea imperialna spajana nienawiścią*" in J. Mysona Byrska and J. Synowiec (eds.), *Nienawiść w życiu publicznym. Sfera społeczna* (Kraków: 2015), 155.

foreign (non-European) influences. Eurasianist ideology, however, is an apologist for the Turanisation of Russia. This is aptly outlined by Jacek Breczko:

> [...] over the centuries [...] as a result of Rus' conquest by the Mongols, this area saw the creation of a peculiar — and yet valuable — national and racial mixture: Mongol-Tatar-Slavic. The Great Russians, therefore, are not Slavs, but mixed (as Yerofeyev put it: 'Scratch a Russian a bit more, and you'll see a Tatar'). Let us imagine that the Mongols were not ultimately driven out by the Principality of Moscow, but were instead absorbed (the Kazan, the Astrakhan, and finally the Crimean Khanates).[70]

These differences in turn effect an entirely different character of relations between citizens and the state. Although on the declarative level the New Right explicitly criticises the ideology of human rights, this does not mean that it supports an authoritative form of government or an absence of individual rights. To the contrary, the critique of the ideology of human rights is dictated by, among other things, the New Right's perspective that such rights ultimately weaken the potential of peoples and ethnic communities to govern themselves and maintain their particularity. Let us recall that in ancient Greece and Rome, the individual enjoyed (compared to the then Eastern despotic states) a relatively large amount of rights and civil freedoms.

In the case of Neo-Eurasianism, the situation is diametrically different. The alternative to the liberalism under critique is a state which, if perhaps not totalitarian, is certainly strongly authoritarian, where the citizen has at most the right to self-organisation "at the bottom", on the local level, while complete and unconditional obedience is demanded of him when it comes to the central government. In this regard, one of the fundamental, ideational (or perhaps rather civilisational) differences between de Benoist and Dugin is that, unlike de Benoist, Dugin is an apologist for the unrestrained cruelty of state power against the

---

70 Ibid.

citizen (which even has a theological origin[71]). This arises from a positive assessment of the reigns of Genghis Khan, Ivan the Terrible, and Joseph Stalin. The very fact that Alexander Dugin's interview in *Fronda* is titled "I'm waiting for Ivan the Terrible" is sufficiently telling.[72]

The next difference between both of these currents is their philosophical toolboxes. Although the New Right and the Fourth Political Theory share many ideational inspirations and often cite the same thinkers, a different distribution of emphases ultimately leads to a far-reaching divergence. This is especially evident in the case of both currents' relation to integral Traditionalism. We can confidently put forth the thesis that Dugin takes up integral Traditionalism as an inventory

---

71 Uspenskij and Zhivov, *Tsar and God*, 7–9: "In 1547 Ivan IV (the Terrible) became the crowned head of the kingdom, and the title of tsar, fixed by sacred rite, became an official attribute of the Russian monarch. In the Russian context this title had different connotations than in Byzantium. In Byzantium calling the emperor 'basileus' (tsar) referred primarily to the imperial tradition; the Byzantine sovereign acted as legal successor to the Roman emperors. In Russia the title of the monarch referred primarily to the religious tradition, and to the texts in which God was called 'tsar'; and in Russia the imperial tradition was not relevant. Thus if in Byzantium the name tsar (basileus) was perceived as describing the office of supreme ruler (which metaphorically could be applied to God), in Russia the same title was perceived, in essence, as a proper name, as one of the divine names; in these circumstances, calling a person a tsar could take on mystical meaning. [...] Thus having taken the place of the Byzantine basileus, the Russian tsar, in the opinion of his subordinates, as well as his own, acquired special charismatic power. One might presume that this perception developed gradually and was not universal. However, it is very clear that the first Russian tsar, Ivan the Terrible, believed that he himself unconditionally possessed such special charisma. It was precisely this perception that led Ivan to believe that his actions were not liable to human judgment. [...] The tsar's acts are not subject to review or in need of justification, just like those of God; to his subordinates the tsar acts as God, and it is only in his relations with God Himself that his human nature manifests itself. [...] For Ivan, to the contrary, these excesses may serve as the mark of his charismatic exceptionalism. No canon of charismatic behavior existed, so that Ivan could interpret his new status as permission for complete license."

72 Dugin, "*Czekam na Iwana Groźnego*", 133.

with all the benefits (the existence of the Primordial Tradition is accepted as an axiom). Thus, it can be argued that the Fourth Political Theory is a sufficiently consequential political concretisation of integral Traditionalism. In its critique of modernity, materialism, liberalism, rationalism, etc., it is extreme, uncompromising, absolutist, and it approaches the achievements of modern science with far-reaching suspicion. To quote Krzysztof Karczewsk: "Dugin [...] stands on the ground of uncompromising anti-liberalism, anti-occidentalism, anti-materialism, and anti-rationalism, instead advocating the 'sacred', tradition, organic society, and the East [...]. Of course, this means that the Fourth Political Theory must be based on the language of Tradition as the most consequential irrationalism".[73] Alain de Benoist, for his part, although he draws some inspiration from integral Traditionalism (specifically Evolian), he treats it with decisively more reservation. He does not recognise the existence of a Primordial Tradition that would be a one and only tradition ("spiritual wellspring") that is the source of all existing religious beliefs. If we can speak of any "ontology" of de Benoist, then it would to a greater extent and decisively be Heideggerianism rather than integral Traditionalism. In Dugin's case, it is the opposite. Moreover, this Russian thinker is undoubtedly closer to René Guénon's version of Traditionalism (*ex Oriente lux* and emphasising the first Dumézilian function), whereas de Benoist exhibits a greater ideational affinity with Julius Evola's Traditionalism (appreciating the Western, pre-Christian heritage and emphasising the second Dumézilian function).

It also bears paying attention to the differences in both currents' views of religion. Dugin sees Orthodox Christianity (and more specifically, the Old Believers movement[74]) as the religion that is the most authentic crystallisation of the spirituality of the

---

73 Karczewski, *Tradycja, imperium, geopolityka*, 420.
74 Dugin himself feels closest to the Bezpopovtsy, and more particularly the Netotovtsy. This should be seen as the origin of his apocalyptic language, his emphasis on the "holiness" of "Rus' the Third Rome", as well as his conviction

Primordial Tradition.[75] At the same time, he appreciates the Eastern or "Eurasian" religions (Islam, Buddhism, Siberian shamanism, etc.) as manifestations of Tradition, albeit not as fully as Orthodoxy. On the other hand, the Russian thinker regards Western religiosity, bound up with rationalism and materialism, to have been the germ of modernity. For him, Catholicism is the "first accord of humanity on the way to modernity".[76] In other words, he regards Western religiosity to be a negation of Tradition. Dugin strongly underscores the differences between Catholicism and Orthodoxy.[77] Following René Guénon, he distinguishes between tradition as a broader notion and religion as a narrower notion. Catholicism is seen as a religion, whereas Orthodoxy is a tradition.[78] Tradition is supposed to have the capacity to absorb elements of other beliefs, whereas religion enters into conflict with them. Thus, Orthodoxy was able to embrace old pagan beliefs without conflict, whereas Catholicism reacted with hostility and persecution.[79]

---

that Russia is the *katechon* against the Antichrist of the West. See Dugin, "*Czekam na Iwana Groźnego*", 142.

75 Karczewski, *Tradycja, imperium, geopolityka*, 221–222: "Orthodoxy in its traditional form from before Nikon's reforms is the religion that is the most faithful concretisation of Tradition, Land, and the East, hence true tellurocratic civilisation must be based on Orthodoxy and must be based on Byzantinism. Of course, only Russia-Eurasia, the Eurasian Byzantium, is this civilisation, as it brings together the spiritual foundation of Orthodoxy and the Mongol imperial heritage. This Russian-Eurasian civilisation of the East, Land, and Tradition is expressed by the formula 'Moscow is the Third Rome', which points to Russia-Eurasia's messianism as God-bearing, that is, as the one chosen by God."

76 Ibid., 435.

77 Ibid., 437. According to Dugin, individualism and rationalism are the main traits that differentiate Catholicism from Orthodoxy.

78 Ibid., 432.

79 Ibid., 433: "The teaching of the Cappadocian and the Palamites do not totally conflict with pagan norms; they only transformed pre-Christian archetypes within Orthodox contexts. Orthodoxy is something greater than a religion, both vertically, as it incorporates paganism, and horizontally, a it is open to the metaphysics that completely disappeared in post-Scholastic Catholicism."

The New Right, as a movement focused on the history of Europe (not Eurasia), does not devote particular attention to Orthodoxy. For Alain de Benoist, the main line of dispute on the religious level is between paganism and Christianity (regardless of which version, although attention is focused on Catholicism). Christianity itself is not particularly appreciated by de Benoist, although he has certain dose of respect for Catholic social teaching. In de Benoist's opinion, liberalism, modernity, and individualism are of Christian origin, not only strictly Catholic provenance. The fact that Western individualism never took shape in Russia might be seen (as Dugin does) as a trait of Orthodoxy itself, but it could equally be regarded as an effect of the Russian people's "civilising" along the Mongol-Tatar model.

It is also worth recalling the differences in method, style of thinking, and language. Dugin speaks in a biblical, apocalyptic, mystical, even messianistic language. He speaks of "Holy Rus", sacred geography, and identifies Western civilisation with the Anti-Christ. He values the mysticism of the East over the scienticity of the West.[80] He applies the "National-Bolshevik method", which compels him to regard Stalin

---

80 Breczko, "*Eurazjatyzm — rosyjska idea imperialna spajana nienawiścią*", 155: "Spirituality tending towards mysticism comes from Asia, while the true faith, Orthodoxy, comes from Europe, and more precisely from Byzantium [...]. In this way, Orthodoxy — strengthened by Eastern mysticism — is deepened and internalised by the Russian people and fused with the structures of the centralised and compact state [...]. After the betrayal of Rome and the fall of Constantinople, Moscow as the 'Third Rome' and Russian Orthodoxy become the depository of the true faith, defending the world against the Antichrist which is identified with the religious reverse of Orthodoxy, that is, the religion of the West: Catholicism and its offspring, Protestantism. The greatest threat comes from Latinism, which through its apparent similarity to Orthodoxy can deeply penetrate and harm the foundation of Russian and Eurasian culture. This already signalled dislike, or rather 'anti-Catholic phobia', is further justified by the disastrous impact that has been exerted on Western European culture [...]. Other religions, such as Buddhism and Islam, are neither a threat nor harmful, for they come from the East and have, like Orthodoxy, a deep spirituality, and therefore they deserve tolerance and belong to the *sobor* of faiths."

as a conservative and to interpret Sovietism as "red Byzantinism".[81] Alain de Benoist, in turn, has the temperament of a typical scholar. His books apply a broad scientific method, and he studies religious traditions with the cold eye of an analyst. The language of the New Right is the language of contemporary science and scientific methodology, completely stripped of any turbid mysticism, messianism, or geographical determinism.

In discussing the differences between the New Right and the Fourth Political Theory, it is necessary to recall the personal differences between these currents' main representatives. Alain de Benoist has the temperament of a scholar and analyst. Alexander Dugin has the temperament of a chaplain and prophet. De Benoist appeals to reason, Dugin appeals to emotion. De Benoist applies "lenses and eyes", Dugin applies "incense". De Benoist analyses, Dugin enchants.

---

81 Karczewski, *Tradycja, imperium, geopolityka*, 237.

CONCLUSION

THE *Nouvelle Droite* is an intellectual current which, without a doubt, goes completely against the stream of the dominant intellectual, cultural, and political trends not only of recent years but of the past dozen centuries. On the political level, the *Nouvelle Droite* stands in opposition to liberalism; on the philosophical level, against individualism; and on the religious level, against Christianity. In this respect, it is no surprise that the movement has been stubbornly opposed by very different milieux. On the other hand, it is just as necessary to note that the *Nouvelle Droite* is not a strictly political movement, and it has no ambition of quickly gaining popularity. The aim that this current set before itself is seizing cultural hegemony, for only such can enable radical change in any desired direction. To this end, Alain de Benoist, in co-founding the *Nouvelle Droite*, traversed a path ranging from political to intellectual activity. Creating an intellectual counter-culture, one that could pose an alternative to post-Christian and modern liberal currents, was indispensable.

It might be tempting to adopt the thesis that the *Nouvelle Droite* emerged as a response to what could be defined as the crisis of the culture of the West or the spiritual exhaustion of the West.[1] The *Nouvelle Droite* developed a rather coherent array of views, if not a comprehensive worldview, that encompasses religious, philosophical, as well as political questions. In attempting to summate the totality of the *Nouvelle Droite*'s ideas, the simplest way would be to define it as radically anti-monotheistic. The current sees in monotheism

---

1 Krzysztofek and Szczepański, *Zrozumieć rozwój*, 263.

the destructive factor *par excellence*. Hence, it could be said that the *Nouvelle Droite* mobilises all creative forces in order to create a comprehensive worldview capable of competing with the 1,500-year-old heritage of monotheism in Europe — this is a task that is just as ambitious as it is backbreaking, if not outright utopian.

To this end, the current has worked out a specific vision and interpretation of history that is derived from its views on religion. History is the proper field for ideological and cultural battle. Reinterpreting history is one of the key threads running throughout the *Nouvelle Droite*'s system. According to Olivier Moos, such a selective exploration of European history is a double task. First, it answered the need for a "scientific" basis to construct an "authentically" European (implicitly non-Christian) memory and identity. Second, it is directed towards the European elites with the aim of propagating a new, "right" transvaluation of the heritage of European "paganism".[2] In this peculiar reconstruction of history, Europe's cultural roots and identity are found in ancient Greece, Rome, and the barbarian peoples of the North; at the same time, the foreignness of Christianity to the indigenous spirituality and mentality of Europe is brought into relief. Despite many centuries of the Christianisation of European peoples, the Indo-European structures of thought have endured, and this is interpreted in terms of how religion (in the case of pre-Christian spirituality) is seen as inseparably bound up with the *modus vivendi* of a given culture and its worldview. In turn, cultures are seen as irreducible beings, *ergo* the proper subjects of history. This vision enables an absolutist view of history as a clash between the (Indo-)European mentality, which is "authentic" for European peoples, and the Judeo-Christian, "Middle Eastern", monotheistic mentality. The obvious goal of this intellectual operation is to attempt to separate Christianity from European identity by way of "unmasking" it as a religion that is fundamentally alien to *Homo europaeus*.

---

2   Moos, *Les intellectuels de la Nouvelle Droite et la religion*, 93.

Instead of Christianity, "paganism" is put forth as the proper religion that aligns with the European spirit. Of course, this is a certain kind of anachronism, since there has *de facto* never been any single, homogenous "paganism" in history. In order to impart their conception with scholarly credibility, the *Nouvelle Droite*'s thought turns to Indo-European studies, which are treated as instrumental and indisputable. Georges Dumézil's trifunctional structure occupies a symbolic and central place in the *Nouvelle Droite*'s system, as it is seen as the matrix of "simultaneously historical and mythical, authentic European identity".[3] This structure is taken to be the common denominator of the particular religions of the European peoples. It allows for speaking of "paganism" as such as well as a heritage of "Indo-European tradition". Whether one can speak in this context of an actual "tradition" (uninterrupted over several dozen centuries) or of an Indo-European legacy remains highly debatable — on this point, Eric Hobsbawm and Terence Ranger's concept of "invented tradition" immediately comes to mind.[4]

---

3   Ibid., 94.
4   According to the British historian Eric Hobsbawm, "invented tradition" is "a set of practices, normally governed by overtly or tacitly accepted rules and of a ritual and symbolic nature, which seek to inculcate certain values and norms of behaviour by repetition, which automatically implies continuity with the past". The invention of a tradition consists in formalisation and ritualisation. Hobsbawm names three types of invented traditions: "a) those establishing or symbolizing social cohesion or the membership of groups, real or artificial communities, b) those establishing or legitimizing institutions, status or relations of authority, and c) those whose main purpose was socialization, the inculcation of beliefs, value systems and conventions of behaviour". In the context of the *Nouvelle Droite*, the following passage is especially interesting: "It is clear that plenty of political institutions, ideological movements and groups — not least in nationalism — were so unprecedented that even historic continuity had to be invented, for example by creating an ancient past beyond effective historical continuity, either by semi-fiction [...] or by forgery [...]. Yet it may be suggested that where they are invented, it is often not because old ways are no longer available or viable, but because they are deliberately not used or adapted. Thus, in consciously setting itself against tradition and for radical innovation,

The preceding considerations are not, however, exclusively of historical value. Although the Christian religion no longer fulfils the role of Berger's "sacred canopy"[5] in the Western world, this does not mean that its impact and influence has ended. Let us recall that Alain de Benoist discerned the origin of modern political structures in Christian theology. Christianity was the first to pull up man's "ontological anchor" in social existence, instead placing the weight on the soul, which marked the beginning of seeing man as an individual entity independent of socio-cultural context. This anthropology prepared the ground for Western individualism and liberalism. Monotheistic-universalistic conceptual clichés led to modern Western political structures being seen as having no alternative, which in turn led the states of the Western cultural circle to aspire for the whole world to adjust to their model of development as the "only right" and "only correct" one. Any alternatives that call into doubt the cardinal ideas of the modern Western *ordo* (such as those which do not take into account or are outright against the idea of human rights) are automatically identified with regress, barbarism, or, in the best case scenario, an earlier stage of development (which implicitly has only one possible direction and end). In other words, the mentality of the old Christian

---

the nineteenth-century liberal ideology of social change systematically failed to provide for the social and authority ties taken for granted in earlier societies, and created voids which might have to be filled by invented practices. [...] The long-term inadaptability of pre-industrial ways to a society revolutionized beyond a certain point is not to be denied, but is not to be confused with the problems arising out of the rejection of old ways in the short term by those who regarded them as obstacles to progress or, even worse, as its militant adversaries." Eric Hobsbawm and Terence Ranger (eds.), *The Invention of Tradition* (Cambridge: Cambridge University Press, 2013), 7–8, 9.

5   See Peter Berger, *The Sacred Canopy: Elements of a Sociological Theory of Religion* (New York: Anchor Books, 1967); Grace Davie, *The Sociology of Religion: A Critical Agenda*, 2nd ed. (New York: SAGE, 2013).

missionary coloniser still persists in the minds of European political elites, albeit in secular form.[6]

In connection with the above, Alain de Benoist proposes to view politics in a "polytheistic" way, i.e., less Eurocentrically and less arrogantly, more modestly and more restrainedly, with a greater inclination towards really, rather than merely declaratively, accepting the cultural differences that influence the operativeness of political structures differing from those which in the Western world are taken to be "common sense" and the only right ones. The pluralism that de Benoist posits on different levels is a reflection of the idea of polytheism as a positive, normative model. This finds application on the global level (the "pluriverse" — a multipolar world) as well as on the local level, as in the praise for regionalism and deep scepticism towards any political centralisation that leads to the erosion of those local cultural specificities which, in the *Nouvelle Droite*'s perspective, are good in and of themselves. Furthermore, this deep scepticism towards centralist ("monotheistic") impulses is supposed to be the best safeguard against totalitarianism.

For similar reasons, de Benoist expresses a critical stance towards global capitalism, which is seen as an (anti-)cultural steamroller that levels everyone and everything down to a monolithic model of consumerism, destroying any and all cultural particularities. Global capitalism, making its way into ever more and ever new markets, destabilises local socio-economic "ecosystems", which in the final analysis causes mass pauperisation as well as the erosion of social ties and the weakening of local institutions. In this regard, de Benoist proposes that the countries of the Third World reorient their local economies

---

6   de Benoist and Molnar, *Éclipse du sacré*, 216–217: "In my eyes, the West was born out of a certain tension between two contradictory sources. It is based on a certain identity crisis whose resolution came, over the centuries, to consist in exporting its own dilemmas to the world and constantly asserting its identity by destroying other identities and ubiquitously propagating the 'civilisation of emptiness' that is ethnocidal in its very essence."

first and foremost to the needs of their local societies instead of attempting to restructure themselves at any cost to meet the demands of the global market.

The entire West finds itself at an indisputably high level of scientific, technological, and economic development, but, in de Benoist's opinion, it exhibits symptoms of exhaustion when it comes to the cultural, religious, and spiritual levels. Christianity is no longer the "driving force" or "axiological pillar" of the West. This place remains empty. According to de Benoist, no unbridled consumption, individual self-realisation, or "warm running water" is sufficient to fill this hole. To put it in even simpler terms, the contemporary European is spiritually hollow and has problems with his own identity. The sources of this problem are not political — and, as follows, they cannot be solved by political means. The problem lies in the spiritual, moral, and cultural sphere — the European has been alienated from his own indigenous identity and has lost a feeling for what Europeanness really is. In Moos' opinion, this is the "obsession" of the *Nouvelle Droite*'s intellectuals, who strive to answer the questions "Who am I?" and "Where do I come from?".[7] In summary, the entire mission of the *Nouvelle Droite* boils down to attempting to give Europeans a clear answer to these fundamental questions. The solutions that the *Nouvelle Droite* proposes are clear: Europe's roots lie in its "pagan", polytheistic, Indo-European spiritual heritage. Regaining this lost heritage is the key to a cultural and spiritual renaissance of European civilisation.

The function of religion in the New Right and Alain de Benoist's thought can be defined as fundamental. It fulfils a paradigmatic role and is the cardinal point of reference. Religion manifests itself as the basic civilisation-creating factor. All particular considerations stem from acknowledging religion to the be the proper basis of social and political phenomena.

---

7   Moos, *Les intellectuels de la Nouvelle Droite et la religion*, 111.

In de Benoist's works, the concept of (Judeo-)Christianity plays an important, symbolic role. It is treated as a source of subversion and the basic cause of the mental and anthropological revolution that has taken place within European civilisation. Christianity is the cause of Europeans' alienation from their original, pre-Christian, Indo-European, "pagan" identity. Christianity is what brought homogenising egalitarianism, world-alienating dualism, and deep intolerance into the European mentality.

The religious question occupies the central place in the structure of the whole and conditions all other issues. The entire system is built on and constructed around it. The *Nouvelle Droite* is not a movement with strictly political changes as its aim. It is a movement striving for paradigmatic changes. The point is not for the "right" (no matter how understood) to seize power. Rather, the point is to end the "egalitarian cycle" and begin a new era in the history Europe. The point is to bring about (by way of "metapolitics") the complete dismantling of the socio-cultural system built on Christianity and egalitarianism and to endeavour to build a new Europe on the foundation of the pagan, polytheistic mentality and axiology by way of (re-)attaining the Indo-European sources of spirituality. The ultimate aim is a cultural renaissance of Europe, that is, of Europe *sensu proprio* (not the creation of another, better "West"). In order to realize this, the "original, substantial identity of Europeans and their ethno-cultural identity"[8] needs to be regained.

At the later stage of the development of the *Nouvelle Droite*'s thought (more or less starting in the 1990s), the critique of Christianity faded into the background, to the point of becoming a rather *sui generis* relative indifference. It is difficult to point to a precise moment in which this change came about. It was a rather long-running process that was most likely conditioned by, among other things, the increasing secularisation of French society, the declining role of the Church,

---

8   Taguieff, *Sur la Nouvelle Droite*, 81.

as well as the new generation of GRECEists and the evolution of Alain de Benoist's own thought.⁹ That being said, it bears pointing out that there has been no fundamental change in the *Nouvelle Droite*'s anti-Christian "vulgate". None of their initial theses on the topic of religion have been subject to revision. The matter at hand is rather a question of shifting emphases and concentration onto other topics (turning the edge of critique towards, above all, liberalism and global capitalism). In addition, it bears noting that the *Nouvelle Droite* stressed ideological clarity in its early phase. Over the course of its evolution, the "taste of nuance" and greater balance in judgements increasingly came to the fore.¹⁰ Yet, radical anti-monotheism undoubtedly remains the constitutive feature of the *Nouvelle Droite*.

To summarise, the *Nouvelle Droite* is a current that aims to construct an identity which obviously runs counter to the historical memory of the majority of French (and European) society. This identity, constructed by way of a selective, anti-Christian re-reading of history, claims to exhibit its own legitimacy and bestow its own kind of "authenticity".

---

9   Moos, *Les intellectuels de la Nouvelle Droite et la religion*, 112.
10 Ibid., 114.

BIBLIOGRAPHY

Primary Sources

Benoist, Alain de. "Alain de Benoist answers Tamir Bar-On". *Journal for the Study of Radicalism* 8(1), 2014: 141–168.

Benoist, Alain de. "*Alain de Benoist, à propos des Gilets Jaunes*". [https://www.youtube.com/watch?v=hSbPdzKTw44].

Benoist, Alain de. "Arthur Moeller van den Bruck". [https://s3-eu-west-1.amazonaws.com/alaindebenoist/pdf/arthur_moeller_van_den_bruck.pdf].

Benoist, Alain de. *Au bord du gouffre. La faillite annoncée du système de l'argent.* Paris: 2011.

Benoist, Alain de. *Au-delà des droits de l'homme: pour défendre les libertés.* Paris: 2016.

Benoist, Alain de. *Beyond Human Rights: Defending Freedoms.* Trans. Alexander Jacob. London: Arktos, 2011.

Benoist, Alain de. *Carl Schmitt Today: Terrorism, 'Just' War, and the State of Emergency.* Trans. Alexander Jacob. London: Arktos, 2013.

Benoist, Alain de.*C'est-à-dire. Entretiens — Témoignages — Explications*, vol. 1. Paris: 2006.

Benoist, Alain de. *C'est-à-dire. Entretiens — Témoignages — Explications*, vol. 2. Paris: 2006.

Benoist, Alain de. "Comment peut-on être païen?". *Éléments pour la civilisation européenne* 89, 1997.

Benoist, Alain de. *Comment peut-on être païen?.* Dublin: 2009.

Benoist, Alain de. *Communisme et nazisme. 25 réflexions sur le totalitarisme au XX siècle (1917–1989).* Paris: 1998.

Benoist, Alain de. "Contre tous les racismes". *Éléments pour la civilisation européenne* 8–9, 1974–1975: 13–23.

Benoist, Alain de. "Czas Rewolucji Duchowej. Rozmowa z Alainem de Benoist". *Szczerbiec* 151, 2016: 11–13.

Benoist, Alain de. *Critiques — Théoriques*. Lausanne: 2002.
Benoist, Alain de. *Europe, Tiers Monde, même combat*. Paris: 1986.
Benoist, Alain de. "*Hayek: la loi de la jungle*". *Éléments pour la civilisation européenne* 68, 1990: 5–14.
Benoist, Alain de. "*Imigracja — armia rezerwowa kapitału*". *Nacjonalista.pl*. [https://www.nacjonalista.pl/2011/08/25/alain-de-benoist-imigracja-armia-rezerwowa-kapitalu/].
Benoist, Alain de. "*Immigration, l'armée réserve du capital*". *Éléments pour la civilisation européenne* 139, 2011: 5–14.
Benoist, Alain de. "*Imperium — kwestionariusz*". *Trygław* 16, 2015: 5–8.
Benoist, Alain de. "*Intelektualna pustka starej prawicy*". *XPortal*. [https://xportal.pl/?p=11030].
Benoist, Alain de and Bryan Sylvain. "Interview with Alain de Benoist". In: Johnson, Greg (ed.). *North American New Right*. San Francisco: Counter-Currents, 2012: 69–86.
Benoist, Alain de. "*Jak liberalizm uprowadził demokrację*". *Do Rzeczy*. [https://dorzeczy.pl/swiat/106566/jak-liberalizm-uprowa-dzil-demokracje.html].
Benoist, Alain de. *Jésus et ses frères et autres écrits sur le christianisme, le paganisme et la religion*. Paris: 2006.
Benoist, Alain de. "*La Condition Féminine*". In: Vial, Pierre (ed.). *Pour une renaissance culturelle: Le GRECE prend la parole*. Paris: 1979: 103–119.
Benoist, Alain de. "*L'addition n'a pas été payée*". *Éléments pour la civilisation européenne* 36, 1980.
Benoist, Alain de. "Monotheism vs. Polytheism". In: Sunic, Tomislav. *Postmortem Report: Cultural Examinations from Postmodernity*. Shamley Green: 2010: 20–27.
Benoist, Alain de. "*La religion de l'Europe*". *Éléments pour la civilisation européenne* 36, 1980: 5–20.
Benoist, Alain de and Guillaume Faye. "*La religion des droits de l'homme*". *Éléments pour la civilisation européenne* 37, 1981: 5–21.
Benoist, Alain de and Thomas Molnar. *L'éclipse du sacré*. Paris: 1986.
Benoist, Alain de. "*Le 'communautarisme' n'est plus rien d'autre que la caricature de l'esprit communautarien*". *Terre et Peuple* 18, 2003: 24–26.
Benoist, Alain de. "*L'Église, l'Europe et le Sacré*". In: Vial, Pierre (ed.). *Pour une renaissance culturelle: : Le GRECE prend la parole*. Paris: 1979: 193–230.
Benoist, Alain de. "*Le massacre des Saxons païens de Verden*". *Krisis* 47, 2017: 70–102.
Benoist, Alain de. *L'empire intérieur*. Cognac: 1995.
Benoist, Alain de. "*L'ennemi principal*". *Éléments pour la civilisation européenne* 41, 1982: 37–48.
Benoist, Alain de. *Les Idées à l'endroit*. Paris: 1979.

Benoist, Alain de. "*Les métamorphoses du colonialisme*". *Éléments pour la civilisation européenne* 48–49, 1983–1984: 5–14.

Benoist, Alain de. "*L'idéologie ethnocidaire de l'Occident. Droits de l'homme et droits des peuples*". *Éléments pour la civilisation européenne* 109, 2003: 28–36.

Benoist Alain de and Charles Champetier. "*Manifeste. La Nouvelle Droite de l'an 2000*". *Éléments pour la civilisation européenne* 94, 1999: 11–23.

Benoist, Alain de and Charles Champetier. "Manifesto for a European Renaissance". In: Sunić, Tomislav. *Against Democracy and Equality: The European New Right*. London: Arktos, 2011: 207–243.

Benoist, Alain de. *Mémoire vive*. Paris: 2012.

Benoist, Alain de. "*Nowoczesność jako wróg tożsamości*". *Szczerbiec* 151, 2019: 9–10.

Benoist, Alain de. *On Being a Pagan*. Trans. Jon Graham. Atlanta: Ultra, 2004.

Benoist, Alain de. *Orientations pour des années décisives*. Paris: 1982.

Benoist, Alain de. "*Pour le Tiers monde, quelles solutions?*". *Éléments pour la civilisation européenne* 48–49, 1983–1984: 33–46.

Benoist, Alain de. *The Problem of Democracy*. Trans. Sergio Knipe. London: Arktos, 2011.

Benoist, Alain de. *Przeciw liberalizmowi*. Warsaw: 2022.

Benoist, Alain de. *Quatre figures de la révolution conservatrice allemande: Werner Sombart, Arthur Moeller van den Bruck, Ernst Niekisch, Oswald Spengler*. Paris: 2014.

Benoist, Alain de. "*Sacré païen et désacralisation judéo-chrétienne du monde*". In: Théiraios, D. (ed.). *Quelle religion pour l'Europe?*. Geneva: 1990: 29–76.

Benoist, Alain de. "The New Right: Forty Years After." In: Sunić, Tomislav. *Against Democracy and Equality: The European New Right*. London: Arktos, 2011: 15–29.

Benoist, Alain de. "*Un mot en quatre lettres*". *Éléments pour la civilisation européenne* 95, 1999: 18–22.

Benoist, Alain de. "*Vers une démocratie organique*". *Éléments pour la civilisation européenne* 52, 1985: 33–35.

Benoist, Alain de. *Vu de droite: Anthologie critique des idées contemporaines*. Paris: 2001.

Benoist, Alain de. "What is Sovereignty?". *New European Conservative*. [https://neweuropeanconservative.files.wordpress.com/2012/11/what-is-sovereignty.pdf].

Benoist, Alain de and Paweł Bielawski. "*Wywiad z Alainem de Benoist*". *Trygław* 16, 2015: 31–36.

Herte, Robert de (Alain de Benoist). "*Le réveil de l'Islam*". *Éléments pour la civilisation européenne* 53, 1985.

Herte, Robert de (Alain de Benoist). "*Pour un autre tiers-mondisme*". *Éléments pour la civilisation européenne* 48–49, 1983–1984: 21–26.
Faye, Guillaume. *Archeofuturism: European Visions of the Post-Catastrophic Age*. Trans. Sergio Knipe. London: Arktos, 2010.
Faye, Guillaume. "From Dusk to Dawn: Guillaume Faye speaks in Moscow". In: O'Meara, Michael. *Guillaume Faye and the Battle of Europe*. London: Arktos, 2019: 53–62.
Faye, Guillaume. "*La société multiraciale en question*". *Éléments pour la civilisation européenne* 48–49, 1983–1984: 69–76.
Faye, Guillaume. "*Pour une alliance euro-arabe*". *Éléments pour la civilisation européenne* 53, 1985: 10–17.
Faye, Guillaume. "*Soupçons sur la cause des peuples*". *Terre et Peuple* 18, 2003: 27–28.
Faye, Guillaume. *The Colonisation of Europe*. Trans. Roger Adwan. London: Arktos, 2016.
Faye, Guillaume. "The Third World War is About to Begin: An Interview with Guillaume Faye". In: O'Meara, Michael. *Guillaume Faye and the Battle of Europe*. London: Arktos, 2019: 66–72.
Faye, Guillaume. *Understanding Islam*. Trans. Roger Adwan. London: Arktos, 2016.
Haudry, Jean. *The Indo-Europeans*. Lyon: 1994.
Sunic, Tomislav. *Homo Americanus: A Child of the Postmodern Age*. Arlington: 2017.
Sunic, Tomislav. *Homo Americanus: Child of the Postmodern Age*. London: Arktos, 2018.
Sunic, Tomislav and Paweł Bielawski. "*Wywiad z Tomislavem Suniciem*". *Trygław* 16, 2015: 37–48.
Sunic, Tomislav. "*Zachód przeciwko Europie*". *Szczerbiec* 149, 2013: 16–18.
Vial, Pierre. "*L'intégrisme musulman: une vraie révolustion culturelle*". *Éléments pour la civilisation européenne* 48–49, 1983–1984: 77–82.

Secondary Literature

Bar-On, Tamir. "Fascism to the *Nouvelle Droite*: The Dream of Pan-European Empire". *Journal of Contemporary European Studies* 16(3), 2008: 327–345.
Bar-On, Tamir. *Rethinking the French New Right: Alternatives to Modernity*. New York: 2013.
Bar-On, Tamir. *Where Have All the Fascists Gone?* London/New York: 2016.
Bielawski, Paweł. "„Bolszewizm starożytności", czyli chrześcijaństwo jak „rewolucja". Perspektywa Nowej Prawicy Alaina de Benoista — wybrane aspekty". *Studia Religiologica* 54(2), 2021: 181–194.

Bielawski, Paweł. "*Bunt przeciwko jednobiegunowemu światu, czyli antykolonializm „z prawa"*. Perspektywa Nowej Prawicy Alaina de Benoist". Społeczeństwo i Polityka 3(64), 2020: 5–21.
Bielawski, Paweł. "*Demokracja organiczna Alaina de Benoist jako alternatywa dla globalistycznej demokracji liberalnej*". Politeja 46(61), 2019: 481–502.
Bielawski, Paweł. "*Prawa człowieka — religia obywatelska Zachodu. Perspektywa Europejskiej Nowej Prawicy*". Athenaeum 66, 2020: 138–149.
Cleary, Collin. *Summoning the Gods: Essays on Paganism in a God-Forsaken World*. San Francisco: 2011.
Dziermant, A. "*Europejska Nowa Prawica i perspektywa białoruska*". Pressje 22–23, 2010: 132–146.
François, Stéphane. *Les paganismes de la Nouvelle Droite (1980-2004)*. PhD dissertation, 2005. [https://theses.hal.science/tel-00442649/].
Griffin, Roger. "Between metapolitics and apoliteia : The *Nouvelle Droite*'s strategy for conserving the fascist vision in the 'interregnum'". *Modern and Contemporary France* 8(1), 2010: 35–53.
Konopko, M. "*Nowa Prawica, Nowa Kultura, Nowe Pogaństwo*". Fronda, 1997: 57–64.
Moos, Olivier. *Les intellectuels de la Nouvelle Droite et la religion. Histoire et idéologie d'un antichristianisme de droite (1968-2001)*. Freiburg: 2005.
Mozgol, R. "*Wybieramy „trzecią drogę". Alain de Benoist o „dekolonizacji" Europy*". Templum Novum 11/12, 2011–2012: 7–9.
O'Meara, Michael. *Guillaume Faye and the Battle of Europe*. London: Arktos, 2019.
O'Meara, Michael. *New Culture, New Right: Anti-Liberalism in Postmodern Europe*. London: Arktos, 2013.
Sheehan, Thomas. "Myth and Violence: The Fascism of Julius Evola and Alain de Benoist". *Social Research* 48(1), 1981: 64–65.
Spektorowski, Alberto. "The French New Right: Differentialism and the Idea of Ethnophilian Exclusionism". *Polity* 33(2), 2000: 283–303.
Spektorowski, Alberto. "The New Right: Ethno-regionalism, ethno-pluralism, and the emergence of a neo-fascist 'Third Way'". *Journal of Political Ideologies* 8(1), 2003: 110–130.
Stobiecki, J. "*Alain de Benoist i Francuska Nowa Prawica — twórcy prawicowej strategii metapolitycznej*". Przegląd Politologiczny 2, 2003: 27–36.
Sunić, Tomislav. *Against Democracy and Equality: The European New Right*. London: Arktos, 2011.
Sylvain, Bryan. "Interview with Alain de Benoist". In: Johnson, Greg (ed.). *North American New Right*. San Francisco: Counter-Currents, 2012: 69–86
Taguieff, Pierre-André. *Sur la Nouvelle Droite*. Paris: 1994.

Tomasiewicz, Jarosław. *Między faszyzmem i anarchizmem. Nowe Idee dla Nowej Ery*. Pyskowice: 2000.
Tudor, Lucian. *From the German Conservative Revolution to the New Right*. Santiago de la Nueva Extremadura: 2014.
Tyszka-Drozdowski, Krzysztof. "Alain de Benoist. Ponad lewicą i prawicą". *Pressje* 5, 2019: 45–51.
Wielomski, Adam and T Szczepański. "Rozmowa z dr A. Wielomskim". *Odmrocze* 8/9, 2004: 78–81.
Wielomski, Adam. *Zabójcy Zachodu. Prawica i lewica nietzscheańsko-heideggerystyczna*. Warsaw: 2022.

Other

Amin, Samir. *The Liberal Virus: Permanent War and the Americanization of the World*. New York: Monthly Review Press, 2004.
Amin, Samir. *Wirus liberalizmu. Permanentna wojna i amerykanizacja świata*. Warsaw: 2007.
Assman, Jan. *Moses the Egyptian: The Memory of Egypt in Western Monotheism*. London: 1998.
Assman, Jan. *Of God and Gods: Egypt, Israel, and the Rise of Monotheism*. Wisconsin: 2008.
Assman, Jan. *The Price of Monotheism*. Stanford: 2010.
Bała, P. and A. Wielomski. *Prawa człowieka i ich krytyka: przyczynek do studiów o ideologii ponowożytnych*. Warsaw: 2016.
Bartyzel, J. "Louis Rougier". [http://myslkonserwatywna.pl/louis-rougier/].
Bartyzel, J. "Metapolityka". [www.legitymizm.org/ebp-metapolityka].
Bartyzel, J. "Prawica". [http://www.legitymizm.org/ebp-prawica].
Bartyzel, J. "Próba teoretyzacji pojęcia 'prawica'". In: Łętocha, R. (Ed.). *Religia, Polityka, Naród*. Kraków: 2010: 47–69.
Beniuszys, P. "Ocena demokratycznego ładu w myśli liberalizmu". *Studia Gdańskie. Wizje Rzeczywistości* 9, 2012: 201–215.
Berger, Peter. *The Sacred Canopy: Elements of a Sociological Theory of Religion*. New York: Anchor Books, 1967.
Berger, Peter. *Święty baldachim. Elementy socjologicznej teorii religii*. Kraków: 2005.
Bielawski, Paweł. "Arthura Moellera van den Brucka konserwatywno-rewolucyjna krytyka liberalizmu". *Pro Fide Rege et Lege* 2(80), 2018: 186–196.
Birch, Nicholas. "'Islamism is an interpretation of Islam in step with the modern world': An Interview with Professor Ismail Kara". *New Age Islam*, 18 July 2010. [https://www.newageislam.com/interview/islamism-interpretation-islam-step-with/d/3327].

Böckenförde, E.W. "*Teoria polityki a teologia polityczna. Uwagi na temat ich wzajemnego stosunku*". *Teologia Polityczna* 3, 2005–2006: 301–309.
Breczko, J. "*Eurazjatyzm — rosyjska idea imperialna spajana nienawiścią*". In: Mysona Byrska, J. and J. Synowiec (eds.). *Nienawiść w życiu publicznym. Sfera społeczna*. Kraków: 2015.
Brzechczyn, J. "*Patriotyzm — nacjonalizm — oikofobia w myśli Rogera Scrutona*". *Przegląd Filozoficzny — Nowa Seria* 1(113), 2020: 51–62.
Cousin, R. "*Europe-Action*". [https://www.memoiresdeguerre.com/article-europe-action-43458265.html].
Crépon, Pierre. *Religie a wojna*. Gdańsk: 1994.
Christiansen, Eric. *Krucjaty Północy*. Poznań: 2009.
Christiansen, Eric. *The Northern Crusades*. New York: Penguin, 1997.
Chung, J. Y. "Globalization and the Crisis of Liberal Democracy: The Political Dynamics of Neoliberalism and Populism". *The Journal of Inequality and Democracy* 2(1), 2019: 46–63.
Condorcet, A.N. *Szkic obrazu postępu ducha ludzkiego poprzez dzieje*. Warsaw: 1957.
Condorcet, Nicolas de. *Outlines of an Historical View of the Progress of the Human Mind*. Philadelphia: M. Carey, 1796.
Czarnecki, M.J. "*Człowiek wobec świata. Gnoza nowożytna Erica Voegelina*". *Dialogi Polityczne* 8, 2007: 155–167.
Dante. *Monarchia*. Kęty: 2002.
Davie, Grace. *The Sociology of Religion: A Critical Agenda*. 2nd ed. New York: SAGE, 2013.
Davie, Grace. *Socjologia religii*. Kraków: 2010.
Dembiński, B. *Zagadnienie skończoności w ontologii fundamentalnej Martina Heideggera*. Katowice: 1990.
Dorn, L. "*Na Zachodzie alarm. Kończy się świat jaki znamy*". *Magazyn TVN24*. [[https://tvn24.pl/magazyn-tvn24/na-zachodzie-alarm-kon- czy-sie-swiat-jaki-znamy,151,2652]].
Dugin, Aleksandr. "*Czekam na Iwana Groźnego*". Interview by G. Górny. *Fronda* 11/12, 1998: 130–146.
Dumézil, Georges. *Mitra-Varuna: An Essay on Two Indo-European Representations of Sovereignty*. New York: 1988.
Dumézil, Georges. *Na tropie Indoeuropejczyków. Mity i epopeje. Z Georges'em Dumézilem rozmawia Didier Eribon*. Warsaw: 1996.
Edling, J. "*Czas i historia epifanem Boga w ujęciu św. Augustyna*". *Warszawskie Studia Teologiczne* IX, 1996: 81–104.
Eliade, Mircea. *Historia wierzeń i idei religijnych*, vol. 1, Warsaw: 1988.

Eliade, Mircea. *A History of Religious Ideas — Volume I: From the Stone Age to the Eleusinian Mysteries*. Trans. Willard R. Trask. Chicago: University of Chicago Press, 1978.
Eliade, Mircea. *Patterns in Comparative Religion*. Trans. Rosemary Sheed. Lincoln: University of Nebraska Press, 1996.
Eliade, Mircea. *The Quest: History and Meaning in Religion*. Chicago: University of Chicago Press, 1969.
Eliade, Mircea. *Sacrum a profanum. O istocie sfery religijnej*. Warsaw: 2008.
Eliade, Mircea. *The Sacred and the Profane: The Nature of Religion*. Trans. Willard R. Trask. New York: Harvest, 1987.
Eliade, Mircea. *Traktat o historii religii*. Warsaw: 2009.
Eliade, Mircea. *W poszukiwaniu historii i znaczenia religii*. Warsaw: 1997.
European Parliament. "Democracy and human rights". [https://www.europarl.europa.eu/about-parliament/en/democracy-and-human-rights].
Evola, Julius. "„Cywilizacja" amerykańska". [https://tradycjonalizm.net/juliusevola/zrodla/cywilizacja-amerykanska].
Evola, Julius. *Etyka aryjska*. Chorzów: 1993.
Evola, Julius. *Men Among the Ruins: Post-War Reflections of a Radical Traditionalist*. Trans. Guido Stucco. Rochester: Inner Traditions, 2002.
Evola, Julius. *Orientacje*. Chorzów: 1991.
Evola, Julius. *Na antypodach modernizmu. Pisma wybrane*. Biała Podlaska: 2014.
Evola, Julius. *Revolt Against the Modern World*. Trans. Guido Stucco. Rochester: Inner Traditions, 1995.
Freeman, Michael. *Human Rights: An Interdisciplinary Approach*. Cambridge: Polity, 2002.
Freeman, Michael. *Prawa człowieka*. Warsaw: 2007.
Frerraresi, F. "Julius Evola: Tradition, Reaction, and the Radical Right". *European Journal of Sociology* 28(1), 1987: 107–151.
Fukuyama, Francis. *The End of History and the Last Man*. New York: Free Press, 1992.
Fukuyama, Francis. *Koniec historii i ostatni człowiek*. Kraków: 2017.
Gadamer, Hans-Georg. *Prawda i Metoda*. Warsaw: 2007.
Gadamer, Hans-Georg. *Truth and Method*. 2nd ed. Trans./ed. Joel Weinsheimer and Donald G. Marshall. London: Bloomsbury, 2020.
Galarowicz J. *Martin Heidegger — genialny myśliciel czy szaman?*. Kraków: 2014.
Ganowicz-Bączyk, A. "Narodziny i rozwój etyki środowiskowej". *Studia Ecologiae et Bioethicae* 13(4), 2015: 39–63.
Gibbon, Edward. *Zmierzch Cesarstwa Rzymskiego*, vols. 1–2. Warsaw: 1995.
Giełżyński, W. *Trzeci Świat — dwie trzecie świata*. Warsaw: 1984.

Gieysztor, A. *Mitologia Słowian*. Warsaw: 2006.
Grott, B. "*Funkcja wiedzy religioznawczej w badaniach politologicznych. Rozważania w kontekście wybranych doktryn nacjonalistycznych*". In: Grott, B. and O. Grott (eds.). *Wiedza religioznawcza w badaniach politologicznych*. Radzymin: 2015: 9–34.
Heidegger, Martin. *Introduction to Metaphysics*. 2nd ed. Trans. Gregory Fried and Richard Polt. New Haven: Yale University Press, 2014.
Heidegger, Martin. "Letter on 'Humanism'". Trans. Frank A. Capuzzi. In: Heidegger, Martin. *Pathmarks*. Ed. William McNeill. Cambridge: Cambridge University Press, 1998.
Heidegger Martin. "*List o humanizmie*". In: Heidegger, Martin. *Budować, mieszkać, myśleć*. Warsaw: 1977: 77–127.
Heidegger, Martin. "*Pytanie o technikę*". In: Heidegger, Martin.*Odczyty i rozprawy*. Warsaw: 7–38.
Heidegger, Maritn. *The Question Concerning Technology and Other Essays*. Trans. William Lovitt. New York: Harper Perennial, 2013.
Heidegger, Martin. *Wprowadzenie do metafizyki*. Warsaw: 2000.
Hobsbawm, Eric and Terence Ranger (eds.). *The Invention of Tradition*. Cambridge: Cambridge University Press, 2013.
Hobsbawm, Eric and Terence Ranger (eds.). *Tradycja wynaleziona*. Kraków: 2008.
Hoły-Łuczaj, M. *Radykalny nonantropcentryzm. Martin Heidegger i ekologia głęboka*. Warsaw: 2018.
Jasiński, K. "*Liberalizm a dobro wspólne*". *Studia Koszalińsko-Kołobrzeskie* 23, 2016: 305–319.
Kara, Ismail. "*Islamizm kontra islam*". Interview by Nicholas Birch. *Znak*, 2011. [https://www.miesiecznik.znak.com.pl/6692011-nicholas-birch-islamizm-kontra-islam/].
Karczewski, K. *Miecz i Krzyż. Doktryna polityczna Trzeciej Pozycji i jej geneza na tle zjawiska terceryzmu*. Warsaw: 2019.
Karczewski, K. *Tradycja, imperium, geopolityka. Eurazjatyzm w ujęciu Aleksandra Dugina jako alternatywa wobec liberalizmu oraz demokracji liberalnej*. Toruń: 2017.
Kelly, R.E. "No 'return to the state': dependency and developmentalism against neoliberalism". *Development in Practice* 18(3), 2008: 319–332.
Kłodkowski, P. "*Polityczna misja islamu*". *Teologia Polityczna*, 2016 [https://teologiapolityczna.pl/piotr-klodkowski-polityczna-misja-islamu-2].
Kołakowski, L. *Główne nurty marksizmu*, vol. 3. Warsaw: 2009.
Komorowski, P. "*Koncepcja historii Edwarda Gibbona*". *Analecta* 7/2(14), 1998: 71–106.

Konik, M. *Filozofia polityczna Dantego w świetle traktatu 'De monarchia'"*. Państwo i Społeczeństwo 1, 2008: 209–224.

Kownacki, P. *Trzeci Świat a polityczny aspekt globalizacji gospodarczej*. Warsaw: 2006.

Kozieł, B. "Sacrum et profanum — Integralny Tradycjonalizm a idee Nowej Prawicy". [https://tradycjonalizm.net/juliusevola/artykuly/sacrum-et-profanum-integralny-tradycjonalizm-a-idee-nowej-prawicy].

Krasnodębski, Z. "Genealogia idei postępu". [http://www.omp.org.pl/stareomp/index19e4.php?module=subjects&func=viewpage&pageid=732].

Krasnodębski, Z. *Upadek idei postępu*. Warsaw: 1991.

Krzysztofek, K. and M.S. Szczepański. *Zrozumieć rozwój. Od społeczeństw tradycyjnych do informacyjnych*. Katowice: 2005.

Kubas, S. "Globalny nieład demokratyczny — współczesne perspektywy". Studia Krytyczne 5, 2017: 14–47.

Kula, L. "Pojęcie φύσις w interpretacji Martina Heideggera". Kwartalnik Filozoficzny XL, 2012: 41–57.

Kulesza, R. *Ateny Peryklesa*. Warsaw: 1991.

Kulesza, R. "Demokracje antyczne i współczesne". In: Fiktus, P., H. Malewski, and M. Marszał (eds.). *"Rodzinna Europa": europejska myśl polityczno-prawna u progu XXI wieku*. Wrocław: 2015: 17–28.

Kuśmirek, A. "Żydzi w Ewangelii Jana". Studia Theologica Varsaviensia, 30(2), 1992: 121–135.

Kuź, M. "Globaliści vs. Lokaliści". Nowa Konfederacja, 3(57), 2015: 3–9.

Lakomy, M. "Czynnik kulturowy w relacjach francusko-amerykańskich". Horyzonty Polityki 1(1), 2010: 39–48.

Lengauer, W. *Religijność starożytnych Greków*. Warsaw: 1994.

Lohmann, G. "Różne kultury — dlaczego więc uniwersalne prawa człowieka?". Principia 57–58, 2014: 121–139.

Lovejoy, A.O. *Essays in the History of Ideas*. Baltimore: 2019.

Lovejoy, A.O. "Reflections on the History of Ideas". Journal of the History of Ideas 1(1), 1940: 3–23.

Löwith, K. *Historia powszechna i dzieje zbawienia*. Kęty: 2002.

Łętocha, R. "Chrześcijaństwo i współczesny kryzys ekologiczny". Nowy Obywatel 32(83), 2020: 112–127.

Łętocha, R. "Polityczne dziedzictwo Reformacji". In: Pilarczyk, K. and W. Gajewski (eds.). *Dziedzictwo kulturowe Reformacji w perspektywie polskiej i europejskiej: w 500-lecie wystąpienia Marcina Lutra*. Kraków: 2017: 191–211.

Łętocha, R. (ed.). *Religia, Polityka, Naród*. Kraków: 2010.

Łysiak, D. "Znaczenie i rozumienie w historii idei. Program Quentina Skinnera". *Przegląd Prawniczy Uniwersytetu Warszawskiego* 2/2018, 2018: 58–78.
MacIntyre, Alasdair. *Dziedzictwo cnoty*. Warsaw: 1996.
Maistre, Joseph de. "Nicość republiki francuskiej". In: Trybusiewicz, J. (ed.). *De Maistre*. Warsaw: 1968: 134–138.
Małek, M. "Liberalizm etyczny J.S. Milla: współczesne nawiązania i kontynuacje (analiza poglądów Johna Graya i Petera Singera". PhD dissertation. Katowice: University of Silesia, 2007.
Maszkiewicz, M. "Hermeneutyka i teoria intertekstualności jako metodologia badań modernizmu w poezji serbskiej drugiej połowy XX w. na przykładzie cyklu „Deset soneta nerođenoj kćeri Ivana V. Lalicia"". *Adeptus. Pismo Humanistów* 6, 2015: 2–10.
Matczak, P. *Problemy ekologiczne jako problemy środowiskowe*. Poznań: 2000.
Mead, Margaret. *Płeć i charakter w trzech społecznościach pierwotnych*. Warsaw: 1986.
Mead, Margaret. *Sex and Temperament in Three Primitive Societies*. New York: 2001.
Michalski, F. (trans./ed.). *Hymny Rigwedy*. Warsaw, 1971.
Miętek, A. "Spór liberałów z komunitarystami". *Dialogi Polityczne* 7, 2007: 101–111.
Miklaszewska, J. "Liberałowie i komunitaryści o wolności i sprawiedliwości". *Prakseologia* 158(2), 2016: 15–33.
Mikołejko, Z. *Mity tradycjonalizmu integralnego. Julius Evola i kultura religijno-polityczna prawicy*. Warsaw: 1998.
Milza, P. *Fascisme français. Passé et présent*. Champs: 1987.
Mishan, E. *Spór o wzrost gospodarczy*. Warsaw: 1986.
Mounk, Y. "Stracone złudzenia". *Kultura liberalna* [https://kulturaliberalna.pl/2019/09/17/yascha-mounk-lud-kontra-demokracja-ksiazka-wprowadzenie/].
Niekisch, Ernst. "Prawo Poczdamu". In: Kunicki, W (ed.). *Rewolucja konserwatywna w Niemczech 1918–1933*. Poznań: 1999: 191–204.
Nietzsche, F. *Wiedza radosna*. Łódź/Wrocław: 2010.
Nowak, L. "Kontrooświeceniowe korzenie antyamerykanizmu". *Studia Politologiczne* 14, 2009.
Pawłowski, Z. "Metoda historyczno-krytyczna i analiza narracyjna w perspektywie założeń hermeneutycznych". *Biblica et Patristica Thoruniensia* 11, 2018: 159–176.
Polanyi, Karl. *The Great Transformation: The Political and Economic Origins of Our Time*. Boston: Beacon Press, 2001.
Polanyi, Karl. *Wielka Transformacja*. Warsaw: 2010.
[Polska Times]. "Kim był samobójca z Notre Dame? Dominique Venner: Nacjonalista, który wybrał śmierć samuraja". *Polska Times*. [https://polskatimes. pl/

kim-byl-samobojca-z-notre-dame-dominique-venner-nacjonalista-ktory-wybral-smierc-samuraja/ar/901651/2].

Prószyńska, M. "*Schmittiańskie pojęcie polityczności. Neutralizacja w ogniu krytyki*". *Teologia Polityczna*. [https://teologiapolityczna.pl/magdalena-pruszynska-schmittianskie-pojecie-politycznosci-neutralizacja-w-ogniu-krytyki].

Przybyszewski, K. *Prawa człowieka w kontekstach kulturowych*. Poznań: 2010.

Rakusa-Suszczewski, M. "*Prawa człowieka — między krytyką i apologią europejskiego modelu politycznego*". *Studia Europejskie* 1, 2016: 11–33.

Rémond, R. *Les Droites en France*. Mayenne: 1999.

Roger, Philippe. "*Généalogie de l'antiaméricanisme français: Entretien avec Philippe Roger*". *Esprit* 287(8/9), 2002: 176–194.

Rostow, Walt. *The Stages of Economic Growth: A Non-Communist Manifesto*. Cambridge: 1991.

Rougier, L. *Le conflit du christianisme primitif et de la civilisation antique*. Paris: 1977.

Russell, James C. *The Germanization of Early Medieval Christianity: A Sociohistorical Approach to Religious Transformation*. Oxford: Oxford University Press, 1994.

Ruthann, M. *Islam: A Very Short Introduction*. New York: 1997.

Sawczuk, T. "*Czy demokracja może być liberalna?*". *Rocznik Historii Socjologii* 8, 2018: 131–138.

Schmitt, Carl. *Teologia polityczna i inne pisma*. Warsaw: 2012.

Schmitt, Carl. *Political Theology: Four Chapters on the Concept of Sovereignty*. Trans. George Schwab. Chicago: University of Chicago Press, 2005.

Schmitt, Carl. "Land & Sea, Part I". [https://counter-currents.com/2011/03/carl-schmitts-land-sea-part-1/].

Schmitt, Carl. *The Leviathan in the State Theory of Thomas Hobbes: Meaning and Failure of a Political Symbol*. Trans. George Schwab and Erna Hilfstein. Chicago: University of Chicago Press, 2008.

Schmitt, Carl. *Lewiatan w teorii państwa i Thomasa Hobbesa*. Warsaw: 2008.

Selwyn, B. and S. Miyamura. "Class Struggle or Embedded Markets? Marx, Polanyi and the Meanings and Possibilities of Social Transformation". *New Political Economy* 19(5), 2014: 639–661.

Skinner, Quentin. "Meaning and Understanding in the History of Ideas". *History and Theory* 8(1), 1969.

Skinner, Quentin. "*Znaczenie i rozumienie w historii idei*". *Refleksje* 9, 2014: 129–168.

Sosenko, K. "*Komuntarianizm i liberalizm. Uwagi w związku z prawami człowieka*". *Prakseologia* 158(2), 2016: 53–74.

Spengler, Oswald. *The Decline of the West — Volume I: Form and Actuality*. Legend Books, 2024.

Spengler, Oswald. *The Decline of the West — Volume II: Perspectives of World-History*. Legend Books, 2024.
Spengler, Oswald. *Historia, kultura, polityka*. Warsaw: 1990.
Spengler, Oswald. *The Hour of Decision: Germany and World-Historical Evolution*. Legend Books, 2023.
Spengler, Oswald. *Lata decyzji*. Warsaw: 2015.
Spengler, Oswald. *Zmierzch Zachodu*. Warsaw: 2014.
Stachowski, Z. (ed.). *Leksykon religioznawczy*. Przegląd Religioznawczy 3–4(189–190), 1998.
Stawrowski, Z. "*Czym jest teologia polityczna?*". Chrześcijaństwo — Świat — Polityk a 22, 2018: 189–198.
Stawrowski, Z. "*Liberalizm a demokracja*". Ośrodek Myśli Politycznej. [https://omp.org.pl/artykul.php?artykul=26].
Stępniak, K. "*Koncepcja jurydyzacji czwartej generacji praw człowieka w międzynarodowym systemie ochrony*", Przegląd Sejmowy 2(151), 2019: 97–121.
Sykulski, L. "*Koncepcja radykalnego podmiotu i 'Czwarta Teoria Polityczna' Aleksandra Dugina w kontekście bezpieczeństwa Polski i Unii Europejskiej*". Przegląd Geopolityczny 8, 2014: 229–242.
Szahaj, A. "*Nie-demokratyczny kapitalizm*". Dziennik Gazeta Prawna. [https://edgp.ga- zetaprawna.pl/e-wydanie/57254,24-kwietnia-2020/70499,Dziennik-Gazeta-Prawna/718830,Niedemokratyczny-kapitalizm.html].
Szymaniec, P. "*Condorcet i religia postępu*". Wrocławskie Studia Erazmiańskie, 2007: 64–77.
Śpiewak, P. *Gramsci*. Warsaw: 1977.
Taguieff, Pierre-André. "*Le néo-racisme differentialiste*". Langage et société 34, 1985: 69–98.
Tomasiewicz, J. "*Wojna światów. Wokół teorii zależności*". Nowy Obywatel. [https://nowyobywatel.pl/2019/12/22/wojna-swiatow-wokol-teorii-zaleznosci-2005/].
Tomasiewicz, J. "*W poszukiwaniu istoty faszyzmu*". Historia i Polityka 2–3(9–10), 2009–2010: 122–138.
Tomasiewicz, M. "*Przedaugustyńska filozofia dziejów — wybrane koncepcje*". Krakowskie Studia z Historii Państwa i Prawa 9(2), 2016: 169–186.
Tondera, M. "*Inna, dziwna prawica*". [https://klubjagiellonski.pl/2018/02/07/inna-dziwna-prawica/].
Trybusiewicz, J. "*Idea wolności w myśli Benjamina Constant*". Archiwum historii filozofii i myśli społecznej 13, 1967: 5–48.
"Universal Declaration of the Rights of Peoples". [https://permanentpeoplestribunal.org/algiers-charter/?lang=en].

Urban, J. "*Co Martin Heidegger rozumie pod pojęciem 'technika'? Na ile jest ona poddana roszczeniu zasady, że wszystko ma swoją przyczynę?*". Studia Redemptorystowskie 2, 2004: 163–172.
Uspenski, Boris and Wiktor Żywow, *Car i Bóg*. Warsaw: 1992.
Uspenskij, Boris and Victor Zhivov. *Tsar and God and Other Essays in Russian Cultural Semiotics*. Trans. Marcus C. Levitt, David Budgen, and Liv Bliss. Boston: Academic Studies Press, 2012.
Veyne, Paul. *Początki chrześcijańskiego świata*. Warsaw: 2009.
Veyne, Paul. *When Our World Became Christian*. Trans. Janet Lloyd. Cambridge: Polity, 2010.
Voegelin, Eric. *From Enlightenment to Revolution*. Durham: Duke University Press, 1975.
Voegelin, Eric. *The New Science of Politics: An Introduction*. Chicago: University of Chicago Press, 1987.
Voegelin, Eric. *Nowa nauka polityki*. Warsaw: 1992.
Voegelin, Eric. *Od Oświecenia do rewolucji*. Warsaw: 2011.
Weber, Max. *Racjonalność, władza, odczarowanie*. Poznań: 2004.
Walker, Michael. "Spotlight on the French New Right". *The Scorpion* 10, 1986.
Wasyluk, P. "*Kategorie filozofii dziejów*". Kultura i Edukacja 4, 2007.
Wielomski, Adam. *Faszyzmy łacińskie. Sen o rewolucji innej niż w Rosji i w Niemczech*. Warsaw: 2011.
Wielomski, Adam. *Konserwatyzm*. Warsaw: 2007.
Wielomski, Adam. *Nacjonalizm francuski 1886–1940. Geneza, przemiany, i istota filozofii politycznej*. Warsaw: 2007.
Wróbel, M. *Antyjudaizm a Ewangelia według św. Jana. Nowe spojrzenie na relację czwartej Ewangelii do judaizmu*. Lublin: 2005.
Zaidman, L. *Grecy i ich bogowie*. Warsaw: 2008.
Zemmour, É. "*Europa Wschodnia przypomina nam czym powinna być Europa*". Wszystko co najważniejsze. [https://wszystkoconajwazniejsze.pl/eric-zemmour-europa-wschodnia-przypomina-nam-czym-powinna-byc-europa/].
Zinn, Howard. *Ludowa historia Stanów Zjednoczonych. Od roku 1492 do dziś*. Warsaw: 2016.
Zinn, Howard. *A People's History of the United States*. New York: 2015.
Żelazna, J. "*Idea postępu, pojęcie rozwoju. Kilka uwag i pytań*". Humaniora. Czasopismo Internetowe 3(19), 2017: 73–83.

OTHER BOOKS PUBLISHED BY ARKTOS

VIRGINIA ABERNETHY	*Born Abroad*
SRI DHARMA PRAVARTAKA ACHARYA	*The Dharma Manifesto*
JOAKIM ANDERSEN	*Rising from the Ruins*
WINSTON C. BANKS	*Excessive Immigration*
STEPHEN BASKERVILLE	*Who Lost America?*
ALFRED BAEUMLER	*Nietzsche: Philosopher and Politician*
ALAIN DE BENOIST	*Beyond Human Rights*
	Carl Schmitt Today
	The Ideology of Sameness
	The Indo-Europeans
	Manifesto for a European Renaissance
	On the Brink of the Abyss
	The Problem of Democracy
	Runes and the Origins of Writing
	View from the Right (vol. 1–3)
ARMAND BERGER	*Tolkien, Europe, and Tradition*
ARTHUR MOELLER VAN DEN BRUCK	*Germany's Third Empire*
MATT BATTAGLIOLI	*The Consequences of Equality*
KERRY BOLTON	*The Perversion of Normality*
	Revolution from Above
	Yockey: A Fascist Odyssey
ISAC BOMAN	*Money Power*
CHARLES WILLIAM DAILEY	*The Serpent Symbol in Tradition*
RICARDO DUCHESNE	*Faustian Man in a Multicultural Age*
ALEXANDER DUGIN	*Ethnos and Society*
	Ethnosociology
	Eurasian Mission
	The Fourth Political Theory
	The Great Awakening vs the Great Reset
	Last War of the World-Island
	Politica Aeterna
	Political Platonism
	Putin vs Putin
	The Rise of the Fourth Political Theory
	The Trump Revolution
	Templars of the Proletariat
	The Theory of a Multipolar World
DARIA DUGINA	*A Theory of Europe*
EDWARD DUTTON	*Race Differences in Ethnocentrism*
MARK DYAL	*Hated and Proud*
CLARE ELLIS	*The Blackening of Europe*
KOENRAAD ELST	*Return of the Swastika*
JULIUS EVOLA	*The Bow and the Club*
	Fascism Viewed from the Right
	A Handbook for Right-Wing Youth
	Metaphysics of Power
	Metaphysics of War
	The Myth of the Blood

OTHER BOOKS PUBLISHED BY ARKTOS

	Notes on the Third Reich
	Pagan Imperialism
	Recognitions
	A Traditionalist Confronts Fascism
GUILLAUME FAYE	*Archeofuturism*
	Archeofuturism 2.0
	The Colonisation of Europe
	Convergence of Catastrophes
	Ethnic Apocalypse
	A Global Coup
	Prelude to War
	Sex and Deviance
	Understanding Islam
	Why We Fight
DANIEL S. FORREST	*Suprahumanism*
ANDREW FRASER	*Dissident Dispatches*
	Reinventing Aristocracy in the Age of Woke Capital
	The WASP Question
GÉNÉRATION IDENTITAIRE	*We are Generation Identity*
PETER GOODCHILD	*The Taxi Driver from Baghdad*
	The Western Path
PAUL GOTTFRIED	*War and Democracy*
PETR HAMPL	*Breached Enclosure*
PORUS HOMI HAVEWALA	*The Saga of the Aryan Race*
CONSTANTIN VON HOFFMEISTER	*Esoteric Trumpism*
	MULTIPOLARITY!
RICHARD HOUCK	*Liberalism Unmasked*
A. J. ILLINGWORTH	*Political Justice*
INSTITUT ILIADE	*For a European Awakening*
	Guardians of Heritage
ALEXANDER JACOB	*De Naturae Natura*
JASON REZA JORJANI	*Artemis Unveiled*
	Closer Encounters
	Erosophia
	Faustian Futurist
	Iranian Leviathan
	Lovers of Sophia
	Metapolemos
	Novel Folklore
	Philosophy of the Future
	Prometheism
	Promethean Pirate
	Prometheus and Atlas
	Psychotron
	Uber Man
	World State of Emergency
HENRIK JONASSON	*Sigmund*
EDGAR JULIUS JUNG	*The Significance of the German Revolution*

OTHER BOOKS PUBLISHED BY ARKTOS

Ruuben Kaalep & August Meister	*Rebirth of Europe*
Roderick Kaine	*Smart and SeXy*
James Kirkpatrick	*Conservatism Inc.*
Ludwig Klages	*The Biocentric Worldview*
	Cosmogonic Reflections
	The Science of Character
Andrew Korybko	*Hybrid Wars*
Pierre Krebs	*Guillaume Faye: Truths & Tributes*
	Fighting for the Essence
Julien Langella	*Catholic and Identitarian*
John Bruce Leonard	*The New Prometheans*
Diana Panchenko	*The Inevitable*
Stephen Pax Leonard	*The Ideology of Failure*
	Travels in Cultural Nihilism
William S. Lind	*Reforging Excalibur*
	Retroculture
Pentti Linkola	*Can Life Prevail?*
Giorgio Locchi	*Definitions*
H. P. Lovecraft	*The Conservative*
Norman Lowell	*Imperium Europa*
Richard Lynn	*Sex Differences in Intelligence*
	A Tribute to Helmut Nyborg (ed.)
John MacLugash	*The Return of the Solar King*
Charles Maurras	*The Future of the Intelligentsia &*
	For a French Awakening
John Harmon McElroy	*Agitprop in America*
Michael O'Meara	*Guillaume Faye and the Battle of Europe*
	New Culture, New Right
Michael Millerman	*Beginning with Heidegger*
Dmitry Moiseev	*The Philosophy of Italian Fascism*
Maurice Muret	*The Greatness of Elites*
Brian Anse Patrick	*The NRA and the Media*
	Rise of the Anti-Media
	The Ten Commandments of Propaganda
	Zombology
Tito Perdue	*The Bent Pyramid*
	Journey to a Location
	Lee
	Morning Crafts
	Philip
	The Sweet-Scented Manuscript
	William's House (vol. 1–4)
John K. Press	*The True West vs the Zombie Apocalypse*
Raido	*A Handbook of Traditional Living* (vol. 1–2)
P R Reddall	*Towards Awakening*
Claire Rae Randall	*The War on Gender*

OTHER BOOKS PUBLISHED BY ARKTOS

Steven J. Rosen	*The Agni and the Ecstasy*
	The Jedi in the Lotus
Nicholas Rooney	*Talking to the Wolf*
Richard Rudgley	*Barbarians*
	Essential Substances
	Wildest Dreams
Ernst von Salomon	*It Cannot Be Stormed*
	The Outlaws
Werner Sombart	*Traders and Heroes*
Piero San Giorgio	*Giuseppe*
	Survive the Economic Collapse
	Surviving the Next Catastrophe
Sri Sri Ravi Shankar	*Celebrating Silence*
	Know Your Child
	Management Mantras
	Patanjali Yoga Sutras
	Secrets of Relationships
George T. Shaw (ed.)	*A Fair Hearing*
Fenek Solère	*Kraal*
	Reconquista
Oswald Spengler	*The Decline of the West*
	Man and Technics
Richard Storey	*The Uniqueness of Western Law*
Tomislav Sunic	*Against Democracy and Equality*
	Homo Americanus
	Postmortem Report
	Titans are in Town
Askr Svarte	*Gods in the Abyss*
Hans-Jürgen Syberberg	*On the Fortunes and Misfortunes of*
	Art in Post-War Germany
Abir Taha	*Defining Terrorism*
	The Epic of Arya (2nd ed.)
	Nietzsche is Coming God, or the
	Redemption of the Divine
	Verses of Light
Jean Thiriart	*Europe: An Empire of 400 Million*
Bal Gangadhar Tilak	*The Arctic Home in the Vedas*
Dominique Venner	*Ernst Jünger: A Different European Destiny*
	For a Positive Critique
	The Shock of History
Hans Vogel	*How Europe Became American*
Markus Willinger	*A Europe of Nations*
	Generation Identity
Alexander Wolfheze	*Alba Rosa*
	Globus Horribilis
	Rupes Nigra

www.ingramcontent.com/pod-product-compliance
Lightning Source LLC
Chambersburg PA
CBHW030851170426
43193CB00009BA/564